Harriet Wilson's New England

Revisiting New England: The New Regionalism

SERIES EDITORS

Siobhan Senier   *University of New Hampshire*
Darren Ranco   *Dartmouth College*
Adam Sweeting   *Boston University*
David H. Watters   *University of New Hampshire*

This series presents fresh discussions of the distinctiveness of New England culture. The editors seek manuscripts examining the history of New England regionalism; the way its culture came to represent American national culture; the interaction between that "official" New England culture and the people who lived in the region; and local, subregional, or even biographical subjects as microcosms that explicitly open up and consider larger issues. The series welcomes new theoretical and historical perspectives and is designed to cross disciplinary boundaries and appeal to a wide audience.

For a complete list of books in this series, please visit
www.upne.com and www.upne.com/series/RVNE.html

Harriet Wilson's New England

Race, Writing, and Region

EDITED BY

JerriAnne Boggis

Eve Allegra Raimon

Barbara A. White

University of New Hampshire Press

DURHAM, NEW HAMPSHIRE

Published by
University Press of New England

HANOVER AND LONDON

University of New Hampshire Press
Published by University Press of New England,
One Court Street, Lebanon, NH 03766
www.upne.com

LIBRARY OF CONGRESS CATALOGING-IN-PUBLICATION DATA

Harriet Wilson's New England : race, writing, and region / edited by
JerriAnne Boggis, Eve Allegra Raimon, Barbara A. White.
    p.   cm. — (Revisiting New England: the new regionalism)
Includes bibliographical references and index.
ISBN-13: 978–1–58465–641–8 (alk. paper)
ISBN-10: 1–58465–641–7 (alk. paper)
ISBN-13: 978–1–58465–642–5 (pbk. : alk. paper)
ISBN-10: 1–58465–642–5 (pbk. : alk. paper)
1. Wilson, Harriet E., 1825–1900 — Criticism and interpretation.
2. Wilson, Harriet E., 1825–1900 Our Nig. 3. Women and literature —
United States — History — 19th century. 4. African American women
authors. 5. Race in literature. 6. Religion and literature. 7. New England —
Intellectual life — 19th century. 8. New England — In literature. I. Boggis,
JerriAnne. II. Raimon, Eve Allegra, 1957– III. White, Barbara Ann, 1942–
PS3334.W39Z69   2007
813'.3 — dc22   2007025151

THIS BOOK WAS PUBLISHED WITH THE SUPPORT OF:
Harriet Wilson Project
Office of the Provost, University of Southern Maine
The Provost's Office, University of New Hampshire
The UNH Center for the Humanities and Center for New England Culture

TO THE MEMORY OF OUR GRANDMOTHERS

Lillian Taylor Creary

Josephine Rosenblum

Martha Jones Busacker

Contents

Foreword

Henry Louis Gates, Jr.

The Revolutionary War has been occupying a considerable part of my attention these days. In the course of a project on *another* revolution — that is, the
revolutionary effects of recent developments in DNA research on African
American genealogical and historical research — I came to see, starkly and
vividly, that the role African Americans played as patriots fighting alongside
their white counterparts and against the British for the independence of this
country has been not only simply grossly underestimated by historians but
also very often rendered nearly, if not entirely, invisible in the historical record
of this country.

That there is more than one historical record of this country has been
known to me for some time, and Harriet Wilson was one of my first textual
teachers of that important lesson. When I first discovered Harriet Wilson's
Our Nig in the early 1980s, I was already a student in good standing of African American literature. I was part of the first generation of scholars that
was studying this field of American writing systematically and in deadly ear-
nest. We had slave narratives (Frederick Douglass), we had magisterial political and sociological writing (W. E. B. Du Bois), we had brilliant literary
stylists (the Harlem Renaissance), and we had novelists and poets who transformed literature in the second half of the twentieth century (Ralph Ellison,
Toni Morrison). We read all of these texts, rightly, as beautiful and audacious
triumphs of literacy, self-representation, and self-empowerment. And we also
read them, for the most part, as coming up from slavery, which at the time
meant the South.

But Wilson's novel (more on that designation later) showed us that slavery and racism existed in New England, just a short journey from Boston and
Concord, those hotbeds of Abolition and freethinking that have long been
considered the foundation of the American literary tradition. *Our Nig* turned
my understanding of New England on its head.

Harriet Wilson's New England: Race, Writing, and Region is a major contribution to the scholarship on Harriet Wilson and *Our Nig*. JerriAnne Boggis,

Eve Allegra Raimon, and Barbara A. White, the volume's editors, have assembled a collection that represents the tremendous industry that has sprung up around Wilson over the past two decades and also points toward new directions of inquiry and exploration for future scholars.

Part I, "New Hampshire's 'Shadows': Context and History," recreates, as no other volume has, the world a black woman in mid-nineteenth-century New Hampshire would have experienced. Taken as a whole, the five essays that make up this section suggest constant movement and instability in Wilson's life: she moved from house to house as a domestic and traveled around New Hampshire and parts of Massachusetts as an itinerant seller of hair products. Other blacks put down firmer roots than Wilson, perhaps, by buying and farming their own land, but even they somehow fell out of the dominant history of New England. It is only through the efforts of historians like those in this volume that their names and histories are being resurrected.

The archival research and data collection that went into this first group of essays is meticulous and truly astounding. By tracking Wilson's circuit as a peddler of hair tonics and dyes in "Of Bottles and Books: Reconsidering the Readers of Harriet Wilson's *Our Nig*," Eric Gardner offers a fascinating account of why Wilson's readers were not who we think they should have been. A black woman writing in New England in the 1850s should have been the toast of that region's Abolitionists. But instead we find the book's sales poor in Boston, and most of the owners of the extant first editions traced to points in southern New Hampshire and west central Massachusetts. Hair tonic labels with Wilson's name on them can be traced to many of these same areas. Gardner puts together these two disparate bodies of evidence — owners' names and bottle labels! — and finds that they converge in the route she follows selling her wares. This article provides the useful service of identifying owners and suggesting Wilson's connection with them. But it also recreates the mid-century itinerant marketplace in a way that is, to me, breathtaking. Wilson's readership was, it seems, determined more by her own personal travels and connections than by (what we think of as) the politics of the day.

Barbara A. White, one of the collection's editors, is one of our most established authorities on Harriet Wilson. In "Harriet Wilson's Mentors: The Walkers of Worcester," White locates the scene of Wilson's advanced education in Worcester (deviating from my own supposition of Ware, Walpole, or Westborough), with the family of Mrs. Ann Mattie Walker. White's findings about Wilson's education (in both "straw sewing" and books) are of great consequence in putting together more of the puzzle of Wilson's identity, of who she was and what made her. But in addition to enhancing what we know of Wilson's life, White also carefully reconstructs the life of Mrs. Walker's son,

Gilbert Walker, who was a very successful businessman, professed Abolition-ist, and noted public figure in Worcester. That a man of such stature would disappear from the public record reveals a great deal about the status of blacks contemporary with Harriet Wilson, and also about the state of the histor-ical record. Despite racism, poverty, and piecemeal education, many blacks were vital parts of their communities. But in an effort to erase the memory of slavery and the lingering effects of racism from New England's history, these dynamic black communities and lives were also too often erased from the his-torical record: if New England is a white region, then the problem of racism must not exist here.

Or so the thinking has gone. Reginald H. Pitts, a genealogist who has made great inroads into the reconstruction of Wilson's life in previous schol-arship with Gabrielle Foreman (another contributor to this volume), illumi-nates for us the lives of George and Tim Blanchard, free blacks in Milford, New Hampshire—lives of work, land ownership, financial success, and ulti-mately financial decline with which Wilson, whose father was in their employ as an itinerant laborer, would have been familiar. George Blanchard's ser-vice in the Wilton, New Hampshire, militia, during the Revolutionary War, and then his settling and successful veterinary business in Milford, stemmed from the fact that he resisted the "warning out" that was typical treatment by whites for blacks who sought their livelihoods in New Hampshire towns. Many blacks fled these towns, fearful of the open animosity of their residents. Blanchard stayed and laid down good roots: his son, Tim, inherited his busi-ness, purchased more land, and built a school (and ultimately lost most of it, either from native poor business sense or generally bad economic conditions in the late 1830s), and his daughters settled as independent dressmakers in the vibrant black community of Salem, Massachusetts. But even good roots can be covered over, and New England has tended to cover over its black history. The efforts of genealogists like Pitts undo the effects of this burial.

David H. Watters writes the history of another African American who, like George Blanchard, was a veteran of the American Revolution who put down roots in New Hampshire. In "'As Soon as I Saw My Sable Brother, I Felt More at Home': Sampson Battis, Harriet Wilson, and New Hampshire Town History," Watters illuminates the ways in which African American life after slavery was largely self-created, despite the efforts of white New Eng-landers to represent the region as white and free of the black mark of slavery. Many literary critics have written about the ways in which *Our Nig* subverts sentimental and novelistic tropes of the mid-nineteenth century (in fact, we see excellent examples of this in this collection). Watters goes farther, to argue that the book also "disrupts the narrative formulas of New England historiography." He puts the case well: "Remembering Sampson Battis reconnects Wilson's life to a complex, interracial community with roots in the colonial era, but it also forces recognition that New Hampshire cannot pass as a state with only white roots."

While Pitts and Watters focus on individual men, Valerie Cunningham performs a similar type of excavation for an entire community in her essay, "New Hampshire Forgot: Blacks in Portsmouth." Portsmouth housed a large African American community during Harriet Wilson's lifetime (in fact, the Portsmouth Black History Trail is the first of its type in New Hampshire, followed in this decade by the Milford Black Heritage tour), and it is from such a community that we can reconstruct both the social practices of African Americans in New England and their lives in slavery in the region in the earlier decades of the nineteenth century. Though there is no record of Wilson's visiting Portsmouth, she would have absorbed many stories of life in slavery from the African American social network into which she was born. Scholars such as Gardner, White, Pitts, Watters, and Cunningham re-create the specifically African American life of the region, and in so doing, they help us to understand the world in which Harriet Wilson lived as a worker and a writer.

Part II of the volume, "'Sketches from the Life of a Free Black': Genre and Gender," expands the literary critical and theoretical reception that has been given *Our Nig* since I published my edition of it in 1983. When I announced my authentication of Harriet Wilson's racial identity, I identified the book as a novel, which is clearly the genre to which it belongs. The novelists Ralph Ellison and Alice Walker, to whom I sent the text and who blurbed this edition, emphatically agreed. Since then, dozens and dozens of sophisticated scholars and critics have identified it as a novel. Despite its decidedly autobiographical elements — some of which I identified and which Barbara White, Gabrielle Foreman, and Reginald Pitts have brilliantly expanded upon — *Our Nig* hews *precisely* to the widely held and commonplace definition of a novel: a long-form narrative that offers a realist portrait of a particular social world and the individuals who inhabit it, in a fictionalized form. Wilson imagines and represents scenes to which she had absolutely no access — such as the "courting" and marriage of her parents — and quite obviously fictionalizes many other autobiographical experiences to which she did have access but which merely provide the basis for an imaginative, novelistic rendering. No one in the history of the novel has ever barred a text from this genre because it was autobiographical! To do so would be limiting at best and preposterous at worst.

In the vast secondary literature on *Our Nig* since 1983, its designation as a novel has been questioned only by a few scholars, most recently in the publication of *The Curse of Caste* by Julia Collins, edited by William L. Andrews and Mitch Kachun. Andrews and Kachun claim that *Our Nig* is autobiography; hence, Collins gets to wear the "first novel" crown. I do not dispute calling Collins's work a novel: in fact, I discovered it and published it as such in 1989, on microfiche, as part of my "Black Periodical Literature Project," on whose editorial board Andrews generously served. Chapters of *The Curse of Caste* had been published in a very important nineteenth-century serial called *The Christian Recorder*, but Andrews's and Kachun's work, happily, has made it widely available to students and scholars of the African American literary tradition who are *not* dusting off manuscripts and sifting through archives. But *The Curse of Caste* is not the first novel published by an African American woman; Harriet Wilson's *Our Nig*, as splendidly and deliciously autobiographical as it is, is first and last a novel. As Sven Birkerts gently commented in his *New York Times* review of the new edition of *The Curse of Caste*, attempts to elevate this book to "first novel" status are puzzling and indeed misguided, if the presence of autobiographical elements is taken to be an exclusionary condition for a text to be defined as a novel.

One of the most interesting and indeed useful things to me about pitting Collins and Wilson against each other (which this disagreement has invariably done) is that it has given us a more detailed view of the history of black publishing and makes us see yet again how much Wilson stands apart from the tradition of black writing, even as she is now considered a foundational figure for it. *Our Nig* was not embraced by either whites or blacks in the Abolitionist community, and it was not considered suitable for moral teaching, as was Collins's book. Wilson published it herself and struggled to sell it, and seems something of a solitary figure, even as she stands at the head of a tradition.

In her essay in this volume, "*Our Nig* and the Politics of Harriet Wilson's Recovery, or, Sketches of the Life of a Free Black and Eloquent Colored Spiritualist," Gabrielle Foreman suggests that my initial categorization of *Our Nig* as a novel says more about the marketplace of literary and historical recovery than it does about the book itself. Even if I do not agree with Foreman's claim (as is evident from the above paragraphs), I love the fact that she makes it! Both Foreman's argument and the controversy over *The Curse of Caste* make us work harder to define our generic terms: when is self-fashioning autobiographical, and when is it fictional? Who has a right to determine genre when the author herself has not? In what ways does genre identification enable and disable reading? These are just a few of the questions opened up in this debate. Foreman reviews these questions skillfully and reminds us how crucial they are to the study not only of *Our Nig* but to all of the magnificent acts of the written word that comprise the African American literary tradition. If this first part of the essay serves as a reminder of what we should be thinking about as literary scholars, the second part provides us with something entirely new: a careful reconstruction of a crucial phase of Wilson's life, when she was an active participant in Boston's Spiritualist movement. The prominence that Wilson could not find as a writer among her contemporaries was apparently available to her as a frequent member of the Spiritual lecture and conference circuit. If Wilson was not necessarily representative of black religious, social, and business communities, her life as a Spiritualist still demonstrates the wide range of what blacks could experience in this time and place.

Lisa E. Green's essay, "The Disorderly Girl in Harriet E. Wilson's *Our Nig*," argues that Wilson appropriates a common figure from sentimental fiction — the disorderly girl, the wild child (think of Pearl in *The Scarlet Letter*) — and re-invents her as a key figure in the transmission of the particular and, in Green's word, "unsanctioned" story of racial abuse in the North. Where white authors contemporary to Wilson tend to represent the restraint of the disorderly girl as a positive and necessary social force, Wilson represents attempts to suppress Frado as largely failed: Frado's recurring playfulness, her sass, and her "disorderliness" are signs of her resourcefulness and are absolutely necessary to her survival. In Green's reading of *Our Nig*, the girl's disorderliness transmogrifies into the woman's victimization: this is, after all, a realist novel, and Wilson does not see her way to creating a triumphant conclusion for Frado as a woman. Green shows us that it is not just the distinction between novel and autobiography that poses a generic question for readers of *Our Nig*: sentimental fiction itself is revised into a unique African American form by Wilson.

Mary Louise Kete moves away from the highly individualized view offered in *Our Nig* toward a fuller, more shaded view of New England racism than what Wilson alone can offer. In "Slavery's Shadows: Narrative Chiaroscuro and *Our Nig*," Kete overlays *Our Nig* with Reverend Thomas Savage's *Memoir of Rev. James C. Bryant, late Missionary of A.M.B.C.F. Missions to South Africa*. Written from the same place (Hillsborough County, New Hampshire) and in the same time, the two texts nonetheless depict radically different landscapes with regard to the existence of racism in New England. In Savage's biography, "New Englanders are hard put to see the relationship between racism and slavery," as Kete says: even if racism exists, slavery has no presence in his account, even as a part of New England's past. For Wilson, we know precisely the opposite to be true: "The most important shadows thrown by slavery, those *Our Nig* is intent to show, are the effects of racism in New England." Kete's reading of the two texts together shows that both versions of New England are necessarily incomplete. Savage acknowledges racism in New England without allowing a view of slavery; Wilson, through Frado, shows plainly that slavery preceded the brutal racism that she endures. To read Savage alone is to see the New England of myth, in which slavery (if not racism) is antithetical to its supposedly long-held values. To read Wilson alone is to lack an inside view into the values that shape the majority New England community. To overlay Savage with Wilson is to revive the history that Savage leaves out and that Wilson brings forcefully to her readers' attention.

Cassandra Jackson undertakes a difficult task in her essay, "Beyond the Page: Rape and the Failure of Genre." She argues that the strange silences in *Our Nig*—when Wilson pulls back from the narrative for fear of disturbing her readers with tales too awful to tell, when Frado's speech is denied her by Mrs. Bellmont's wood block—point toward a concealed and in fact impossible-to-narrate history of same-sex sexual abuse. To name an absence as one of a novel's motors is always hazardous, and Jackson's essay certainly will leave some readers unconvinced and bothered. However, her claim about the "failure of genre"—that neither sentimental fiction nor autobiography (nor, I would add, slave narrative and history) can accommodate the sheer brutality of the violence engendered by slavery and racism—is profound and points to the difficulty of the project of recovery and reconstruction that explicating a novel such as *Our Nig* demands.

Eve Allegra Raimon returns to a scene quite visible in the novel but nonetheless regrettably unexplored by other scholars: Miss Marsh's schoolroom, where Frado is educated in a racially integrated setting that looks nothing like what even the most liberal-minded social reformers would have imagined at the time. In "Miss Marsh's Uncommon School Reform," Raimon suggests that Wilson demands a form of social justice that was actually unavailable at the time. I would argue that Wilson here goes beyond the Boston and Concord circles so famous for their progressive thinking. The common school movement in New England (of which Miss Marsh's school is surely a part) sought to provide free education to the increasingly industrial and diversifying population of the region. In Miss Marsh's school, Frado receives respect from both her teacher and her peers and engages as an equal, not an inferior, for the first and only time in the novel. Raimon points out that "As the only personification of the public sphere" in the novel, "the teacher and her school embody the community's great potential to enact a more expansive conception of social justice to include 'Our Nig.'" It is this potential that New England, with its historical revisions and erasures, denies, and that Wilson seeks to reveal in her novel.

In "Feminist Approaches to Teaching Harriet Wilson's *Our Nig*," Helen Frink argues that gender becomes as great a source of oppression as race. Frink rightly points out that this was not my position when I published *Our Nig*, but I hope that I have come to see the intersection of race and gender with more complexity in the two decades since then! *Our Nig*, in Frink's read-ing, echoes the themes in behavior and conflict that run throughout fairy tales and traditional stories about girls' development, tying it still more closely to the genre of sentimental fiction that many of the other scholars in the collec-tion analyze. Frink's reading illuminates a truth about the "market" that is so often at the heart of sentimentalism: *Our Nig* is a young woman's "narra-tive of struggle against poverty and oppression, a struggle predetermined by the economic conditions facing New Hampshire working women in the mid-nineteenth century." In both parts of this collection, then, region occupies a prominent place in determining the stories Wilson tells, how she tells them, and for whom she tells them.

Part III of the collection, "'A Faithful Band of Supporters and Defend-ers': Personal Reflections," offers four accounts of readers discovering Har-riet Wilson. John Ernest, the literary scholar, attributes to Wilson his second education as a scholar: *Our Nig* revised the American literary landscape for him and changed for him the nature of knowledge itself. The Jamaican-born JerriAnne Boggis, despite having a husband and two children in New Hamp-shire, came to think of the New England state as home only after discovering that Wilson was a fellow Milford resident. While still in high school, William Allen learned to educate himself and others about race and racism through Wilson's book. And in a conversation with Gloria Henry, Native American Tami Sanders sees in Wilson not only a story that can connect individuals of various ancestries but also a demand that all citizens of a society, regardless of color or creed, be visible and counted.

I want to devote at least some space to JerriAnne Boggis's creation of the Harriet Wilson Project and the Milford Black Heritage Tour. I say above that her connection to New Hampshire came about through her discovery of Wil-son and *Our Nig*. Without giving away the details of Boggis's fascinating jour-ney, I will say that it has been an honor and a privilege to be involved with the Harriet Wilson Project. From reading an article on Wilson's ties to New Hampshire through ferreting out a hard-to-find copy of *Our Nig* to establish-ing the Harriet Wilson Project and the Milford Black Heritage Tour, Boggis has worked tirelessly to show that New Hampshire is "far more than rolling hills, grazing fields and white ancestors," as she writes at the close of her essay. It is also the landscape which gave birth to an African American writer named Harriet Wilson who was formerly lost to a history whose outlines seemed to hold no place for her. Thanks to JerriAnne Boggis and the other scholars who have contributed their time and talents to the study of Harriet Wilson's work and life, we have a much more detailed and truer picture of this region that I, too, now call home.

Acknowledgments

To borrow from Harriet Wilson, we would like to thank the "faithful band of supporters and defenders" who helped this first collection of essays on the author to reach publication. First, we extend heartfelt thanks to the contributors for their hard work and collegiality. Thanks must go to Ellen Wicklum and all those at the University Press of New England for their advice and assistance throughout the publishing process. Along with these visible participants, we must also thank those less visible collaborators who had a profound impact on this venture. Our sincere gratitude goes to *Milford Cabinet* reporter Peggy Miller for the news story that initially inspired the Harriet Wilson Project. We are in debt to the project's founding members, Gloria Henry, Stasia Millet, Mabelle Barnette, and Claudette Williams. Nancy Amato, Napoleon Jones-Henderson, and Tami Sanders also deserve recognition, as do past members Sumana Northover, Delia Kostner, and Jessica Hejtmanek. Profound gratitude goes to the project's volunteers as well, including Celeste Barnette, Bobbie Bagglie, Kyle Evans, Claudia Everest, Erika Reid, Cindy Stave, and Marci Stetson. In addition, we are deeply indebted to Henry Louis Gates, Jr., for his keynote address at the project's inaugural event, for his foreword, and for his continued support of the project's goals. Joanne Kendell merits special recognition for being a most pleasant, helpful, and diligent gatekeeper. Additionally, Mary V. Dougherty and Mary M. Moynihan offered key editorial help and wise counsel from the sidelines. We also gratefully acknowledge the early and consistent support from Louis Carey and Polly Cote of the Milford Historical Society; Chuck Worchester, Joan Jones, and Judy Parker of the Milford Heritage Commission; Dawn Griska from the Milford Town Hall, and Noreen O'Connor from the Milford Board of Selectmen. We benefited immeasurably from sculptor Fern Cunningham, whose talented hands molded Wilson's indomitable spirit into a piece of clay that will stand as a permanent memorial to the writer in Milford. Thanks also to actresses Nicola Creary-Rivas, Logan Levesque, Christina Gonsalves, Jasmine Gathright, Morgan Stanton, Justianna Andrews, Ashley Gauthier, Stacey Thompson, and Kayla and Amber Rondeau, whose performances in the play "Hearing from Harriet" brought Wilson's willful nature and singular voice to life. We are equally grateful for the support from our colleagues and institutions. In particular, thanks go to Provost Joseph S. Wood at the University of Southern Maine and Provost Bruce Mallory at the University of New Hampshire. Additionally, we benefited from the support of the Center for the Humanities and the Center for New England Culture at the University of New Hampshire. Finally, we extend our gratitude to the financial institutions that so generously supported the creation of the Harriet E. Wilson Memorial. Thanks to the New Hampshire Charitable Foundation, the Northern Utilities Foundation, the Marchasi Foundation, and the Milford Rotary, whose generous contributions have helped to make New Hampshire's black history enduringly visible.

Introduction

Making Space for Harriet E. Wilson

The small town of Milford, New Hampshire, typifies our common image of a "real New England" village. Although it boasts an "oval" rather than a square, Milford features a "compact white village, anchored by a steepled church," as Joseph A. Conforti describes these nineteenth-century constructs.[1] As in other such hamlets, the town hall is one of the structures that dominates the landscape. Its three-story brick frame built in 1869 in the federalist style possesses its own clock tower and flag pole. All manner of town business is transacted inside, of course. Community theater and contra dances provide occasional entertainment as well. It's doubtful, however, that this town meetingplace has ever hosted a public gathering the likes of the one that occurred on June 2, 2004.

On that day, more than 500 townspeople, academics, students, local historians, civil rights activists, and others crowded inside the hall to hear a program titled "Hearing from Harriet." It was the first large local event held in honor of Harriet E. Wilson, a town daughter and the first African American woman to publish a novel in the United States.[2] Henry Louis Gates, Jr., delivered the keynote address about his 1983 rediscovery of the 1859 *Our Nig, or Sketches from the Life of a Free Black*, a fictionalized account of the servitude and hardships of the young Frado, a girl of mixed black and white parentage who was abandoned by her parents and left to the devices of the nefarious Mrs. Bellmont. In addition to Gates's address, the occasion featured entertainment reminiscent of the antebellum years around Milford, when the famous Hutchinson Singers would rally townsfolk behind the abolitionist cause. As well as hearing spirituals the audience watched a play, whose title, "Hearing From Harriet," gave the event its name. The production was performed primarily by area schoolchildren as old as eighteen and as young as six, each representing Frado at different stages of her youth. Much of the dialogue was taken directly from the novel. At play's end, the actors exclaimed in unison: "My name is Harriet E. Adams Wilson, and I was *here*.[3]

What "here" means, precisely, is the central concern of *Harriet Wilson's New England*. What exactly would the young Wilson have encountered in her

Actresses portraying Wilson in the play "Hearing From Harriet," performed May 2, 2004. *Courtesy of Paul F. Johnson*

Town Hall, Milford, New Hampshire (c. 1869). *Courtesy of the Milford (NH) Historical Society*

hometown and in surrounding communities during the antebellum years that might either have helped sustain her through her trials or, conversely, have exacerbated her predicament? What were the prospects for an abandoned biracial girl from a small New England village? Was there a community of color in the region that might have afforded her comfort and to which she might have had access? What would have been the educational climate for a black servant girl in the mid-nineteenth century and what can we surmise about her experience in school assuming that Harriet, like Frado, had the opportunity to attend? While we know that the readership Wilson most explicitly addressed in *Our Nig* is her "colored brethren," who might that "brethren" have been who made up such a makeshift family and who was her actual audience? Who read the work in Wilson's day and in the years that followed its publication? How might they have interpreted it? What is the historic and generic import of Wilson's work today? We also know that after her years in service, the author went on to engage in other ventures, including the manufacture and sale of a hair tonic. Who were her likely customers and what was the commercial market like in the region for such a product produced by a black woman?

Addressing such questions is vital to everyone interested in this enterprising and pathbreaking antebellum writer. More broadly, however, *Harriet Wilson's New England* contributes significantly to our understanding of questions concerning African Americans in New England at midcentury and to what has been termed "the new regional studies." To return to the romantic image of the compact "white" New England village, the adjective describes more than a shade of housepaint.[4] As Conforti asserts in *Imagining New England*, the prevailing vision of the region's cultural and commercial geography is premised upon ethnic and racial exclusions: "New England has been a posted territory," Conforti writes, "where certain people, places, and historical experiences have been excluded or relegated to the cultural margins."[5] The traditional notion of the New England village green has no room for newly arrived Irish immigrants, for example, and certainly none for poor African Americans, no matter how "free." Joanne Pope Melish notes that this "whitewashing" of the population of New England in the early national period is nothing new, nor is it only a thing of the past: "A virtual amnesia about slavery in New England had a history almost as old as the history of slavery itself," Melish contends. "It was an easy leap from the erasure of the experience of slavery to the illusion of the historical absence of people of color generally."[6] *Harriet Wilson's New England* builds on the important recovery work of such historians as Conforti and Melish to help remedy such regional amnesia and erasure as refracted through the cultural lens of Wilson's life and writing.

While other recent contributions to the scholarship on ethnic New England have focused on place, this volume offers readers a glimpse into how New England as a region might have looked to a single and singular African American writer. Moreover, this first-ever collection devoted to Harriet Wilson crosses traditional boundaries between scholarly and popular, academic and personal writing. Such crossover is only fitting for a book that had its genesis in a grass-roots community organization in Milford called the Harriet Wilson Project, founded by JerriAnne Boggis in 2003 to resurrect the author's memory in New Hampshire and afford her the regional recognition she deserves.[7] That spring, the project organized a series of speakers' panels across the state made up of researchers, librarians, social workers, psychologists, and others to ponder questions of the place of Wilson and *Our Nig* in our collective memory of New Hampshire's past. Our hope is that the resulting group of essays will be of use to general readers as much as to Wilson scholars, and to high school students as much as to history teachers. It is perhaps the collaboration among and participation by a range of constituencies that is most distinctive about this volume, and the quality Wilson herself would have most welcomed.

To bridge these sometimes disparate communities of readers *Harriet Wilson's New England: Race, Writing, and Region* is divided into three sections. Part 1, "New Hampshire's 'Shadows': Context and History," contains essays exploring the hidden history of racial diversity in the nineteenth-century New England region. Part 2, "Reading 'Sketches from the Life of a Free Black': Genre and Gender," offers literary-historical interpretations of *Our Nig*, some of which are based on new information about Wilson's life or on topics related to regional history. Part 3, "'A Faithful Band of Supporters and Defenders': Personal Reflections," features stories of the authors' encounters with Harriet Wilson's work and the transformative effect the text had on their lives.

Eric Gardner opens Part 1 with his essay "Of Bottles and Books: Reconsidering the Readers of Harriet Wilson's *Our Nig.*" The article updates the author's 1993 reception study and includes a discussion of the eight newly discovered owners of the book in nineteenth-century New England. Like Wilson's other readers, they tended to be children living in or near her home county. Gardner argues that Wilson's work selling hair tonic "deeply shaped the reception of her book." The other essays in this section deal with specific New England communities. In "Harriet Wilson's Mentors: The Walkers of Worcester," Barbara A. White resurrects the Walker family of Worcester, Massachusetts, which was probably the family who aided the author after she went to Massachusetts. Although Worcester had only a tiny population of African Americans (about 1 percent), the Walkers nonetheless participated in a viable black community. By contrast, the Blanchards of "George and Timothy Blanchard: Surviving and Thriving in Nineteenth-Century Milford," were *the* black family in Milford, New Hampshire. Reginald H. Pitts tells the history of George, a Revolutionary War veteran and veterinarian, and his son, Timothy, who likely employed Harriet Wilson's father in their cooperage, or barrel-making business. However, when Timothy died suddenly in middle age, two of his sons ended up in the poor house and the Blanchards' contributions were quickly forgotten by the town.

This systemic forgetting of the complex racial history of the region, especially in town histories and other local institutions, is the subject of David H. Watters's essay, "'As soon as I saw my sable brother, I felt more at home': Sampson Battis and the Place of New Hampshire African American History." Like many successful black men of the antebellum years, Sampson Battis, an African American from Canterbury, fought in the Revolutionary War. Watters reveals the extent to which local historians effectively erased the racially mixed origins of Canterbury and other New England towns. Local records also failed to note the mixed racial ancestry of town citizens, including Battis's partial Native American heritage. Nonetheless, Watters maintains, Battis endeavored to preserve his story and acted to counter "the cultural matrix of white supremacy." So did the Spring and the Whipple families of Portsmouth, as Valerie Cunningham describes in "New Hampshire Forgot: African Americans in a Community by the Sea." In this essay, Cunningham provides an overview of Portsmouth's black history, also introducing us to such influential local figures as Pomp Spring, who was president of Portsmouth's African Society, and his wife Candace, probably a leader in the Ladies Charitable African Society.

Part 2 of the collection opens with Mary Louise Kete's "Slavery's Shadows: Narrative Chiaroscuro and *Our Nig*." This essay is transitional, both placing Wilson in a regional context and providing analysis of the novel. Kete compares *Our Nig* with the *Memoir of the Rev. James C. Bryant*, the story of a white orphan boy working for a black family at the same time and in the same county as Harriet Wilson. This comparison is meant to complicate popular myths of the region as being outside of or beyond considerations of racial difference. Kete also underscores the extent to which such difference is inextricable from the problems of economic disparity. Many of the remaining readings of *Our Nig* in Part 2 have genre and gender as their focus. The emphasis on genre is not new, as critics have frequently remarked on Wilson's borrowings from such traditions as the sentimental novel, the slave narrative, and the gothic novel.

The generic questions that are part of the politics of recovery come in for re-examination by P. Gabrielle Foreman in "Recovered Autobiographies and the Marketplace: *Our Nig*'s Generic Genealogies and Harriet Wilson's Entrepreneurial Enterprise." Here, Foreman argues that Wilson's narrative may not be a novel at all but rather one of the most important African American autobiographies of its time. Foreman links this discussion with an examination of Wilson's later commercial pursuits manufacturing and selling a hair restoration product. She contends that Wilson's conjoining of her literary and business activities calls for a deeper analysis of nineteenth-century material production and consumption.

In "The Disorderly Girl" in Harriet E. Wilson's *Our Nig*, Lisa E. Green argues that Wilson appropriates the prototypical young heroine of woman's fiction, "the disorderly girl" known for her "outspoken, often angry voice," to legitimate and make palatable a story that few readers of her day wanted to hear. Cassandra Jackson further explores the "relationship between genre and silence" in "Beyond the Page: Rape and the Failure of Genre." Jackson suggests that the "collision of generic practices" in *Our Nig* is indicative of a deeply coded and unutterable evocation of same-sex sexual abuse.

In "Miss Marsh's Uncommon School Reform," Eve Allegra Raimon turns her attention to Frado's teacher and the common school as presented in *Our Nig*. She asserts that in contrast to the increasing racial segregation that often coincided with early school reform Wilson creates a "rare vision of a racially inclusive republic" in brief but "pivotal" scenes in the schoolyard. Finally, Helen Frink adds the fairy tale to the list of Wilson's genre borrowings in her "Fairy Tales and *Our Nig*: Feminist Approaches to Teaching Harriet Wilson's Novel." Frink explores the text's connections to well-known fairy tales about girls' development and interprets *Our Nig* as a "*woman's* narrative" of economic struggle predetermined by the poor conditions facing New Hampshire working women at the time.

Part 3 is devoted to readers' personal reflections on the importance of Wilson's work to their understanding of African American history and literature, their region, and themselves. John Ernest's "Losing Equilibrium: Harriet E. Wilson, Frado, and Me" describes his informal "second graduate education" in African American literature and his experiences "learning how to read" *Our Nig*. The process involved confronting anew the virulent Northern racism that made the book necessary then and now. "Discovering Harriet Wilson in My Own Backyard" is William Allen's recollection of studying *Our Nig* in high school after having grown up on the site of the Milford Poor Farm. He recounts how the book gave meaning to the "remnants from the past" he found in his yard as a child. Indeed, reading *Our Nig* influenced him to join the work of getting the text into New Hampshire high schools. In "A Conversation with Tami Sanders," Gloria Henry, a founding member of the Harriet Wilson Project, interviews another member about Sanders's identification with Wilson's mixed-race heroine. Growing up as a person with Mi'Kmaq and Cree ancestors along with Scotch and Irish heritage, Sanders relates *Our Nig* to her life as a young person in Nashua when early education meant assimilation and cultural forgetting. The last article of the collection, "Not Somewhere Else, but Here," recounts the provocative events that prompted JerriAnne Boggis to found the Harriet Wilson Project in 2003. A Milford resident, Boggis explains how her work on the Harriet Wilson Project helped her establish new and more lasting roots in her hometown. Her efforts also led to this volume, a contribution to the work now being undertaken by community leaders and professional historians to restore to the region its rich racial and ethnic inheritance.

References to the text of *Our Nig* are to Henry Louis Gates, Jr.'s, landmark 1983 edition, revised in 2002. Many of the contributors to this collection, however, refer to information in P. Gabrielle Foreman and Reginald H. Pitts's 2005 edition, in which they present their exciting findings about Harriet Wilson's life after *Our Nig*. Students of the novel would be well advised to consult both editions, as the introductions, notes, and chronologies are full of information not available elsewhere. Indeed, the third edition in print, R. J. Ellis's British edition, published by Trent in 1998, also has a worthy introduction.

NOTES

1. Joseph A. Conforti, *Imagining New England: Explorations of Regional Identity from the Pilgrims to the Mid-Twentieth Century* (Chapel Hill: University of North Carolina Press, 2001), 123. For an influential study of the constructed image of the New England village, see Joseph S. Wood, *The New England Village* (Baltimore: Johns Hopkins University Press, 1997).

2. In this volume, Foreman raises questions about *Our Nig*'s generic classification as a novel, as does William L. Andrews and Mitch Kachun in their edition of Julia Collins, *Curse of Caste or, the Slave Bride* (Oxford: 2006). This newly discovered work was serialized in 1865 in the *Christian Recorder*. Since questions about *Our Nig*'s genre are ongoing, many essays in this collection recognize Henry Louis Gates, Jr.'s, original designation of the work as a fictionalized account of events based in fact, and thus refer to it as the first novel by a black woman published in the United States. Indeed, a definitive explanation has not been offered to date as to why Wilson changed so many facts about her life with the Hayward family. The notion that the author was trying to disguise her association with the family fails to explain why she would create the "maiden sister" character of Aunt Abby, for example, or why she

would make two composite characters out of the Hayward sons. Such decisions are more typically the work of fiction writers. Moreover, John Ernest has questioned the very act of applying twentieth-century standards for generic classifications to nineteenth-century works (American Literature Association remarks, May 25, 2006).

3. JerriAnne Boggis and Gloria Henry, *Hearing From Harriet, A Live Adaptation of Harriet Wilson's Novel, Our Nig,* The Harriet Wilson Project, unpublished manuscript.

4. Conforti notes that the color white was an outgrowth of the neoclassicism of much nineteenth-century central village architecture, and was a self-conscious sign of prosperity: "White paint was more expensive to produce than colored paint; it was recognized as the tint of wealth" (*Imagining New England*, 129).

5. Conforti, 7.

6. Joanne Pope Melish, *Disowning Slavery: Gradual Emancipation and "Race" in New England, 1780–1860* (Ithaca: Cornell University Press, 1998), xiii, xiv.

7. Here, we have in mind several recent studies in the "Revisiting New England" series, published by the University Press of New England. These include Joseph A. Conforti, ed., *Creating Portland: History and Place in Northern New England* (2005); Mark J. Sammons and Valerie Cunningham, *Black Portsmouth: Three Centuries of African-American Heritage* (2004); Maureen Elgersman Lee, *Black Bangor: African Americans in a Maine Community, 1880–1950* (2005). Also see *Salem: Place, Myth, and Memory*, eds. Dane Anthony Morrison and Nancy Lusignan Schultz (Boston: Northeastern University Press, 2004).

PART I

New Hampshire's "Shadows":
Context and History

Of Bottles and Books

Reconsidering the Readers
of Harriet Wilson's *Our Nig*

Eric Gardner

IN MY 1993 STUDY of the journey of Harriet Wilson's *Our Nig* from its printer to its first owners (based on a survey of thirty-four extant copies of the book's first edition), I argued that, in spite of the abolitionist ties of both printer George C. Rand and one owner, William Lloyd Garrison, Jr., the book's reception was highly localized around Wilson's home in Hillsborough County, New Hampshire, and included a disproportionately high number of young readers.[1]

Since my original study, scholars such as P. Gabrielle Foreman, Reginald H. Pitts, and Barbara White have given us a much fuller sense of what Harriet Wilson did before and after *Our Nig* was published. Further, improved access to a range of records has allowed me to clarify and expand my understanding of the circumstances of the book's publication, and, more important, to locate eight more copies of the first edition.[2] This essay enriches our knowledge of Wilson's work before *Our Nig*—especially her work making and selling hair tonic—and views this work through the lens of a fuller reception study based on consideration of all forty-two extant copies, which yield a total of twenty names associated with original owners. In addition to detailing additional owners, I offer here new information on some of the owners noted in my original study. While this sampling of owners remains admittedly small, the patterns that emerge are suggestive—and highlight the need for students of *Our Nig* to reconsider what has been called "the problem of no audience."[3] Specifically, the essay argues that we need to recognize that Wilson's audience was very different from that expected by literary critics of today, and that this fact may have been related as much to Wilson's life—and especially her time selling bottled hair products—as to the book's content.

OF BOTTLES

Though our understanding has progressed significantly, we still know precious little of Harriet Wilson in the years immediately preceding the publication of *Our Nig*. She married Thomas Wilson in Milford on October 6, 1851, and the couple had their only child, George Mason, the next year. Thomas Wilson was a sailor, and probably also (like Frado's husband in *Our Nig*) a con-man, who was often away, died in mid-1853, and seems to have left the small family destitute. Hillsborough County Poor Farm records and the Milford Poor List show Harriet Wilson and her son occasionally throughout the 1850s. Foreman and Pitts suggest that George Wilson was probably taken in by an area family — perhaps Joshua and Irene Fisher Hutchinson — in what, to Wilson, must have painfully echoed her own childhood. They suggest that Wilson traveled around "central and western Massachusetts and southern New Hampshire working as a seamstress, house servant, or selling hair products, contingent on her health."[4]

In short, Wilson, like many free blacks of the period, was often teetering on the brink of poverty and had limited occupational options. Sewing and doing domestic work were among the few readily open to free black women in New England. The catch-all "house servant" likely meant being hired on an as-needed basis by women of the middle class when they had extra money — and meant that Wilson was probably assigned some of the most onerous tasks, including the immensely taxing job of laundress.[5]

Wilson's work selling hair products, though, will cause some excitement among historians looking for forebears of Madam C. J. Walker (aka Sadie Breedlove) — especially given Foreman and Pitts's discovery of bottles from the period from Manchester, New Hampshire, that are embossed with "Mrs. H. E. Wilson's Hair Dressing / Manchester, N.H.," "Tewksbury & Wilson / Mrs. H. E. Wilson's Hair Regenerator / Manchester, N.H.," and "Henry Wilson & Co. / Mrs. H. E. Wilson's Hair Restorer / Manchester, N.H."[6]

Foreman and Pitts are correct that they are almost certainly *her* bottles. *Our Nig*'s account of Frado's travels provides key textual evidence: "In one of her tours, Providence favored her with a friend who, pitying her cheerless lot, kindly provided her with a valuable recipe, from which she might herself manufacture a useful article for her maintenance."[7] Further, "Allida," in her letter in *Our Nig*'s appendix, notes that "The heart of a stranger was moved with compassion, and bestowed a recipe upon" Wilson "for restoring gray hair to its former color" (137).

Beyond, this, though, the phrasing of Wilson's name on the bottles — "Mrs. H. E. Wilson" as opposed to, for example, the use of her full first name —

echoes *Our Nig*'s copyright page as well as the 1860 death notice of Wilson's son.[8] More to the point, while there were a handful of people named "H. Wilson" in the Manchester area, I have found no other people named "H. E. Wilson" during this period in the state who were married or widowed women (women who would be labeled "Mrs.").[9] At least one bottle collecting expert dates the bottles to the antebellum period — though they seem to be occasionally advertised after the Civil War.[10]

That expert, Donald Fadely, notes that, in addition to "Mrs. H. E. Wilson," two variants suggest a connection to Henry Wilson, a white druggist in Manchester, New Hampshire, who sometimes worked alone and sometimes in partnership with Dr. G. J. Tewksbury.[11] The druggist Henry Wilson, though, did not carry the middle initial "E," and his wife's name was Mary. Based on my survey of literature on the history of bottles, it also seems unlikely that Henry Wilson would have had the facilities to produce his own bottles. Thus, he may well have served as a middleman between Harriet Wilson and one or more of the several area glassworks.[12]

Whatever the circumstances surrounding the manufacture of the bottles, we do know — from both the text of *Our Nig* and the history of hair care products during this period — that she almost certainly planned to sell her "valuable recipe" herself, fully aware of the complexity of such a venture.[13] She was also, though, deeply proud; she describes Frado's selling of hair products in these words: "And thus, to the present time, may you see her busily employed in preparing her merchandise; then sallying forth to encounter many frowns, but some kind friends and purchasers. Nothing turns her from her steadfast purpose of elevating herself" (129–30).

Wilson would also have been well aware — especially from her experiences with the Hayward family, who seem to have been, at times, obsessed with appearances — that antebellum white American culture was fascinated with hair. Most domestic manuals and cookbooks of the 1820s and 1830s offered advice on hair care, but, as Kathy Peiss points out, "women's access to information about cosmetics expanded even more with the publishing boom of the 1840s and 1850s" coupled with "a growing commerce in herbs, oils, and chemicals" that "enabled women to secure formerly exotic and costly substances."[14] Erasmus Wilson's *Healthy Skin: A Popular Treatise on the Skin and Hair* went through two quick American editions in the 1850s after being first published in Great Britain, and William Edward Coale's *Hints on Health*, which included a substantial section on hair, went through three American editions in the same period.[15] So significant was the personal care industry to the new sense of the druggist that one firm, A. I. Matthews of Buffalo, actually published a book-length guide to the field, *Hints on Various Subjects Connected with Our Business*, in 1856.[16] And by the mid-1850s, Wilson might have heard the nationally popular Stephen Foster tune, "[I Dream of] Jeanie with the Light Brown Hair."[17] In short, the world that allowed the seven Sutherland Sisters to make a fortune with their bottled "Hair Grower" in the later nineteenth century — complete with singing, appearances with P. T. Barnum, and the slogan "It's the hair and not the hat that makes a woman attractive" — was entering a fast-paced adolescence.[18]

This white fascination with hair certainly functioned in dialogue with broader conceptions of whiteness. For many health advocates and for the pseudo-science surrounding race during the period, hair was a key marker of racial difference: witness Peter A. Browne's 1850 publication *The Classification of Mankind; by the hair and wool of their heads, with an answer to Dr. Prichard's assertion, that 'the covering of the head of the negro is hair, properly so termed, and not wool.' Read before the American Ethnological Society, November 3, 1849*.[19] Scholars like Peiss, Noliwe Rooks, Ayana Byrd, and Lori Tharps have discussed how "black hair" — and other "black" features — became the antithesis of America's growing beauty culture, leading not only to advertising campaigns that constructed specific types of whiteness later in the century, but also, arguably, to more than a century of abusive hair care products, treatments, and advertising aimed at black women.[20] We need look no further than the pages of *Our Nig* to understand the racial dimensions of hair and vanity: Frado initially has "long, curly black hair"; when Jack, after being absent for a time, returns, he asks "Where are your curls, Fra?" only to have Frado reply "Your mother cut them off" (17 and 70).

Still, for all this, hair care ironically offered key socio-economic opportunities for African Americans, both pre- and post-bellum. The long tradition of barbering by elite free blacks in the antebellum period has been regularly noticed by historians — though its social and political dimensions remain understudied — and there were, indeed, barbers in some of the towns Wilson passed through.[21]

Nonetheless, black barbering was largely male-dominated. Though a few women made important inroads in specific areas — especially Sarah Parker Remond's sisters Caroline, Cecilia, and Marchita, whose wig-making operation complemented a successful beauty parlor and a tonic business ("Mrs. Putman's Medicated Hair Tonic," carrying Caroline's married name) — such women came from families with the capital and the local connections necessary to start and maintain such businesses.[22]

Wilson had neither the money nor the connections of the Remonds. She did, though, by the mid-1850s, have an obvious familiarity with southern New Hampshire and west-central Massachusetts and an understanding of how to travel and live cheaply. She had also clearly established some connections among area whites—though certainly not whites with socio-economic powers like the patrons of the Remond sisters or hairdresser Eliza Potter.[23] In essence, she had some skills that would be of great benefit to a peddler.

Wilson would certainly have had a basic understanding of peddlers. As historians like David Jaffee have pointed out, peddlers changed the face of the Northern economy in the first half of the nineteenth century by bringing hitherto unavailable commodities into rural communities throughout the Northeast—and, in so doing, also changed practices of making and distributing items from clocks to books.[24] Most important, as Peiss points out, "peddlers and traders even carried the cheaper brands" of personal care products "into distant farming and frontier communities," and "self-help manuals often advised would-be entrepreneurs to peddle cosmetics; these wares could 'command a quick sale and insure a full pocket.'"[25] Wilson would undoubtedly have seen such peddlers in both her childhood and her early travels; she must also have recognized that, as Jaffee points out, "for many young [white] townspeople, itinerancy proved to be a stage in the life cycle as well as a method of social mobility in the fluid social world of the early republic."[26] She would probably not have thought of peddling seriously until the "valuable recipe"— for a product already associated with African Americans—came to her, as she would have been excluded from most itinerant selling because of her race and gender.

Pragmatically, that "valuable recipe" was probably also an excellent product for an itinerant. Its manufacture probably didn't demand significant funds; chemical analyses done of later nineteenth-century hair tonics generally showed high concentrations of various alcohols and botanical ingredients, many of which would have been readily and cheaply available.[27] It is even possible that Wilson traveled with empty—and so, much lighter—bottles and made batches of the recipe as she traveled. The bottles themselves would not have cost a great deal, either, given the number of glassworks in New Hampshire—even if she had to go through middlemen like Wilson and Tewksbury. And, of course, there is also the possibility that Tewksbury and Wilson might have agreed to take a small stock of her recipe.[28]

Foreman and Pitts note that Wilson was initially successful—building from both Wilson's comments that Frado found making and selling hair tonic "a more agreeable, and an easier way of sustenance" and from Allida's sense that "She availed herself of this great help, and has been quite successful. . . ."[29] But the reality, more probably, was that the business simply allowed her some level of self-sufficiency, given that she and her son were in and out of the few charitable enterprises designed for those in deepest poverty during this period.[30]

That limited success would have come at a price. Wilson, who certainly never had funds to set up a free-standing shop—had to go *to* her customers—the very circumstance that proved so liberating for young, white, unmarried male peddlers. Wilson was tied to a specific geographic area because of her love for her son (that she never abandoned him, and that, even near his death, she was consistently trying to raise funds to reunite with him is a testament to such love). Within that area, racial prejudice would have limited not only her customer base, but also her choices for travel, lodging, and a host of daily living issues—and so probably forced her into a fairly regular circuit of customers who, if the product failed, would have been none too happy. New England winters would have destroyed most of the potential for traveling—and so for sales—for more than a quarter of each year (the quarter in which heating costs alone could cause financial stress). And, of course, Wilson's health was already fragile from the years of abuse she suffered in the Hayward home.

Her health may well have been a central factor in Wilson's decision to leave—at least temporarily—the hair tonic business; Allida's letter in the appendix of *Our Nig* says that Wilson's "health is again falling, and she has felt herself obliged to resort to another method of procuring her bread—that of writing an Autobiography" (137). Other factors, though, would have weighed in, too. Wilson entered the New England peddling industry at a period of notable shift in its character: the barely regulated peddlers of her childhood were made less and less necessary by advances in production and distribution and by the increase of free-standing shops that came with area population growth.[31] In the face of these factors, the number of itinerants nonetheless increased greatly between 1850 and 1860, intensifying the competition in an already-tight market.[32]

These shifts meant that buyers had many more options for purchasing products that competed directly with Wilson's—products probably more attractively promoted, products that offered a richer range of choices, and, bluntly, products that didn't call on racially-biased customers to deal with a free African American.

Shop-owners grew more and more vocal, too, about competition from outside their own communities, and battles for local licensing that had begun in the 1820s and 1830s became much more heated. By the time Wilson began peddling, Massachusetts had already passed a Hawkers and Peddler's Act (1846), which considerably toughened earlier legislation and, according to Jaffee, "established a graded level of licenses based on 'morals and citizenship'" that "extended from town licenses for general merchandise peddlers, which would locate peddlers for one year 'upon a certain course of travel' where the itinerant could always be found and 'held to any just accountability for his conduct,' to state licenses for wholesaler peddlers."[33] Other states followed suit.

The legislation New Hampshire passed on June 25, 1858 — a date too close to the publication of *Our Nig* to be dismissed as simply coincidental — would have severely hampered Wilson. It required all peddlers to be licensed; application for such licenses was to be made to the clerk of the court of common pleas in the peddler's home county and had to include evidence that the peddler "sustains a good moral character; that he had been two years a citizen of the United States and of this State; [and] that he has resided the year previous . . . in some town in this State." In addition to the $50 fee for the license, he — and all of the language in the act uses the male pronoun — would have to produce an additional dollar for the clerk's costs as well as "a certificate of good moral character from the municipal officers of the town where such applicant may reside at the time of making such application." Such licenses lasted for only a year. Unlicensed peddlers in New Hampshire could not only be fined — between $50 and $200 — but could have their belongings confiscated until all fines were paid. Failure to exhibit a license was deemed to be evidence of guilt. Finally, peddlers were required to paint "in some conspicuous place upon any carriage, box, trunk, valise" they carried "the word 'Licensed.'" The xenophobic intent of the act is clear; its gendered language only slightly less clear in intent; and its implied racism is only a step away in logic. Like most regulation of individual participation in certain occupations, this legislation would enable formalized harassment of an African American peddler like Wilson. Even if she were able to obtain a license — which is doubtful — the act, which could be enforced by "any justice of the peace," could cause her to waste valuable time and resources. If Wilson continued to sell hair products after the passage of the act — as suggested by her report that Frado was "to the present time" (129) — it must have been under significantly changed and limited circumstances.[34]

Perhaps already recognizing that peddling hair products would not allow her enough stability — in terms of either finances or location — to reunite with her son, Wilson seems to have begun composing *Our Nig* as she traveled, and, when the book was near completion, moved to Boston.

OF BOOKS

It remains unclear just when Wilson went to Boston — a city well outside her established traveling patterns — though it is now almost certain that the Harriet Wilson listed in a handful of Boston records between 1855 and 1860, marked as being Virginia-born and initially thought to be the author of *Our Nig*, was likely a different Harriet Wilson altogether.[35] But we do know that the author Harriet Wilson did go to Boston herself because she filed copyright papers for the book in the Massachusetts District office.[36]

We can only speculate on what led her to the printers George C. Rand and Abraham Avery. If she came to the pair through books, it might have been because she noticed the printers' names on a copy of *Uncle Tom's Cabin* or any one of a number of cheap tracts associated with a range of reform societies — tracts like those other peddlers would have carried.[37] Word-of-mouth in Boston might have noted Rand and Avery's abolitionist sentiments.[38] As Foreman and Pitts point out, they also published some Spiritualist titles, and Wilson's growing interest in such might also have drawn her to them.[39] But Rand and Avery was also larger and more active in both printing and publishing than previous scholars — myself included — have suggested, and so the firm's size and reputation as a "jobber" (a printer for other publishers, as well as private clients) may have been a factor.[40] Simple location also may have contributed; as I noted in my 1993 study, Rand and Avery's offices were close to the Massachusetts Sunday School Union, the American Sunday School Union, the Massachusetts Temperance Depository, the New England Temperance Depository, the American Tract Society, the American Peace Society, the Massachusetts Anti-Slavery Society, the American Anti-Slavery Society, and *The Liberator* — as friendly a publishing neighborhood as a black woman in America might have found.[41]

But the proximity of Rand and Avery to these liberal efforts — and the fact that they also printed work by activists like Theodore Parker as well as texts for the young house of Thayer and Eldridge[42] — begs the question, asked first by Gates, of just how and why Wilson's text could have been virtually ignored in Boston, a center of radical abolitionism and of African American civil rights efforts. The likely answers to this question have been painful to hear, because they remind us that many white abolitionists were, indeed, the racists that Wilson herself condemns: those "who didn't want slaves at the South, nor niggers in their own houses, North. Faugh! to lodge one; to eat with one; to admit one through the front door; to sit next one; awful!" (129). Simply put, few in the abolitionist community would have seen *Our Nig* as a text that would help the movement, and many would have felt it could hurt abolitionist efforts given that its depiction of suffering free blacks in the North echoed texts like the pro-slavery novels written in response to *Uncle Tom's Cabin*.[43]

Beyond such issues, though, some free blacks found growing difficulty in getting their stories into print — even when those stories strongly supported white abolitionist politics and foci. By the late 1850s, organized abolitionism — embodied in the publications of the American Anti-Slavery Society, for example — leaned heavily on African American lecturers for material for published narratives, and, given Douglass's now-infamous defection to start his own newspaper, seems to have been skeptical about pushing black-authored texts too heavily. The success of *Uncle Tom's Cabin* also created a new sense of just what might sell — and who authors might be; thus the circumstances of publication and distribution of Douglass's first autobiography (published by the Society in 1845) and second autobiography (published by a commercial firm that Douglass had some dealings with) were very different.[44]

Harriet Jacobs, for example, seems to have been boxed out of the few publishing opportunities offered by organized abolition societies — probably in part because of her gender — and commercial publishers demanded a preface by a white abolitionist luminary — a "name" — before they would consider publishing her narrative. While Jacobs's work with Lydia Maria Child led to both a stunning product and a notable friendship, that connection was made only after years of networking and was aided by Jacobs's friendships with other key players in the movement like William Cooper Nell.[45]

We do not know if Wilson attempted the routes that Jacobs did — if she sought out a supporter in the white abolitionist movement or if she attempted to get one of the societies based near Rand's offices to publish her text. As past critics have pointed out, she would have had a harder sell than Jacobs, even though, as Lois Brown's rediscovery of both Susan Paul's *Memoir of James Jackson* (1835) and the *Liberator's* support of that text show, a biographical account of a young, free African American would not have been totally unknown in Boston.[46]

Within this framework, we can guess that Wilson probably, in the end, came to Rand as a printer rather than a publisher. The seemingly small print run and the inexpensiveness of the product suggest that the book might have been a subsidized or a charitable endeavor.[47] Wilson may have paid part or all of the production costs — which would not have been great — and someone like Rand or even the writers of the letters in *Our Nig's* appendix might have aided her. She may have hoped the book might gain some notice in Boston — and perhaps go into a second, larger edition.[48] If she did, these hopes were in vain: more than a decade of searching by scholars has produced no notice or review of the book contemporary with its publication, and only one highly suspect reference to the text has been found among the letters and diaries of abolitionist literati.[49]

Thus, it seems — even more than it did when I completed my original reception study in 1993 — that the "problem of no audience" was a problem of no audience *in Boston*. The preface's call for support from her "colored brethren" makes it clear that Wilson did hope for such an audience — as Boston was the African American center of the region — and, unfortunately, we can only guess at the reasons for her failure.[50] But, as data from extant copies show, there *was* an audience for the book — one with striking similarities in age, region, politics, and class. It was also likely an audience of people who met and talked with Wilson herself. Specifically, though it would have been increasingly difficult given both her health and the regulation of peddlers, it looks as if she distributed the book in much the same way she distributed her hair tonic — going to the same locations and perhaps to the same people.

As I noted in my 1993 study, a significant number of owners were quite young when they received the book. Flora Lovejoy was only two when it was published. George Armstrong Tinker was six. George F. Sawyer was nine, as was Mary A. Whitcomb (she was eleven when she signed her copy). Sarah C. Tompkins, an owner unidentified in my original study, was fourteen when her elder sister gave her a copy as a Christmas gift. Further, John H. Colburn was nine when the book was published and fifteen when he gave a copy to the thirty-seven-year old M. Jennie Moar, and, although neither the Asthes E. Gay nor the Abby Reed who gave him a copy on Christmas 1863 has been identified, the fact that Reed used the title "Mas." — short for "Master" — in her inscription to Gay marks him as a young man, not yet a "Mr." Among the traceable owners, this means that only Garrison, Henry Stiles, and Alonzo Sargent were adults at the time of *Our Nig's* publication.[51]

All of the owners — children and adults — were clustered in a small and exceedingly white geographic area. Five copies trace to owners in Hillsborough County, where Wilson grew up: Flora Lovejoy's copy (Nashua), the Moar/Colburn copy (Nashua), George Sawyer's copy (Nashua), Henry Stiles's copy (Brookline), and the Tinker/Johnson copy (Bedford). With two exceptions, all of the other copies with locatable owners trace to counties adjacent to Hillsborough: Sarah C. Tompkins's copy (Concord, Merrimack County, New Hampshire), Mary Whitcomb's copy (Hampton, Rockingham County, New Hampshire), and Edith D'Orecy's copy (South Gardner, Middlesex County, Massachusetts). Garrison's copy, of course, traces to Boston, and Alonzo Sargent's copy traces to Essex County, Massachusetts, though Sargent may certainly have traveled to Boston or even to New Hampshire.

With the exception of Garrison, none of the owners had notable ties with organized abolitionism. One could hypothesize that at least some of the owners must have been more liberal in terms of thinking about reform generally, and the limited data available support this. Miranda Tompkins Widmer, for example, attended the Troy Female Seminary (now the Emma Willard School) from 1845 to 1848, as did her younger sister Ellen; her younger sister Mary also received some education and was listed in the 1860 census as a "schoolteacher."[52] George Sawyer also came to believe in education for women; his daughter Orra Sawyer taught in Nashua's public schools for more than two decades.[53] Widmer and Henry Stiles were both active in church organizations that emphasized benevolence, and Stiles was active in local government (eventually as a Republican) and supported his son Charles when he joined the Union army.[54] George and Ella Tinker, whose two biological children died in infancy, took in at least ten orphaned children between 1900 and 1930; most were young, most seem to be of immigrant parentage, and most had birthplaces listed only as "unknown."[55] And after the death of Flora Lovejoy's father, her mother, Sarah (French) Lovejoy, seems to have turned to Spiritualism, like Harriet Wilson did: she is listed as a "clairvoyant" in the 1895 Nashua city directory.[56]

All of the owners' families probably fell into the "middling classes." Most biographers of the Garrison family note that they often teetered on the edge of genteel poverty; still, the 1860 census, which listed Garrison, Sr.'s occupation as "editor" tallied property valued at $8,500 — and by 1870, the family's real and personal property was valued at over $35,000.[57]

Flora Lovejoy's father was working as a confectioner when *Our Nig* was published; later, he became an "undertaker's assistant." Though he owned no real estate and little personal property in 1860, by 1870, his combined property was worth over $2,000. Jennie Moar's family is difficult to trace, and it is not certain as to whether Moar was her maiden or married name. By the late nineteenth century, she was living with Elvira (Moore) Dow, a divorcee who was listed as her sister. John H. Colburn (sometimes spelled "Coburn") is easier to trace. John's father, Charles L. Coburn, was listed as a farmer throughout his life, and his assets steadily climbed from $2,000 in 1850 to $19,000 in 1870. John was a younger son of a large family, and so left farming; he is listed as a "teamster" or "contractor — trucking" for most of his life. Like his father, Alonzo Sargent worked as a carpenter, often a ship's carpenter; a set of fairly sloppy census takers in his area failed to record property valuations. George Sawyer's father, Joseph, was listed in both 1850 and 1860 as a "trader," though in 1870 he was listed as a "mechanic." His property valuation rose from $1,700 to $4,500 during the period. George's first job was in a suspender factory; by 1880, he was working as a grocer.

Henry Stiles also worked as a merchant — though he was much more successful. Partnering with Joseph C. Tucker in the late 1840s, he opened a multi-faceted business that included coopering, wholesale lumber sales, and a "large general merchandise" store. The valuation of his property rose from $1,250 in 1850 to $20,000 in 1860. When he sold off his interest in the store, that valuation dropped—to $5,500 in 1870, but he had obtained some prominence in the town and secured a comfortable government job as town postmaster that would see him through his later years. He was also the town clerk for twenty-three years, a position one of his sons took over just before Stiles's death.

Clark Tompkins, father of both Sarah C. Tompkins and Miranda (Tompkins) Widmer, was a successful machinist in Troy, New York, who had amassed some $25,000 in personal and real property by 1860 and, as noted above, saw his children educated. When she purchased a copy of *Our Nig*, Miranda was living in Concord, New Hampshire, with her husband Daniel, a Swiss immigrant who worked as a blacksmith; the young couple boarded at the Flanders family's boarding house, though by 1870 Daniel was working as a "spring maker," the couple was living in their own home with a niece and one of Miranda's younger sisters, and the family's property valuation was $2,900.

Joseph Tinker was listed as a farmer throughout his life; the valuation of his property climbed from $2,000 in 1860 to $7,000 in 1870. George and Ella Tinker lived with the elder Tinker on the family farm, which George and Ella took over on his death. Ella (Gale) Tinker's father had been a farmer and blacksmith; her stepfather was also a blacksmith. Mary Whitcomb would later work as a "shoe stitcher" as a teenager; for most of her life, her father, Jared P. Whitcomb, worked as a grocer—though when Whitcomb received her copy of *Our Nig*, he was the proprietor of the Union House, a hotel and sometime-tavern in Hampton that he purchased c. 1859, renovated, named, and operated into the early 1860s. His property valuation in 1860 was $8,000.[58]

Still, while certainly not wealthy, many of the families of the owners of *Our Nig* had established places in the region: the Lovejoy, Moar, Colburn, Sargent, Sawyer, Stiles, Tinker, and Gale families had all been in the area for generations.[59] In part because of this and in part because of the massive number of Hutchinson and Hayward relatives in this section of New Hampshire, it is not surprising that the families of owners of *Our Nig* had some interaction with people bearing these surnames. Henry Stiles's second wife, Hattie L. Seaver, for example, was the daughter of Asa and Rebecca (Hutchinson) Seaver, though this line of the Hutchinsons is different from the ancestors of "she-devil" Rebecca Hutchinson Hayward.[60] The family of a John and Margaret Hayward boarded with the Lovejoys in 1860, and John Hayward seems to have trained under Lovejoy, because he is later listed—bafflingly, with the first name "Ariel"—as a "candy maker." I have not been able to determine the ancestry of this John/Ariel Hayward.[61]

Perhaps more importantly, though, many of the owners' families were in occupations that might have lent themselves to connections to Wilson. Henry

Stiles and Joseph Sawyer, of course, were shopkeepers who might have dealt directly with Wilson and might have purchased her hair tonic. Charles Love-joy, like most confectioners, may well have also had connections to area apoth-ecaries. And in addition to dealing with a clientele who would have wanted ready hair products, hotel-keeper Jared Whitcomb would later become a gro-cer. Further, many of the parents of owners of *Our Nig* were of an age where gray hair might begin to bother them.[62]

In short, then, it seems likely that Wilson's life as a peddler of hair tonic deeply shaped the reception of her book — and gave her an audience where there might not otherwise have been one. Wilson's peddling offers a workable explanation for the region (and so race), seeming liberality, class, and occupa-tional status of the families of initial owners.

Whether Wilson intended the book as a "children's book" — as suggested by the ages of most of the initial owners — is open to debate; a full consider-ation of such is beyond the scope of this essay. Still, it is worth noting that the phrase "children's book" signified differently in the antebellum period than it does now and included a much wider range of texts (it would be easy to argue that many sentimental novels could and were designed in part to be read by children) — and that many women writers who considered race (and who ad-vocated abolition) wrote "children's texts."[63]

But explaining the book's *deployment* as a children's text is easier. While would-be publishers and reviewers would have read the full manuscript before ultimately deciding to publish or review the book, book buyers would have be-haved quite differently. Specifically, while they might have scanned the book's title page or first chapter — or even appendix — before purchasing the book, they would not have read it all. Instead, they would most probably have been guided by Wilson, who may have made each sale personally.

What did she say? It seems unlikely that she would have claimed any sim-ilarities to the widely circulating slave narratives — at least, if she told would-be buyers that she was the author. A free black woman of limited economic status and even more limited social connections simply would have been ex-ceedingly unlikely to tramp around post–Fugitive Slave Law New England claiming to have any connection to slavery, as to do so was to risk abduction and abuse.[64] Thus, she probably said things like, "It is the story of a young girl . . ." or "It tells of my early life . . ." or "It is an autobiography I wrote to help my young child . . ." In short, almost all of the descriptions of the book that she could give to would-be buyers would eventually come back to the fact that most of the book is not only the story of a child, but a story written to sup-port a child.

Given that she would have been using such language to sell the book to adults, she might well have emphasized the book's power as a moral teaching tool — and, given the emphasis that Frado places on values like self-sufficiency, hard work, and love of her child at the book's end (all echoing Wilson's preface), such a pitch would not have been far from the truth.

And the likely book-buyers might have been more familiar with the stories of young black children designed to morally educate young people. By 1859, the myriad corruptions of Stowe's Topsy were everywhere — but so, too, were stories of black children by abolitionists and by religious and missionary societies in the form of tracts and small books that looked and felt very much like *Our Nig*.[65] Such texts may even have influenced the writing of *Our Nig*, and it may not be a coincidence that Rand and Avery did a brisk business producing cheap children's books of similar size, shape, and quality.[66]

If the first buyers of the book bought it expecting a tale designed to tell of a pious black child's move toward God, they must have been surprised by *Our Nig*'s complex and troubling treatment not only of organized religion, but also of politics, race, and gender. But we do know that at least some readers seem, nonetheless, to have found the book of value. Miranda Tompkins, for example, would have known about the power of books to instruct young women and the care needed in choosing books for young readers from her time at the Troy Female Seminary.[67] It would seem likely that she read it before giving it to her younger sister as a Christmas gift. The same may well be true of other copies given as gifts — especially those given to children, like the Gay/Reed copy. And, of course, Henry Stiles wrote the phrase "a good book" twice in his copy.[68]

Our Nig, then, did find an audience — a small, localized one, shaped deeply by the circumstances of its distribution by an author who had area ties, peddling experience, and a text that was about — among several subjects — children. What may be curious to modern readers, then, is not so much that *Our Nig* did not find an audience in Boston or even that many of its original readers were children. Given Foreman and Pitts's work, the next logical question would seem to be: if Wilson lived for forty years after the book, moved back to Boston, and gained some level of fame, why did she not bring her book along?

The answer to this question may not be much further than the book's preface: Wilson says, quite directly, that the book is designed to aid herself *and* her child. As Gates demonstrated in his rediscovery of the book, George Mason Wilson died only a few months after *Our Nig* was copyrighted.[69] In the most pragmatic sense, at her son's death, Wilson would have seen both that the immediate utilitarian purpose of the book had been lost and that, even if she wanted such, the book was gaining no entry into Boston's reform communities. And given that the book was not simply tied to children but was for *her* child, continuing to carry *Our Nig* from place to place to sell it to readers she hoped would, in her prefatory words, support and defend her might simply have been too strong a reminder of all that she had lost.

But while her son's death may well have lessened Wilson's desire to try to expand the book's audience beyond the small group of mainly New Hampshire–based acquaintances, it may also have been the event that most propelled her toward Spiritualism, a movement focused on connections between the living and the dead. In the light of Foreman and Pitts's reports of Wilson communing with — and celebrating — the spirits of both her father and her son,[70] we may understand her embrace of Spiritualism, along with her concurrent and ardent advocacy for neglected and abused child laborers, as giving her, on the one hand, a solace the book could not — and, on the other, an outlet for both the personal and social justice concerns that have so drawn modern readers to *Our Nig.*

APPENDIX A

Extant Copies of Harriet Wilson's *Our Nig* (1859) with Ownership Markings

Primary Name	Associated Name(s)	Notes	Location
M. W. Chandler	Mrs. C. B. Blake	Gift from Blake to Chandler	University of California–Berkeley
Edith M. D'Orecy	R. S——— [or R. S. M———]	Gift to D'Orecy	Historical Society of Pennsylvania (Balch)
[William Lloyd Garrison, Jr.]	n/a	Ownership determined from provenance records	Smith College
Asthes E. Gay	Abby Reed	Gift from Reed to "Mas." Gay dated "Dec 25, 1863"	University of Texas (Ransom Center)
M. D. Gilman	n/a	No other markings	Library Company of Philadelphia
Flora M. Lovejoy	n/a	No other markings	University of Wisconsin
M. Jennie Moar	John H. Colburn	Gift from Colburn (of Nashua) to Moar on "Feb 16th 1865"	Ohio State University
Alonzo Sargent	n/a	"Annisquam / Mass / 1860"	Huntington Library
George F. Sawyer	n/a	"Nashua, N. H."	University of California–Los Angeles
Henry Stiles	n/a	Signed three times, with "P.M." following; also "a good book" written twice	Dartmouth College
George Armstrong Tinker	Ella Tinker, Edgar Johnson	Childlike "George Armstrong / Book / Bedford, N.H."; later "Presented to / Mr. Edgar Johnson / By Ella Tinker"	New York Public Library
Sarah C. Tompkins	Miranda [Tompkins Widmer]	"Sarah C. Tompkins / from Miranda / Concord Dec. 25 / 59"	Cornell University
Mary A. Whitcomb	n/a	"Miss Mary A. Whitcomb / Hampton, N.H. / February 1, 1861"	Gates Copy A

APPENDIX B

Extant Copies of Harriet Wilson's *Our Nig* (1859) without Ownership Markings

American Antiquarian Society
Atlanta University Research Center
Berea College
Boston Public Library
Boston University
Brown University
Columbia University
Donnelly College
Duke University
Fisk University
Free Library of Philadelphia
Grand Valley State University
New York Historical Society Library
Newberry Library
Northwestern University
Private Copy: Gates Copy B
Private Copy: Unnamed owner
Temple University
University of California at Santa Barbara
University of Chicago
University of Delaware
University of Illinois at Urbana Champaign
University of Iowa
University of Minnesota
University of North Carolina at Chapel Hill (missing)
University of Virginia
Virginia State Library (Library of Virginia)
Yale University Copy A
Yale University Copy B (in mylar encapsulation)

NOTES

The author wishes to thank Jodie Gardner, P. Gabrielle Foreman, Rhondda R. Thomas, and Nina Baym for discussing issues considered in this essay, as well as the Interlibrary Loan Department of Saginaw Valley State University's Library, Zelda Moore at the New Hampshire State Library, Nancy Iannucci at the Emma Willard School, and librarians and archivists at the libraries listed in the appendixes that own copies of the first edition of *Our Nig*.

1. Eric Gardner, "'This Attempt of Their Sister': Harriet Wilson's *Our Nig* from Printer to Readers," *New England Quarterly* 66.2 (1993): 226–46.

2. The single largest advance has been the development of WorldCat, which allows diverse and complex searches of an incredibly large group of libraries in ways simply not possible in 1993. The increase in individual libraries providing both online catalogs and online reference, as well as the massive developments in technologies for genealogists (especially fully searchable indexes to censuses), are also worth note. Undoubtedly, additional copies will surface—especially as Wilson's work becomes better known (through, for example, the efforts of the Harriet Wilson Project).

3. On this term, see especially Ellen Pratofiorito, "'To Demand Your Sympathy and Aid': *Our Nig* and the Problem of No Audience," *Journal of American and Comparative Cultures* 24.1 (2001): 31–48.

4. See especially P. Gabrielle Foreman and Reginald H. Pitts, apparatus to *Our Nig* by Harriet Wilson (New York: Penguin, 2005). For earlier work, see Henry Louis Gates, apparatus to *Our Nig* by Harriet Wilson (New York: Vintage, 1983); Gates, apparatus to *Our Nig* by Harriet Wilson (New York: Vintage, 2002); and Barbara A. White, "'Our Nig' and the She-Devil: New Information about Harriet Wilson and the 'Bellmont' Family," *American Literature* 65.1 (1993): 19–52. References to *Our Nig* use the Gates 2002 edition and are hereafter cited in text.

5. On domestic work and laundry specifically, see Tera Hunter, *To 'Joy My Freedom: Southern Black Women's Lives and Labors After the Civil War* (Cambridge: Harvard University Press, 1997). Though Hunter's text focuses on the postbellum years, it remains one of the best accounts of black women's domestic work. See also Susan Strasser, *Never Done: A History of American Housework* (New York: Henry Holt, 2000).

6. On the bottles, see Foreman and Pitts, apparatus to *Our Nig*, ix, xxx, xlviii, 101–102.

7. Harriet Wilson, *Our Nig*, eds. P. Gabrielle Foreman and Reginald H. Pitts (New York: Penguin, 2005), 72.

8. *Farmer's Cabinet*, February 29, 1860.

9. Indeed, the only other likely candidate in the entire region seems to be a Hannah E. Wilson, whose father was a "botanic druggist," but who lived in Boston and Chelsea, Massachusetts. Besides the fact that she was unmarried, there would be no reason for her to travel all the way to Manchester and then stamp that location

on bottles, given the number of glassworks closer to her and given her father's likely business connections with other area apothecaries and glassworks. On this Hannah Wilson, see 1860 Federal Census of Chelsea, Suffolk County, Massachusetts, 222.

10. Donald V. Fadely, "Mrs. Wilson's Hair Preparations," in *Hair-Raising Stories* (self published), 164, also cited in Foreman and Pitts. The first reference to the bottles in bottle collecting literature seems to be Richard E. Fike's brief description in *The Bottle Book* (Gibbs M. Smith, Inc., 1987), 126. Fike notes an ad for Wilson's bottled product in *Drugs, Chemicals, and Medicines* (Chicago: Van Schaack, 1871), n.p., which is also cited by Fadely, Foreman, and Pitts. The bottles are also noted in Bill Hunt's massive "Medicine Bottle Glass Index," available from the Midwest Archaeological Center online at <http://www.cr.nps.gov/mwac/bottle_glass/index.html>, and a selection of the most recent editions of the now famous *Kovell's* guides. One of the bottles, dated to "1840–1860" was sold as part of a lot in 2003 from the Norman C. Heckler and Company *Auction 60 Online Catalog*; see <http://www.hecklerauction.com>.

11. Ibid; see also Foreman and Pitts, apparatus to *Our Nig*, xlviii.

12. In addition to the sources mentioned above, other texts that are useful but that do not specifically note Wilson's bottles include: John P. Adams, *Bottle Collecting in New England* (Somersworth, N.H.: New Hampshire Publishing Company, 1969); Virginia T. Bates and Beverly Chamberlain, *Antique Bottle Finds in New England* (Peterborough, N.H., 1968); William C. Ketchum, Jr., *A Treasury of American Bottles* (Indianapolis: Bobbs-Merrill, 1975); Helen McKearin and Kenneth M. Wilson, *American Bottles and Their Ancestry* (New York: Crown, 1978); Mike Russell, *The Collector's Guide to Civil War Period Bottles and Jars* (self-published, 1992). On Henry Wilson, see, among other sources, the 1860 Federal Census of Manchester, New Hampshire, 655.

13. For context, see especially Kathy Peiss, *Hope in a Jar: The Making of America's Beauty Culture* (New York: Henry Holt, 1998). For Wilson's discussion of Frado's work, see *Our Nig*, 129–30.

14. Peiss, *Hope in a Jar*, 14 and 16.

15. See, for example, Erasmus Wilson, *Healthy Skin* (Philadelphia: Blanchard and Lea, 1854), and William Edward Coale, *Hints on Health* (Boston: Ticknor and Fields, 1867).

16. A. I. Matthews, *Hints on Various Subjects* (Buffalo: Thomas and Lathrops, 1856).

17. Stephen Foster, "Jeanie with the Light Brown Hair" (New York: Firth, Pond, and Co., 1854).

18. On the Sutherland sisters, see Clarence O. Lewis, *The Seven Sutherland Sisters* (Lockport, N.Y.: Niagara County Historical Society, 1965). More generally, see Peiss, *Hope in a Jar*.

19. Peter A. Browne, *The Classification of Mankind* (Philadelphia: A. Hart, 1850). Alexander Rowland, *The Human Hair, Popularly and Physiologically Considered*

(London: Piper, Brothers, and Co., 1853), with a section on the hair of "Africa — The Negro or Ethiopian Race," also saw circulation in the United States.

20. In addition to material in Peiss, *Hope in a Jar*, see Ayana D. Byrd and Lori L. Tharps, *Hair Story: Untangling the Roots of Black Hair in America* (New York: St. Martin's, 2001), and Noliwe M. Rooks, *Hair Raising: Beauty, Culture, and African American Women* (New Brunswick: Rutgers University Press, 1996). Shane White and Graham White's "Slave Hair and African American Culture in the Eighteenth and Nineteenth Century," *The Journal of Southern History* 61.1 (1995): 45–76, though it does not pertain directly to Wilson's circumstances, is also informative.

21. Foreman and Pitts, apparatus to *Our Nig*, 101–102, note both William H. Montague of Springfield, Massachusetts, and Phillip O. Ames of Nashua. Closer to Wilson's original home, we should also note Nashua's Zimri Johnson (1850 Federal Census of Nashua, New Hampshire, 259), as well as Manchester's George Bundy (who worked with another black barber, William Cole; 1850 Federal Census of Manchester, New Hampshire, 152–53) and John C. Dunlop (who worked with two other black barbers, Robert H. Gibson and Abraham Roper; 1850 Federal Census of Manchester, New Hampshire, 153). There is also, as per Barbara A. White's "Harriet Wilson's Mentors" (in this volume), the Walker family of Worcester.

22. See, generally, Byrd and Tharps, *Hair Story*, and Rooks, *Hair Raising*; for material specifically on the Remonds, see Dorothy Sterling, ed., *We Are Your Sisters: Black Women in the Nineteenth Century* (New York: W. W. Norton, 1984).

23. On Potter, see Eliza Potter, *A Hairdresser's Experience in High Life* (Cincinnati: For the Author, 1859; republished New York: Oxford University Press, 1988).

24. David Jaffee, "Peddlers of Progress and the Transformation of the Rural North, 1760–1860," *The Journal of American History*, 78.2 (1991): 511–35. On book peddlers specifically, see David Paul Nord's study of colporteurs, "Religious Reading and Readers in Antebellum America," *Journal of the Early Republic* 15.2 (1995): 241–272.

25. Peiss, *Hope in a Jar*, 21.

26. Jaffee, "Peddlers," 522.

27. See, generally, Peiss, *Hope in a Jar*.

28. In a broad sense, Jaffee, "Peddlers," 523, notes that "the relationship of peddlers with their suppliers ranged along a spectrum of increasing independence: the salaried employee, the commissioned agent, those who worked on credit (the clock peddler) or on their own account, and finally, the independent artisan who produced his or her own wares (the itinerant portrait maker." Distributive relationships probably ran a similar gamut.

29. Wilson, *Our Nig*, 129 and 137; Foreman and Pitts, apparatus to *Our Nig*, ix.

30. Generally on this, see Foreman and Pitts as well as White, "'Our Nig' and the She-Devil."

31. Generally on this, see Jaffee, "Peddlers." According to the Federal Census, the tiny Milford rose to a population of 2,159 by 1850 and 2,223 by 1860; Nashua, rid-

ing a manufacturing boom, went from a population of 5,820 in 1850 to 10,065 in 1860; industrial Manchester experienced similar growth.

32. Jaffee, "Peddlers," 522.

33. Ibid, 533, and, more generally, 531–35.

34. Material in this paragraph is drawn from "An Act in Relation to Hawkers and Peddlers," *Laws of the State of New Hampshire* (Concord, N.H.: John F. Brown, 1858), 1991–1992).

35. Gates, lxxix–lxxx, was the first to discuss this Harriet Wilson; see also the Boston Athenaeum's BOSBLACK database. I share Foreman and Pitts's sense that the author Harriet Wilson may be the woman listed as a white 28-year-old living in Manchester and working as a weaver in 1860; see 1860 Federal Census of Manchester, New Hampshire, 174.

36. Wilson, *Our Nig*, copyright page, and copyright form filed at the District Office.

37. Under various names, Rand printed not only the first edition of *Uncle Tom's Cabin* (for publisher John P. Jewett), but also material for, for example, the American Tract Society, the Massachusetts Sunday School Union, and the Tremont Street Baptist Church.

38. Rand's ties to abolitionism supposedly began with his setting into type a placard that led to the mob action against the Boston Female Anti-Slavery Society in 1835. He was later a friend to the Garrison family. See Gardner, "'This Attempt,'" 228–30.

39. Foreman and Pitts, apparatus to *Our Nig*, 80–81; Ann Braude, *Radical Spirits: Spiritualism and Women's Rights in Nineteenth Century America* (Bloomington: Indiana University Press, 2001), 73.

40. Much improved search capabilities through sources like WorldCat allow us to understand that Rand worked under a variety of firm names — "George C. Rand and Avery," "Geo. C. Rand and Avery," "Rand and Avery," etc. — during this period. Through conducting a wide array of such searches, I have determined that Rand and Avery dealt with at least 100 book projects in 1859 alone.

41. Gardner, "'This Attempt,'" 229.

42. Theodore Parker, *Theodore Parker's Experience as a Minister* (Boston: R. Leighton, Jr., 1859). Thayer and Eldridge took not only the radical *Song of Myself* for its 1860 edition (which Rand printed), but had also agreed to publish Harriet Jacobs's *Incidents in the Life of a Slave Girl* before bankruptcy prevented them from doing so. On the connection to Jacobs, see Jean Fagan Yellin, *Harriet Jacobs: A Life* (New York: Basic Civitas, 2004), 140–43.

43. See Foreman and Pitts for a useful synthesis of critical opinion on this issue. Texts like Caroline Lee Hentz's *The Planter's Northern Bride* (Philadelphia: A. Hart, 1854) devoted significant energy to discussing the suffering of Northern free blacks — though in racist terms designed to argue for slavery and against Northern texts like *Uncle Tom's Cabin*.

44. An examination of most bibliographies and collections of slave narratives —

including the massive *Documenting the American South* website — confirms this. On Douglass vis-à-vis the leaders of the Garrisonian wing of abolitionists, see, for example, Henry Mayer, *All on Fire* (New York: St. Martin's Griffin, 1998), and William McFeely, *Frederick Douglass* (New York: W. W. Norton, 1991), especially 91–200.

45. On Jacobs, see Yellin, *Harriet Jacobs*, 117–53.

46. Susan Paul, *Memoir of James Jackson* (Boston: James Loring, 1835; republished with an introduction by Lois Brown (Cambridge: Harvard University Press, 2000).

47. See Gardner, "'This Attempt,'" 231–32.

48. This speculation is based in part on Foreman and Pitts's claim that Wilson might have met African American lecturer Thomas H. Jones in 1850. Jones initially published his narrative in 1854, lectured actively, and began to advocate for a new edition of his narrative, which was eventually published in 1862, with a third edition in 1865. Douglass's similarly enlarged autobiography was published in 1855.

49. Foreman and Pitts summarize this search, which began as part of Gates's original search for information on the novel. Gates, *Figures in Black* (New York: Oxford University Press, 1987), 142–43, speculates that Lydia Maria Child knew of the book and notes a July 9, 1878, letter.

50. Wilson, *Our Nig*, preface; among the large amount of material on Boston's black community, see James Horton and Lois Horton, *Black Bostonians* (New York: Holmes and Meier, 1979). Foreman and Pitts summarize such speculation.

51. On the Lovejoy family, see 1860 Federal Census of Nashua, New Hampshire, 213; 1870 Federal Census of Nashua, New Hampshire, 174; 1880 Federal Census of Nashua, New Hampshire, 542c; George C. Ramsdell, *History of Milford, New Hampshire* (Concord, N.H.: Rumford Press, 1901), 828. On the Tinker family, see 1860 Federal Census of Bedford, New Hampshire, 34; 1870 Federal Census of Bedford, New Hampshire, 38; 1880 Federal Census of Bedford, New Hampshire, 506. On the Sawyer family, see 1850 Federal Census of Nashua, New Hampshire, 249–50; 1860 Federal Census of Nashua, New Hampshire, 102; 1870 Federal Census of Nashua, New Hampshire, 123; 1880 Federal Census of Nashua, New Hampshire, 528B; 1900 Federal Census of Nashua, New Hampshire, 14A. On the Whitcomb family, see 1860 Federal Census of Hampton, New Hampshire, 38; 1870 Federal Census of North Reading, Massachusetts, 249. On the Tompkins family, see 1850 Federal Census of Troy, New York, 185–86; 1860 Federal Census of Troy, New York, 139; 1870 Federal Census of Troy, New York, 198; 1880 Federal Census of Oakland, California, 182c. On the Colburn family, see 1850 Federal Census of Nashua, New Hampshire, 451; 1860 Federal Census of Nashua, New Hampshire, 24; 1870 Federal Census of Nashua, New Hampshire, 85; 1880 Federal Census of Nashua, New Hampshire, 413c; 1900 Federal Census of Concord, New Hampshire, 18A; 1910 Federal Census of Concord, New Hampshire, 84B; 1920 Federal Census of Concord, New Hampshire, 13A. On the Moar/Moore family, see 1900 Federal Census of Nashua, New Hampshire, 23A; 1880 Federal Census of Nashua, New Hampshire, 426D; 1870 Federal Census of Peterborough, New Hampshire, 265. I have been unable to locate fur-

ther information on either Asthes E. Gay or Abby Reed. On Stiles, see 1860 Federal Census of Brookline, New Hampshire, 259; E. E. Parker, *History of Brookline* (Gardner, Mass.: Meals Printing, 1914), *passim*. On Sargent, who was twenty-five when the book was published, see 1850 Federal Census of Gloucester, Massachusetts, 125; 1860 Federal Census of Gloucester, Massachusetts, 527; 1870 Federal Census of Gloucester, Massachusetts, 465; 1880 Federal Census of Gloucester, Massachusetts, 537B. I have been unable to trace biographical information on owners M. W. Chandler (or the Mrs. C. B. Blake who gave a copy to him/her), Edith M. D'Orecy (or the R. S. M——— who gave a copy to her), and M. D. Gilman. For a full listing of extant copies of *Our Nig* with their owners, see the appendix to this chapter.

52. In addition to sources listed in note 51, see, for material on Sarah Tompkins's sister Miranda Tompkins Widmer (who purchased the book), 1860 Federal Census of Concord, New Hampshire, 193; 1870 Federal Census of Concord, New Hampshire, 451; 1880 Federal Census of Concord, New Hampshire, 121A. Also see Mrs. A. W. Fairbanks, ed., *Emma Willard and Her Pupils, or 50 Years of the Troy Female Seminary* (New York: Mrs. Russell Sage, 1898), 402; *Catalogue of the Officers and Pupils of the Troy Female Seminary for the Academic Year Commencing September 17, 1846, and ending August 5, 1847* (Troy: Prescott and Wilson, 1847), 13.

53. See 1930 Federal Census of Nashua, New Hampshire, 1A, as well as Nashua city directories throughout the early twentieth century.

54. On Widmer, in addition to material in note 52, see *History of Merrimack County, New Hampshire* (Philadelphia: J. W. Lewis, 1883), 78. On Stiles, see material cited in note 51.

55. In addition to material in note 51, see 1900 Federal Census of Bedford, New Hampshire, 7B; 1910 Federal Census of Bedford, New Hampshire, 45B; 1920 Federal Census of Bedford, New Hampshire, 3A–3B; 1930 Federal Census of Bedford, New Hampshire, 12B; and the marriage record (October 30, 1877) listed in *History of Bedford, New Hampshire* (Concord, N.H.: Rumford Printing, 1903). Ella's given name seems to have been Mary Ella Gale.

56. *Nashua Business Directory for 1895*, 305.

57. 1860 Federal Census of Boston, Massachusetts, 188; 1870 Federal Census of Boston, Massachusetts, 407.

58. Material in this paragraph and the three preceding paragraphs comes from sources listed in notes 51, 52, 54, and 55, as well as 1850 Federal Census of Danbury, New Hampshire, 186; 1860 Federal Census of Danbury, New Hampshire, 20; 1870 Federal Census of Danbury, 343; John M. Holmes, "Hampton's 'Hotel Whittier,'" available online at <http://www.hampton.lib.nh.us>.

59. A perusal of indexes of texts like Ramsdell's *History of Milford* yields several such references.

60. On the Hutchinsons related to the "She-Devil," see Perley Derby, *The Hutchinson Family; Or, the Descendants of Barnard Hutchinson* (Salem, Mass.: Essex Institute Press, 1870). This text does not list Hattie L. Seaver's parents, grandparents, or great-grandparents.

61. See 1860 Federal Census of Nashua, New Hampshire, 213; 1870 Federal Census of Cambridge, Massachusetts, 604; 1880 Federal Census of Salem, Massachusetts, 605D. The Hayward ancestry is more difficult to trace, especially given John/Ariel Hayward's name change. I have not been able to determine his parentage, and he, his wife, and his children are all absent from genealogies that discuss the Nehemiah Hayward family. See, for example, Matthew A. Stickney, *The Stickney Family* (Salem, Mass.: Essex Institute Press, 1869).

62. Additionally, Jaffee, "Peddlers," cites farmers' wives as key customers of peddlers.

63. See, for example, Deborah C. De Rosa, *Domestic Abolitionists and Juvenile Literature, 1830–1865* (Albany: SUNY Press, 2003). Beyond the texts discussed in De Rosa, one thinks especially of the protagonists of Maria Susanna Cummins's *The Lamplighter* and Susan Warner's *The Wide, Wide World*.

64. Wilson, *Our Nig*, 129, notes such fears.

65. On these issues, see De Rosa, *Domestic Abolitionists*.

66. I have located over fifty books for children published or printed by various incarnations of Rand and Avery in the 1850s, including works by Jacob Abbott, Walter Aimwell, R. M. Ballantyne, "Cousin Mary," Eliza Follen, Josephine Franklin, Charlotte M. Higgins, Laura Winthrop Johnson, Harvey Newcomb, and Daniel Wise, among others.

67. See *Catalogue of the Troy Female Seminary*, 17–19, for discussion of curriculum and moral philosophy.

68. See note 51 and Appendix A.

69. *Farmer's Cabinet*, February 29, 1860; Gates, apparatus to *Our Nig*, lxxxi–lxxxii.

70. See Foreman and Pitts, apparatus to *Our Nig*, xi–xii and xl–xlii, as well as Foreman's forthcoming work on *Our Nig*.

Harriet Wilson's Mentors
The Walkers of Worcester

Barbara A. White

IN THE NEXT-TO-THE-LAST chapter of *Our Nig*, Harriet Wilson recounts the struggles of her heroine to support herself after leaving service with the Milford, New Hampshire, family to whom she was indentured. For a time Frado sews and does housework, but her health has been broken by years of mistreatment. She succumbs to "three years of weary sickness" until she feels strong enough "to take care of herself, to cast off the unpleasant charities of the public."[1] Frado hears that in some Massachusetts towns, girls earn a living by making straw hats. "But how should *she*, black, feeble and poor, find any one to teach her. But God prepares the way, when human agencies see no path" (124). In Massachusetts she "found a plain, poor, simple woman, who could see merit beneath a dark skin; and when the invalid mulatto told her sorrows, she opened her door and her heart, and took the stranger in" (124). Frado becomes an expert straw sewer and lives contentedly in her new home until the last chapter of the book when she meets a professed fugitive from slavery and leaves to marry him.

The reader learns more about the plain woman who taught straw sewing in the first and longest appendix to *Our Nig*, by "Allida." Allida writes that the author of the book was brought by an "itinerant colored lecturer" to the "ancient town" of W———, Massachusetts. "Here she was introduced to the family of Mrs. Walker, who kindly consented to receive her as an inmate of her household, and immediately succeeded in procuring work for her as a 'straw sewer'" (133). Harriet quickly acquired the art of making straw bonnets but was still subject to bouts of illness. Mrs. Walker thus gave her a room adjoining her own and cared for her. Harriet told Allida that she had lacked a mother since her own mother abandoned her in Milford; now with Mrs. Walker she had "at last found a *home*, — and not only a home, but a *mother*" (133).

It has been suggested that "Allida" might be Harriet Wilson herself, who wrote her own appendixes — that is to say, the appendixes may not be the straightforward testimonials they seem.[2] It is certainly possible that Harriet masqueraded as Allida, but in either case "Mrs. Walker" was most likely a real person of that name. Wilson did not have the same motivation to change this name as she did with the names in the narrative itself. In 1859, when she published *Our Nig*, Wilson had to worry about the reactions of two members of the family who abused her — her "she-devil" mistress's daughter Betsy, who still lived in Milford, and her son Jonas, who had become rich and powerful. Mrs. Walker, on the other hand, was presented in a positive light in *Our Nig* and posed no threat to Wilson. Wilson tended to be truthful in her narrative whenever there was no substantial reason for disguise. As I noted in my 1993 article, it was by assuming her truthfulness, in this case that the "she-devil"'s brother was a doctor, that I discovered the family's identity as the Nehemiah Hayward family of Milford, New Hampshire.[3]

But granted that "Mrs. Walker" was real, why (beyond our obvious desire to document Wilson's life as fully as possible) is it important to know more about her? The reason, I think, is that Mrs. Walker is key to answering the question readers most frequently ask about Wilson's novel: How did Harriet Wilson attain the educational level to write a narrative as sophisticated as *Our Nig*? Native ability would account for Wilson's highly developed irony and sense of humor, but what about the epigraphs she uses and her wide range of citation? In *Our Nig* Frado receives "three months of schooling, summer and winter," for three years (37). She learns to read and spell, mastering the "elementary steps in grammar, arithmetic, and writing" (41). The "she-devil" then pronounces Frado's education complete, and any further learning is purely informal. Frado loves reading the Bible and strives to "enrich her mind" with "school-books," keeping "her book always fastened open near her, where she could glance from toil to soul refreshment" (115).

This desultory self-education is all for Frado until she meets Mrs. Walker. Mrs. Walker proves to be more than an expert straw sewer who can teach a practical skill. She is also a literate woman who greatly values reading and writing. Wilson says that she

> sought also to teach her the value of useful books; and while one read aloud to the other of deeds historic and names renowned, Frado experienced a new impulse. She felt herself capable of elevation; she felt that this book information supplied an undefined dissatisfaction she had long felt, but could not express. (124)

Under the mentorship of Mrs. Walker, Frado applied every leisure moment to "self-improvement" until she left W——— (124–25). Mrs. Walker's parting gift (according to Allida in the first appendix) was a symbolic one — a "porta-ble inkstand, pens and paper" (134). No wonder that, when Wilson needed a new way of supporting herself and son, she turned to writing a book. Who was this "Mrs. Walker" who taught Harriet Wilson her most important lesson — that she was "capable of elevation"? Identifying Mrs. Walker means identi-fying W———, Massachusetts, and since Henry Louis Gates, Jr., brought out the second edition of *Our Nig* in 1983, there have been attempts to do so. Gates himself noted three Massachusetts towns known for their straw goods: Walpole, Ware, and Westborough. He concluded that "Harriet most proba-bly lived in the section of Massachusetts that includes Ware and Walpole, as well as Worcester, which is approximately fifteen miles from Westborough" (xxi). All these towns are directly south of Milford, New Hampshire, where Harriet grew up. In their recent edition of *Our Nig,* P. Gabrielle Foreman and Reginald H. Pitts, who did excellent work in discovering Wilson's where-abouts after she published *Our Nig,* select Ware as "probably the 'W———' that Wilson identifies as her place of refuge."[4] They go on to say that "R. J. Ellis suggests Worcester as the 'W———'; but in the 1860s Worcester was a vibrant city with several thousand people," while Ware was merely a village.[5] Foreman and Pitts note further that there is a Mary Walker (white) in the 1850 Ware census enumerations and a Lewis Marsh teaching school there (in *Our Nig* Frado has a teacher named Miss Marsh).

There are Walkers everywhere, however, just as there are Wilsons, and the names used in *Our Nig* are too common to be restricted to one town. I was the person who suggested Worcester as "W———" to R. J. Ellis when he in-terviewed me for his book.[6] The reason is a letter received by Professor Gates from a Walker descendant.[7] The descendant recalled spending summers of her youth in her grandmother's house in Roxbury, Massachusetts. When she came across a manuscript of *Our Nig,* she was told that an ancestor, "Mother Walker," had once aided the author and provided housing with her family in Worcester, Massachusetts. It is true that Worcester was larger than we might expect from Wilson's references to a "town" and "villagers" (124–25); perhaps she meant "town" in the legal sense. In 1850 (Wilson would have been there some time between June 1850 and October 1851) the population of Worces-ter was about 17,000. The main occupation of the residents had just ceased to be farming and was now manufacturing. There were boot and shoe factories; other workers made agricultural implements. Irish immigration had swelled the population since the last census, and one of every eight Worcester resi-dents had been born in Ireland. Interestingly, though, when the famous Brit-ish writer Charles Dickens visited Worcester in 1842, he described it more as Harriet Wilson did; he called Worcester "a pretty New England town . . .

where all the buildings looked as if they had been built and painted that morning, and could be taken down on Monday with very little trouble."[8]

Whether viewed as vibrant city or pretty town, Worcester was a center for the making of straw hats. Women braided straw in Worcester county starting in about 1820. A decade later they added palm leaf hats to their repertoire but also kept on with straw. The manufacture of straw hats continued until 1870, when machines took over.[9] Worcester also had another characteristic necessary to be Wilson's W———, Massachusetts: it was a likely destination for an "itinerant colored lecturer." Worcester had been an abolitionist stronghold since way back in the eighteenth century; as early as 1767 the town had instructed its representative to the General Court to obtain a law against slavery. In 1781 slavery was officially abolished in Massachusetts because of a suit involving Quok Walker, a former slave from nearby Barre. Walker (probably no relation to the later "Mother Walker") claimed he was free under the new state constitution and prevailed in court. By the 1830s there were two anti-slavery societies in Worcester County and from 1840 to 1860 nearly two hundred subscriptions to William Lloyd Garrison's radical anti-slavery journal the *Liberator*. Garrison was a regular speaker in Worcester, along with black lecturers Frederick Douglass, Charles Remond, and William Wells Brown.[10] These "itinerant colored lecturers" were often joined by the abolitionist Hutchinson Family Singers, the singing group who were blood relatives of Harriet Wilson's former employer and tormenter in New Hampshire.

In the 1850 Worcester census enumerations there is only one appropriate black Walker family, and that is headed by Gilbert Walker. He is a black male barber, thirty-three years old, who was born in Maryland. He lived at the time on Arch St. in Ward 2 with his wife Sarah, age thirty-one, and daughter Sarah Ellen, age five. At first glance Sarah would seem to be "Mother Walker" at a young age, but other information about the Walkers reveals that Sarah Ellen was adopted. A more likely "Mother Walker" is Gilbert's mother Ann Mattie Walker (1793–1873), who would have been fifty-eight when Harriet Wilson lived in Worcester. Ann Walker does not appear in Worcester records until 1858 when the business directory lists her as a laundress; in the 1860 census she is living with her son and his family.

Allida's appendix to *Our Nig* says that the author of the narrative was brought to W———, Massachusetts, and there "she was introduced to the family of Mrs. Walker" (133). The wording is a bit odd here — "the family of Mrs. Walker" rather than just "Mrs. Walker." Perhaps Ann Walker did not reside full time with the family in 1851. She may have had "her own chamber" (133) there and placed Harriet next door yet traveled in Massachusetts and southern New Hampshire. She does not appear in censuses of either state before 1860; in 1854 an Ann M. Walker is listed in the Boston directory. If Mrs. Walker moved around as a seamstress, laundress, and seller of hair products, she would have acted as a mentor to Harriet Wilson in more than one respect. That is to say, she not only introduced Harriet to the life of the mind but also provided a model for earning a living. According to Foreman and Pitts, in the twelve-year period before and after she wrote *Our Nig* (1855–1867) Harriet Wilson worked as an itinerant seamstress, house servant, and vendor of hair products.

There is no direct evidence that Ann Walker sold hair products, but it seems reasonable to assume that Harriet received her recipe for restoring gray hair from the Walkers. Foreman and Pitts note that Wilson's formula "could have been provided by an African-American barber in a town she may have visited — William H. Montague of Springfield, Massachusetts, or Phillip O. Ames of Nashua, for example."[11] But, of course, Harriet visited Worcester, and by 1850 Gilbert Walker was a barber. He had moved to Worcester from New York state in 1841, aged twenty-four, for his wife Sarah hailed from Grafton, a town bordering Worcester. At first the young couple lived "at service" in the family of (white) William Bickford, a "prosperous merchant."[12] Apparently Gilbert performed odd jobs for a few years — he was a coachman, kept a candy store on Main St., and helped Bickford build looms. By the time of the 1850 census the Walkers lived on their own and Gilbert opened shop as a barber; in 1851 he had his own listing in the business directory with separate work and home addresses.

The Walkers' history was this: Ann Mattie, born into slavery in Maryland, married Luke Walker. She and her husband were slaves in Caroline county, an agricultural region on the Eastern shore. The Walkers had fourteen children, six of them, including Gilbert, born into slavery; there were nine boys and five girls. Apparently Luke saved his "young owner," one Fred Pernell, from drowning and was thereby freed. Afterward he succeeded in purchasing the freedom of his family for $1,050. The Walkers came north to Pennsylvania and then New York, where Gilbert met Sarah and moved to Worcester. At some point his mother and at least two of his brothers, Thomas and Allen, followed him. The Worcester encountered by the Walkers was a bastion of abolitionism — there were abolitionist lectures by well-known people every week. But in spite of its anti-slavery past and current activism, the city was overwhelmingly white. In 1850 blacks constituted about 1 percent of the population of Worcester.[13] Harriet Wilson was correct when she said of W——— that "people of color were rare there" (126).

But in spite of the heavy white majority the Walkers moved to a city that had a viable black community — or perhaps it is more accurate to say that the

Walkers helped create one, for it was in the 1840s, as black families like the Walkers migrated from the mid-Atlantic states, that race conditions improved in Worcester. In 1840 railroad cars to Worcester were integrated; in 1846 the high school was integrated (after almost twenty years of separate schools for black children).[14] Most important, although some blacks attended other churches, the African Methodist Episcopal Zion church was established. It began house to house in 1846–47; then until 1848 services were held in the basement of Henry Willard's on Summer St. (two blocks from the Walkers on Arch). The Walkers were active in the AME Zion church, and Josephine Willard is a prime candidate for Harriet Wilson's Worcester friend "Aunt J." In 1848 the congregation began to use a small chapel on Exchange St. (four blocks from Arch) and from that year on had regular pastors.[15] Gilbert Walker's obituary notes that the church "owes its possession of its house of worship on Exchange street to his personal efforts in raising funds to keep it from being sold at one time in its history."[16] As there were not yet "black neighborhoods" (the Walkers' neighbors were all white, and only one other black family lived in their ward), the AME Zion church was a unifying factor. It also sponsored charitable organizations and the first black political group in Worcester, the Anti-Slavery and Temperance Society of Colored Citizens. This organization raised money to help fugitives and attended meetings and demonstrations in Worcester and Boston.[17]

But if there was community support for blacks in Worcester, support that was notably lacking in Harriet Wilson's hometown, it was always difficult to survive economically. Geographic mobility studies of Worcester show that about two-thirds of the male residents aged sixteen and over on the 1850 census do not appear ten years later. Between 1850 and 1860 as many as 100,000 people moved in and out of the city, even though the total population never went above 25,000. People "moved because they had to—because they were pushed out by insecure employment."[18] Even after her son Gilbert became an economic success, Ann Mattie Walker's other son, Allen, left Worcester for New York for long periods. There was so much need for charity that the town's two most famous ministers (and literary men), Edward Everett Hale and Thomas Wentworth Higginson, planned an "Unfortunates' Magazine" which would "print as contributions all the letters received by the two pastors asking their aid."[19] Certainly in 1850–51 when Harriet Wilson was in town Mrs. Walker qualified as "poor" (124), along with her son Gilbert who was beginning his barbering business. Whether he received his knowledge of hair and hair products from his mother, or learned it elsewhere, Gilbert made a tremendous success of his business.

From 1850 to 1855 he kept shop at various places on Main St., including the

Bay State House, Worcester, Massachusetts (c. 1860), where Gilbert Walker had his shop. *From the collections of WORCESTER HISTORICAL MUSEUM, Worcester, Mass.*

spot opposite the courthouse where he had once opened a candy store. In 1856 he moved to a more prestigious address under the Bay State House, a new five-story hotel. The Bay State House, which advertised its name with gilt letters across its granite front, would soon become known as "one of the finest hotels in the country."[20] The hotel had a prime location at the corner of Main and Exchange streets, a central intersection, and it boasted the latest in elegant furnishings and conveniences; among its "modern improvements" was a new contraption called an elevator.[21] Gilbert Walker prospered at the Bay State House. His success is symbolized in the advertisements he placed in the Worcester directory. The year after he moved to the new hotel his name appears in capital letters; by 1860 he is no longer just a barber but a "Fashionable Hair Dresser, and Wig Maker." There was now a separate ladies' entrance to the shop and would soon be a separate head of the Ladies Department. The 1860 ad says "Particular attention paid to Cutting Ladies', Misses and Children's Hair." In the late 1860s Gilbert added the title "Prof." to his name, and it would appear in all subsequent ads. In the early 1870s the advertisements became fancier yet again and also promoted "Walker's Detergent for Removing Dandruff."[22]

   As Gilbert became successful in the 1850s and '60s, he acquired real estate.

In 1855 he bought his house on Liberty St., a block from Arch, and after that continued to add parcels of land. In 1860 a full 82 percent of Worcester's residents possessed no real property at all, so Gilbert was unusual.[23] The Walker entries in the 1860 and 1870 census show his rise in status. In 1850 there was no figure entered in the columns provided for a head of household's real estate worth or personal savings. But in 1860 he has $1,800 in real estate and $1,000 in personal savings; in 1870 these amounts have jumped to $10,000 real estate and $2,500 personal. The Walker family was no longer poor.

Taking into account the small black population of Worcester, Gilbert's clientele must have been predominantly white. Certainly he sought to please his customers, and certainly (as all the information about him shows) he had an outgoing, if not positively exuberant, personality. But did he achieve his success by "kowtowing" to white people? That "Prof." is a troubling addition to his name because it recalls the honorifics like "aunt" and "uncle" that whites often bestowed on blacks in place of "sir" or "madam." Gilbert may have been "Prof." because he couldn't be "Mr." Yet, however he may have acted to promote his business, Gilbert Walker was no buffoon, and he never kept quiet about his radical anti-slavery politics. In 1859 he was chair of a committee of the Anti-Slavery and Temperance Society of Colored Citizens. After white abolitionist John Brown and his interracial band of fighters were hanged for their attack on Harper's Ferry, the committee presented a series of resolutions praising Brown. They resolved that John Brown had been one of the "noblest defenders" of the cause of freedom and that "the colored citizens of Worcester" should raise funds for the bereaved families of Brown and his fellow martyrs. After Walker's resolutions were adopted, his good friend William Brown, an African American who came to Worcester in the 1840s and became a successful upholsterer, added another. Lest people not realize that John Brown's followers included black men, he resolved that "we tender our deepest sympathy to the relatives and friends of those colored patriots who so nobly sacrificed their lives."[24]

Once the Civil War started, Gilbert Walker supported enlisting black men to fight for the North. At age forty-five he was too old to go himself, but when news came in 1862 that the Rhode Island militia would accept blacks he stepped in as a recruiter. The Worcester *Daily Spy* announced that "Prof. Gilbert Walker at the hair dressing rooms corner of Main and Exchange streets, has authority in the matter and has already enlisted 17 men." He and another barber encouraged departing soldiers to call at their shops and "get trimmed up, without charge, before leaving."[25] But again the War Department rejected the use of black troops, and it was not until 1863 that Massachusetts governor John Andrew received permission to raise a black regiment. At that point

Gilbert Walker and William Brown became "important recruiters of black troops."[26]

Apparently Gilbert's role as recruiter was controversial in Worcester and led to his being assaulted in the street. In his book on Amos Webber, an African American diarist who became Walker's neighbor and friend after the war, Nick Salvatore argues that it was probably Gilbert's recruiting that led to the assault.[27] The timing is certainly suggestive. The *Daily Spy* reported on February 19, 1863, that two men were fined in police court for assault and battery on Gilbert Walker, Mrs. Walker, one "C. Mellen," and Gilbert's brother Allen. Some of the men Gilbert Walker and William Brown recruited ended up in the 54th Massachusetts Infantry, where they had to struggle for the regular soldier's pay of $13 a month (Washington in its wisdom fixed the pay for black soldiers at $10). The Massachusetts legislature passed a law providing that the difference of $3 would be made up by the state, but as Brown's wife's cousin, John H. Johnson wrote her, the men refused to accept the state supplement and demanded equal pay from the federal government. Johnson, who frequently asked to be remembered to "Mr. Walker's family," came to a sad end—he was accidentally shot by one of his own men while on picket duty at Morris Island, South Carolina.[28]

After the war was over, Worcester held a huge celebratory parade that was two and a half miles long and took almost an hour to pass a given point. The trades were represented in one section with floats drawn by teams of horses. Gilbert Walker's float merited a full paragraph description in the newspaper:

> Prof. Gilbert Walker came out in style, his commodious hair dressing rooms under the Bay State House being the only one represented in the line. His team was new and well decorated. . . . In the wagon the professor was seen employed cutting a little misses [*sic*] hair, while an assistant was doing the same good office for a gentleman, and a lady assistant was manufacturing wigs. They attracted universal attention.

Perhaps the most interesting part of the float for us today was the bold banner that appeared above it: "The black man has shed his blood for the Union; he claims equal rights before the law."[29] The professor did not mince words.

The year 1865 and the decade after were probably the zenith of Gilbert Walker's career, as these years were also for black men's status nationally. It was 1870 when Gilbert reported an impressive $10,000 in real estate and $2,500 personal wealth. In 1873 Ann Walker died of "bilious fever" at age seventy-nine. She had been able to experience what few black women of the time got to enjoy—retirement. When she befriended Harriet Wilson in 1850, she was a "plain, poor, simple woman," probably an itinerant saleswoman, of fifty-eight

(124). At age sixty-seven she was a laundress, but at sixty-eight she disappears from the Worcester business directory. In the 1860 and subsequent censuses she is listed as living with Gilbert and as being a widow with "no occupation." Most likely, she continued to sell hair products on occasion. It could be a coincidence that the year following Ann's death (1874) is the first year Gilbert advertised "Walker's detergent" in the Worcester business directory. Or, more probably, it was not a coincidence and Gilbert took over one of his mother's formulas that she had previously sold. In 1879, a few years after Ann Walker's death, Sarah B. Walker, Gilbert's wife, also died. I have not been able to find an obituary for either woman. Typically, women are much harder to trace than men in the nineteenth century, as men were allowed to live a more public life — men owned and sold property, appeared in the newspaper, spoke at public meetings, received newspaper obituaries, and so on.

Although we know much more about Gilbert than we do about the female Walkers, it would seem that the women provided the ballast in Gilbert's life. When he lost them, he lost the successes he had accumulated over the years. His newspaper obituary tells the story, making it into a moral homily. Walker's business was flourishing, the obituary states.

> But, like many other men, he could not stand prosperity in his legitimate business, in which he was perfectly at home and able to manage, but engaged in outside affairs, and among other things attempted to breed horses. The result was disastrous to his finances, and he never recovered from the losses he then sustained. In recent years Mr. Walker frequently changed the location of his barber shop, and finally gave up the business. . . .[30]

The timing suggests that it was actually his mother's death that led Gilbert to this belated sowing of his wild oats. She died in 1873, he left the Bay State House in 1876, and he mortgaged his properties in 1877; Sarah Walker did not die until 1879. Gilbert Walker's descent, much like his rise, can be traced through the Worcester business directories. After 1876, his last year at the Bay State House, he dropped to "hairdresser" at various locations. Ultimately, in the mid-eighties, he became a mere "barber," working occasionally at other people's shops. Having sold his house and properties, he boarded elsewhere.

Gilbert Walker lost his health along with his wealth and spent a portion of his last years in City Hospital suffering from "chronic gastritis." He died in 1890 at the age of seventy-two. His obituary tells us that he returned to an old stand-by before his death. He "finally gave up the [barbering] business and peddled a detergent for the hair, which he made from an original recipe."[31] Thus, Gilbert came full circle — from the dizzying heights of business success and land ownership at the time of the 1870 census back to being a peddler like his mother; he must have been thankful for the reliable "original recipe" that was no doubt hers. Her mentorship gave her son something comfortable to depend on in his old age.

By the time of Gilbert's death, Harriet Wilson, whom he and his mother once housed in Worcester, had undergone a status change of her own. She found success as a medium and trance speaker in Boston. She was now known as "Dr. Hattie Wilson" and felt no need of selling hair tonic. Harriet seems to have traced a circle of her own. According to the research of Foreman and Pitts, she ended up in the loving family of a Silas and Catherine Cobb, where she perhaps acted as nurse to Silas. He died in 1900 and Wilson herself soon followed.[32] She had similarly fallen ill after her indenture while working for various families in Milford — and then again while living with the Walkers in Worcester. Ann Mattie Walker had nursed her back to health. Mrs. Walker not only guided her son Gilbert, before and after her death; she also bestowed on Harriet her very best "original recipe," the confidence to move forward with something new. She taught the young Harriet Wilson, yet to write *Our Nig* and become a successful Spiritualist, that she was a person fully "capable of elevation" (124).

NOTES

1. Harriet E. Wilson, *Our Nig; or, Sketches from the Life of a Free Black*, ed. Henry Louis Gates, Jr. (New York: Vintage Books, 2002), 122, 124. Further references are noted in the text.

2. Elizabeth Breau, "Identifying Satire: *Our Nig*," *Callaloo* (Spring 1993): 458–59.

3. See Barbara A. White, "'Our Nig' and the She-Devil: New Information about Harriet Wilson and the 'Bellmont' Family," *American Literature* 65 (March 1993): 19–52. Reprinted in Harriet E. Wilson, *Our Nig; or, Sketches from the Life of a Free Black*, ed. Henry Louis Gates, Jr., iii–liv.

4. Harriet E. Wilson, *Our Nig; or, Sketches from the Life of a Free Black*, ed. P. Gabrielle Foreman and Reginald H. Pitts (New York: Penguin Books, 2005), xiv.

5. Ibid.

6. R. J. Ellis, *Harriet Wilson's 'Our Nig': A Cultural Biography of a 'Two-Story' African American Novel* (Amsterdam: Rodopi Press, 2003), 28.

7. E. M. Clare to Professor Henry Louis Gates, September 9, 1994.

8. Quoted in U. Waldo Cutler, *Jottings from Worcester's History* (Worcester: Worcester Historical Society, 1932), 90.

9. John Nelson, *Worcester County: A Narrative History* (New York: American Historical Society, 1934), v. 2, 414.

10. James Eugene Moody, "Antislavery in Worcester County, Massachusetts: A Case Study" (Ph.D. diss., Clark University, 1971), 77. According to John L. Brooke, "Worcester County's central corridor would develop into one of the most militant Free Soil-Republican regions in the entire North"—*The Heart of the Commonwealth: Society and Political Culture in Worcester County, Massachusetts, 1713–1861* (Cambridge: Cambridge University Press, 1989), 368.

Frederick Douglass (1817?–1895) could have been the "itinerant colored lecturer" who brought Harriet Wilson to Worcester. He visited her hometown of Milford, New Hampshire, frequently and also spent considerable time in Worcester. Douglass spoke in Worcester City Hall in October 1850. The lecturer could also have been Thomas H. Jones (1806–c. 1865), as suggested by Foreman and Pitts (xv). Jones was a fugitive slave from North Carolina who lived in Worcester before he fled to Canada in May 1851 (in the wake of the Fugitive Slave Law).

11. Foreman and Pitts, 101–02.

12. *The Worcester Almanac, Directory, and Business Advertiser, for 1850* (Worcester: H. J. Howland, 1850), 133.

13. By my hand count. A news article is consistent, saying there were 184 blacks living in Worcester in 1850 (the total population was 17,049)—"Black History: A Central Massachusetts Sampling," Worcester *Sunday Telegram*, February 9, 1997, A18. The same percentage held true in 1860 and 1870.

14. Moody, 77; "Desegregation of Worcester's High School Wins by Narrow Vote," clipping file on "Blacks," Worcester Historical Museum. For more information on school segregation/desegregation, see *Worcester Town Records, 1817–1832*, ed. Franklin P. Rice, 342; Art Simas, "A Rich Heritage: Worcester Area Was Leader in Move to Abolish Slavery," Worcester *Telegram and Gazette*, n.d., clipping file on "Blacks," Worcester Historical Museum; and Tilden G. Edelstein, *Strange Enthusiasm: A Life of Thomas Wentworth Higginson* (New Haven: Yale University Press, 1968), 176.

15. See *The Fiftieth Anniversary of the A. M. E. Z[ion] Church, Exchange St.* (Worcester, 1898). The Exchange St. building was later destroyed by fire, whereupon the congregation moved to Belmont St.—"Black History: A Central Massachusetts Sampling," A18.

16. "'Professor' Walker Gone," Worcester *Evening Post*, December 17, 1890. Josephine Willard is not the only candidate for "Aunt J." In the 1855 state census, a Mary J. Johnson, age 41, is living with the Gilbert Walker family.

17. Nick Salvatore, *We All Got History: The Memory Books of Amos Webber* (New York: Random House, 1996), 104.

18. Robert Doherty, *Society and Power: Five New England Towns 1800–1860* (Amherst: University of Massachusetts Press, 1877), 31, 40, 71.

19. Jean Holloway, *Edward Everett Hale* (Austin: University of Texas Press, 1956), 102.

20. Charles Nutt, *History of Worcester and Its People* (New York: Lewis Historical Publishing Co., 1919), 1039.

21. Quoted in Adele Logan Alexander, *Homelands and Waterways: The American Journey of the Bond Family, 1846–1926* (New York: Vintage, 2000), 183.

22. *The Worcester Almanac, Directory, and Business Advertiser, for 1860* (Worcester: H. J. Howland, 1860), 123. *The Worcester Almanac . . . for 1874*, 417.

23. Registry of Deeds, Worcester County Courthouse. Joshua S. Chasan, "Civilizing Worcester: The Creation of Institutional and Cultural Order, Worcester, Massachusetts, 1848–1876" (Ph.D. diss., University of Pittsburgh, 1974), 16.

24. William Brown the upholsterer was not the same William Brown as William Wells Brown, the lecturer and pioneering author of *Clotel* (1853). The resolutions are quoted in Jonathan A. Geller, Michael Goesch, and Eric Pearson, "Chemistry, Success, and John Brown: Events in Mechanics Hall in 1859" (B.S. thesis, Worcester Polytechnic Institute, 1994), 64.

Gilbert's brother, Allen Walker, was also an activist. In 1862 he organized the Worcester celebration of a holiday often recognized by American blacks — the anniversary on August 1 of the emancipation of West Indian slaves — Worcester *Daily Spy*, August 4, 1862.

25. Worcester *Daily Spy*, September 17, 1862. Salvatore, 111.

26. Salvatore, 117.

27. Salvatore, 349.

28. John H. Johnson to Martha Brown, December 31, 1863. Brown Family Papers, 1762–1965, American Antiquarian Society, Worcester, Massachusetts. Johnson was killed before his regiment, the 54th Massachusetts Infantry under Colonel Robert Shaw, made their famous assault on Fort Wagner. The story is told in the film *Glory* (1989).

29. Worcester *Daily Spy*, July 6, 1865.

30. "'Professor' Walker Gone."

31. Ibid.

32. Foreman and Pitts, xliii.

George and Timothy Blanchard

Surviving and Thriving in Nineteenth-Century Milford

Reginald H. Pitts

IN AN EARLY SCENE in Harriet Wilson's *Our Nig; or, Sketches from the Life of a Free Black*, Jim, an African American "hooper of barrels," proposes marriage to Mag, a white woman who becomes the protagonist's mother. Jim pledges to help support her since no one else will. He practices his trade at the farm and blacksmith shop of Peter Greene, described as another black man, who provides cheap boarding at his farm. Historically speaking, the only known African American landowner living in Milford at the time Harriet Wilson lived there was a man named Timothy Blanchard. This account will tell the story of several generations of the Milford Blanchards, a family of veterinarians and farmers whose presence has been neglected in town and regional histories but who would likely have been known to the young Wilson.

This recounting of several generations of a black Milford family reveals the barriers to economic success and civic inclusion faced by African Americans in northern New England. Indeed, historian Lorenzo Johnston Greene has observed that, "The condition of free Negroes in New England was probably no more favorable than elsewhere in Colonial America. Strictly speaking, they were not free because they were persecuted politically, economically, and socially, while the white indentured servant, once free, became a respected member of the community."[1] Despite these obstacles, a few African Americans attempted to better themselves: to learn a trade or develop a way to make a living sufficient to support themselves and their loved ones. Some were able to take root in towns and become respected citizens, taxpayers, and landowners. In fact, we now know that early New Hampshire was home to Amos Fortune of Jaffrey, the Primas Chandler family of Bedford, the Battis family of

Canterbury, and the Pauls, Tashes, Whitfields, and Halls of Exeter.[2] Others struggled to little avail. "Notwithstanding these efforts at self-improvement [Northern free blacks] were socially ostracized because of their color, and were forbidden to marry with whites," Greene continues. "With few exceptions, their children do not seem to have attended the public schools provided for white persons. Because of their low incomes and also because of the attitude of the majority group, they were frequently confined to the most undesirable living quarters of the towns."[3] This dubious history helps explain why town fathers would actively further the diminishment and erasure of local black history from the public record. The story of the Blanchards provides one instance of the pervasive and successive "whitening" by omission of the region in local histories, an illustration that could be multiplied countless times in scores of towns throughout New England. Despite the obstacles, this particular black family managed to flourish briefly even as the young Harriet Wilson suffered the hardships of domestic servitude nearby.

George Blanchard, a Milford veterinarian during Wilson's early childhood, was born in slavery in Andover, Massachusetts, sometime around 1740. Of mixed parentage, he bore the surname of the prolific Blanchard family of New England, and may have been related to them. Blanchard may have been the "George, a Molatto Boy, Servant to the Widow Farnum" who was baptized in Andover in 1747 and may also have been related to Caesar Blanchard, an African American who would, with his wife, Diana, eventually move to Litchfield, New Hampshire, just thirteen miles from Wilton.[4] George could also have been kin as well to a servant named Nancy, who worked for Isaac Cummings, a farmer in the adjacent town of Hudson, just over the Litchfield town line. Cummings deeded over his farm to Nancy, who lived there with her son, Peter Blanchard, "who owned and occupied the place during his life," according to real estate records. After his death, other African American families lived on the property, which local whites dubbed the "Nigger Place."[5]

George Blanchard probably had gained his freedom by the time he first appears in the town of Wilton, New Hampshire, before the beginning of the American Revolution. In 1774, George, with his wife, known only as Hannah, attempted to settle in Wilton. However, the town fathers, worried about transients draining local resources, "warned out" the young couple. That is, town leaders took advantage of a common custom to give the pair official notice that their presence was not wanted in the community. Moreover, if they did decide to stay, the town would not be held responsible for the family's welfare.[6]

Despite such official discouragement, George and Hannah decided to stay in Wilton. Soon after that decision, the British regulars fired on the Minutemen at Lexington and Concord, Massachusetts, and soon those able-bodied residents of surrounding towns and colonies organized to fight the British. The various states mobilized their troops as the Continental Congress named George Washington of Virginia Commander-in-Chief of the Continental Forces. General Washington ordered General John Sullivan, commanding the New Hampshire troops, to send soldiers to winter camp around Boston to watch the British, who still held the town. General Sullivan in turn called out the state militia. Twenty-two Wilton citizens out of 623 total residents — including two "Negroes" — enrolled in Captain Benjamin Taylor's Company of Colonel Jonathan Burnham's Regiment of New Hampshire Militia. The company marched from the Hillsborough County seat of Amherst to "Joyn the Continental Army at Winter Hill" near Boston on December 8, 1775. One of its numbers was thirty-five-year-old George Blanchard.[7]

In less than two months the company returned home. Though some militiamen continued serving in either the state militia or with the Continental Army, George Blanchard appears to have stayed home in Wilton. He soon became a tax-paying citizen, purchasing a forty-acre farm from Nathan Abbot on July 13, 1776.[8] Four years later, he would add to his holdings by acquiring an adjacent thirty-acre parcel.[9] George and Hannah moved onto their new farm and set up housekeeping. On June 22, 1778, their first child was born, a little girl named for her mother. Tragedy struck the family eighteen months later: on December 10, 1779, Hannah Blanchard died, probably from childbirth.[10] With an eighteen-month-old baby to care for, George remarried in less than a year. On November 24, 1780, he married Elizabeth "Bettie" Nichols in Litchfield. It is not clear from the records if Bettie, who was about thirty years of age, was white, African American, or Native American, or a mixture of all three.[11] However, their youngest son became a successful farmer and the town veterinarian when Harriet Wilson was a servant in the Hayward (Bellmont) house in Milford, New Hampshire.

From the family's modest beginnings they became an important animal husbandry resource in the community. George, who gained enough education to at least read a little and to sign his own name, soon became known as an "animal healer," becoming one of the pioneer veterinarians in the region. As can easily be imagined, in the early nineteenth century, veterinarians were considered almost as important as medical doctors. In a farming area, someone with the knowledge George Blanchard possessed could represent the difference between success and ruin for farming families.[12] There is evidence that, in administering to the wellbeing of domestic animals, Blanchard used medicinal compounds made of plants, herbs, and roots. He may also have made use of knowledge derived from area Native Americans, or even further back, ancestral remedies from Africa.

In the succeeding years, "Doctor" Blanchard became well known, traveling through southern New Hampshire and probably into central Massachusetts to administer treatment to sick animals.[13] Meanwhile, probably with the proceeds from his veterinary practice and from working on various farms, George purchased a thirty-acre plot from one James Brown of Wilton on May 17, 1780, and settled his bride and daughter there. The family of George and Bettie Blanchard was growing; they would eventually have ten children, four boys and six girls. Their first child, a son, lived only one month, but the remaining children grew strong and thrived. Thus, from a homeless transient, George Blanchard became a taxpayer and a landowner in the town.[14] The Blanchards would stay in Wilton until at least 1805, when they packed up and moved to a sixty-six-acre plot on the Mason Road within the limits of the adjacent town of Milford.[15]

Timothy Blanchard, the eighth child and youngest son of George and Bettie's ten children, would have been the family patriarch when Wilson began her unhappy years in the Hayward (Bellmont) household. Born at the family homestead in Wilton on October 1, 1791, he was about fourteen when the family moved to Milford, where George set himself up in business as a farmer and a vet. George appears to have schooled his three surviving sons in the care and healing of domestic animals, to the extent that they would sometimes appear in the public record as "Doctor." It seems that the older Blanchard girls never learned to read or write, and no specimens of the handwriting of the two older sons appear to have survived, with one possible exception. However, it is likely that Timothy Blanchard, along with his two younger sisters, Ruth, born in April 1794, and Sarah, called "Sally," almost exactly a year younger, attended the local district school, District Number Four. A generation later, Harriet would attend nearby District School Number Three. As we know from Greene and others, it was a rarity to allow blacks to attend public school. This new evidence of Timothy's admittance offers further indication of Milford's unusual inclusiveness in this regard. Timothy's elder sisters did not have the advantages of an education. They appear to have been put out to service at a relatively young age, and spent their time learning the "domestic arts." Hannah Blanchard, the eldest daughter, spent the whole of her life working in various Wilton households, but the two older daughters, Mary, called "Molly," and the younger Elizabeth, called "Betsey," would make their way to Salem, Massachusetts, almost a hundred miles away. There, they worked as domestics and also set themselves up in business as dressmakers in their own shop. As the years passed, sisters Hepzibah (called "Hipsy"), Ruth, and Sally, and their brother John, would join them and become part of Salem's vibrant African American community.

Even when he was of age, brother "Tim," as he appears to have been called, stayed on at home in Milford with his parents and various family members, including his sister Anna and his older brother George Washington Blanchard. The family was likely joined by a number of transient African Americans passing through who needed a place to stay. With them, he worked the family farm, probably occasionally hiring himself out on other farms in the area. He also assisted his father in his veterinary practice and looked about for other ways to make a living. Just as Tim was establishing himself, his elder brother, George Washington Blanchard, died of an unknown ailment in Wilton on April 10, 1812, at the age of twenty-seven.[16]

At about the same time, his father, the senior George Blanchard, then in his seventies, apparently cut back on his agricultural and veterinary activities and essentially turned everything over to Tim, who was then approaching his twenty-first birthday. Why the remaining Blanchard brother, John, was overlooked is not known. Although he doesn't make much of an imprint in surviving records, what is known is that at times he was a sailor working ships from Salem or other ports—His "Seaman's Protection Certificate," a form of identification confirming that he was an American citizen, exists from an 1807 voyage originating from Salem—and when work was slack, he may have been an itinerant farm laborer or peddler, tramping the dusty farm roads of New Hampshire and Massachusetts.[17]

After George Washington Blanchard's death, Timothy Blanchard starts to appear regularly in legal records. Before his death, however, on November 22, 1813, George Blanchard purchased a tract of sixty-six acres from Milford farmer Simeon Gutterson. The lot was located in the southwestern section of Milford on the Mason Road and may have been originally rented from Gutterson by the Blanchards. A year later, George sold the same tract to Timothy for nine hundred dollars, whereupon Tim granted his father a life estate in the property. The deed declares that George will "hold the aforesaid premises with all the privileges & appurtenances thereunto belonging to him the said George for & during the term of his natural life."[18] Then, significantly, on January 26, 1815, Tim Blanchard, as the leaseholder and owner of the land in question, leased to the "Directors of the Fourth School District of the town of Milford" an acre of his ground so that a schoolhouse could be erected for the children of the district. This is the same building listed on the 1854 Chace map of Hillsborough County as the "P.F. Shedd School." The fact that the younger Blanchard leased the small plot to the town to be used as a school is a measure of the family's active involvement in education generally and schooling for Milford's black population in particular.[19]

Meanwhile, the records show that, while George settled into a well-earned

Site of Shepherd's Mill, where George Blanchard bought a building in 1805.
Courtesy of the Milford (NH) Historical Society

retirement, Tim took over the responsibility for running the farm and the veterinary practice to the extent that some of the tax returns for this period list him as "Dr. T. Blanchard." Although his father was alive at the time of the 1820 Federal Census, it was "Timo. Blanchard" who was listed as the head of the household of six, which included a number of "free people other than Indians" who may not have been related to him, but who may also have been hired help or transients seeking a place of shelter.[20] Clearly, the Blanchard homestead served as an important place of refuge for the small rural community of free African Americans in the antebellum years.

About this time, Tim Blanchard's life underwent fundamental changes. First, on February 26, 1824, the thirty-two-year-old Blanchard was married to twenty-five-year-old Dorcas Hood of Milford. Dorcas, a white woman, was born April 13, 1798, the third of the twelve children of Joseph Hood, a farmer and carpenter of English ancestry, by his first wife Eleanor (Woodbury) Hood.[21] Some two weeks later, on March 10, 1824, eighty-four-year-old George Blanchard died and was buried in the Elm Street Cemetery, alongside his elder son, George Washington Blanchard. The following November, Tim and Dorcas's first child was born and named in honor of his grandfather and uncle, George Walter Blanchard.[22] Now the head of an extended household, Tim Blanchard "succeeded [his father] upon the farm and in the business as a veterinary."[23] There is also evidence that he branched out into other commercial ventures, including a cooperage, a barrel-making shop, probably located on his farm. This business endeavor would probably have been under the direct supervision of his brother-in-law, Jeremiah Hood II, a journeyman cooper in his early twenties. It would have been staffed by a number of skilled and semi-skilled laborers, both black and white. It is likely that one of the workers, a "hooper of barrels," may have named a daughter, born about March of 1825, in honor of Jeremiah Hood's future wife, Harriet E. Elkins.[24] That "hooper" may have been Harriet Wilson's father.

As this evidence shows, the Blanchards weren't the only family of African Americans in Milford, although they appear to have been the sole property owners. They may also have been the only long-term residents besides little Harriet (Hattie) Adams, Wilson's maiden name. Most free blacks were transients and not native to the area; they were farm laborers tramping the roads looking for work. When they found it, they stayed for short periods, and then moved on. Peddlers selling various products from wagons or baskets they lugged were also common, as were entertainers — singers, magicians, buskers, dancers — traversing the dusty roads, walking from town to town looking for crowds to entertain. For example, in the summer of 1773, when the residents of nearby Wilton got together to construct a larger and more commodious meetinghouse, the men working on the building and the women preparing food for them were entertained by an itinerant traveling magician, described only as a "mulatto Man," who delighted the crowd with a show featuring "snappy patter and feats of sleight of hand."[25]

Occasionally, other African Americans passing through the area were able to get into the public record, if only for a moment. Usually, their appearance was related to their being warned out of town, just as George Blanchard had been. Their names and places of birth, or of last residence, were noted. Many wandered in from nearby towns in southern New Hampshire or in neighboring Massachusetts. Pauline Jones Oesterlin's listing of blacks who were warned out of Hillsborough County towns included people from Maine, Vermont, New York, and "Road Island."[26] Sometimes, if blacks called upon the services of the local minister, they would appear in the church register. In addition, the marriages of "strangers" might be recorded, as might their burial in the local churchyard. Frequently, the town Overseers of the Poor would be billed by the local undertaker/carpenter for the cost of disposing of bodies, and the bill and receipt of payment would become part of the public record.[27] These paltry and disparaging markers of the lives of free African Americans contrast sharply with the lengthy and laudatory accounts of a remarkably wide array of white townsfolk in innumerable town histories dating into the twentieth century. Indeed, most black townspeople failed to gain the notice of the town fathers for any reason and slipped through life unknown and unsung, their trails lost. Joshua Green, the young "hooper of barrels" who worked for Jeremiah Hood and evidently lived in Tim Blanchard's house, was remembered only by his devoted daughter, Harriet Wilson. If she had forgotten him, the world would not have known that he had ever existed.[28]

The stories of other African American residents survive only through anecdotes. This is true of one Caesar Parker, originally from Methuen, Massachusetts, and later of Weare, New Hampshire. Although a longtime resident of Mont Vernon, for a time Parker lived in Milford. Parker is a good example of the clown-character typical of white descriptions of free African Americans in antebellum accounts. In this case, the source of Parker's portrait is native son John Hutchinson of the famous anti-slavery Hutchinson Singers. According to Hutchinson, Parker was a town "character," remembered as "Black as the ace of spades." He was "a tall, well-proportioned, athletic, uneducated but witty African" who worked on farms in Milford and Amherst.[29] Hutchinson recalls that Parker was "quite conspicuous on public occasions, like trainings, musters, and holidays, with the 'b-hoys,' who were fond of scuffling and wrestling. He was always brought into the ring under the influence of a glass or two, which was freely furnished him, was sufficiently bold and sprightly, and could bring down to the amusement of all, almost any of those selected to scuffle or wrestle."[30] In fact, Parker appears in two comedic stories recounted by John Hutchinson. In the first, a young white girl, jilted by her lover, is heard to sigh that she would marry the first man that asked her. "Some wag," writes Hutchinson, goes up to Parker, tells him that "Miss So-and-So is very fond of you" and that if he hastens to her and proposes marriage, she would accept: "Consequently, this colored man dressed himself in his best overalls, repaired to the house, and boldly made his proposition; and to his great delight the lady agreed that he should be her suitor. Subsequently they married, and the result was that instead of one black man in our neighborhood, there soon grew up five boys and two girls of a lighter hue." The second story shows Parker out trapping for beaver along the banks of the Souhegan River. It describes his consternation when he found out someone placed a dead house cat in his trap.

In addition to such patronizing anecdotes, public records show that Caesar Parker and Margaret Spear of New Ipswich, New Hampshire, married around 1800 and had five boys and two girls. Although they were remembered as "athletic and dexterous" and "fond of music," the boys felt keenly the sting of being different in homogeneous Milford. While they were able to attend the district schools, there "was observable a notable reservation and withdrawing from the common plays and sports of the children." Later, one of the sons, described as "a very agreeable, pleasant man, speaking familiarly of his relation and his condition, said he would suffer to be skinned alive if he could rid himself of his color."[31]

Clearly, the Blanchards' increasing prosperity over the years afforded them unusual advantages for free blacks. By 1830, Timothy was comfortably in the middle ranks of Milford citizens, a family man who owned his own farm and was involved in a number of business concerns. In less than a decade, however, the family's fortunes would all come to an end. Worse, after his death, his life would be largely forgotten, his property in the hands of others, and his family scattered and impoverished.

However, Timothy's reversal in fortunes began gradually. At the time of the 1830 census, "Timo." Blanchard, heading a household of seven, was taxed for over sixty acres of land in Milford.[32] It's possible that by the middle of the decade he had decided to engage in land speculation. Legal records filed during this period show that he was involved with the sale and purchase of a number of parcels of land. However, the Panic of 1837, a severe economic depression, may have hit him hard, as it did many small speculators and landowners. The records show that, on November 20, 1837, Timothy sold his farm to Mrs. Mary Pearse (Blunt) Shedd who, with her husband, Peter "Pete" Shedd, and their growing young family, had recently moved to Milford from Andover, Massachusetts. Like Blanchard, Pete Shedd was a farmer and veterinarian, originally from Tewksbury, Massachusetts. The family, eventually numbering twelve in all, quickly became established in town and stayed for several years.[33] Meanwhile, Blanchard moved his operations to another location and re-established his farm and his "veterinary."[34] Apparently, however, in an attempt to raise cash to cover outstanding debts and needed expenses, Blanchard started selling off parcels of land or putting up land for collateral for loans.[35]

Then, suddenly, disaster befell the Blanchard household. Two days after his forty-eighth birthday, on October 3, 1839, Timothy died from an unknown cause.[36] He left behind a pregnant widow and five children, the eldest barely fifteen. With Dorcas Blanchard expecting her last child, Milford farmer Moses Foster, Jr., was appointed guardian of those "minors aged under fourteen years"—Tim, Jr. (12), Sara Malysa (9), Elizabeth, called Lizzie (5), and James, about a year old. The oldest boy, George Walter Blanchard, was older than fourteen, thus did not require a guardian.[37] Tragically, Blanchard died without a will, so Hillsborough County Judge of Probate Luke Woodbury appointed three Milford residents—Moses Foster, Jr., Stephen C. Marshall, and Daniel Lakin—to take an inventory of Tim's personal property and appraise its value. The inventory of Blanchard's personal property takes up most of three double-columned ledger pages and shows that, despite any financial troubles, the Blanchard family had lived rather comfortably.[38]

That relative comfort was no longer possible, however. It stands to reason

that, since the rights of the Blanchard children were supposedly being protected, there would be enough set aside for their continued wellbeing. On the
contrary, records reflect just the opposite. From the beginning, it appears that
Dorcas Blanchard was dissatisfied with how the estate was being handled and
how the money designated for her support and that of her children was being
distributed. She was forced to request more to handle her family's immediate needs. In response, Moses Foster, as the administrator of the estate and
the guardian of the children — now including Henry Blanchard, born after
his father's death — started selling off portions of Tim Blanchard's remaining landholdings. According to records, thirteen acres went to Foster himself,
with various other tracts going to Dr. S. S. Stickney and David P. Needham.[39] Moreover, the family home still remained in the hands of the administrators. Nonetheless, Dorcas Blanchard did receive her dower rights in the
family homestead, which specifically delineated property she had ownership
rights in, "together with the privilege of passing and repassing to and from
said woodlot without intruding in crops of grain also the privilege of using the
barn floor for threshing and cutting hay and harvesting grain also the privilege of using the well of water and passing to and from it by the west end of the
house standing on the north side of road."[40]

While the property records are not clear about the details, the funds set
aside for the Blanchard children ran out, either through negligence or deliberate mismanagement by the administrators, or else by Moses Foster as the
children's guardian. Sometime later, Dorcas Blanchard met a farmer from the
nearby town of Mason named Luther Elliot (or Elliott), who was, if census returns are accurate, twenty-one years her junior.[41] It appears that Elliot, although willing to take the hand of the widow Blanchard in marriage, did not
intend to extend his welcome to her mixed-race children. Although the record
is silent, it seems that Dorcas, like Mag in Wilson's narrative, effectively abandoned her six children, the youngest barely a toddler, to become the wife of
Luther Elliot. The 1850 federal census for Hillsborough County reflects this
dispersion of the family. The two oldest sons, George Walter (26), and Tim, Jr.
(22), are enumerated in Milford with their grandfather Joseph Hood, working
as farm laborers. George is also enumerated with his uncle Jeremiah Hood,
where he had evidently been apprenticed as a cooper; he would subsequently
work at that trade.[42] Soon afterward, George Walter Blanchard and Timothy Blanchard, Jr., left Milford to take their chances in the outside world.
Evidence suggests that Tim Blanchard, Jr., eventually wound up in Massachusetts, where he married and died young, leaving two children. However,
George Walter stayed in the area, working as a cooper and a laborer on local
farms. Although he was known to be of partial African American descent, he

was light-skinned enough to pass for white, and soon the public record began to reflect that supposition.[43]

And what of Timothy Blanchard's daughters? As we know, nearly all of his sisters—except the eldest, Hannah, by then an inmate at the Wilton Poor House, where she would stay until she died at ninety, and sister Anna, who lived in Francestown—were living in Salem, Massachusetts. There, they worked as seamstresses, housekeepers, and cooks. Notably, they were active in the black community there and were involved in a number of charitable organizations, mutual aid societies, and "relief" associations. Salem, as a port city, was the home of sailors from all over the globe, and as such was a hospitable place for many African Americans. Besides those born on the North American continent, blacks from the Caribbean, Africa, South America, the Cape Verde Islands, and the East Indies found themselves a home there. The city had long exhibited a reputation for cosmopolitanism and opportunity. John Blanchard, the second surviving Blanchard son, had gone to sea from Salem, although he died back home in Milford in 1828. In the summer of 1804, one London Ruleff (or Roloff) of Salem, a sailor, and a day laborer when ashore, died in his "part of a dwelling house . . . situated in the north fields on a road leading to Danvers." He left behind a wife and several children. When his estate was inventoried—including his house and property, the total valuation from which came to more than two hundred dollars—the task was handled by three men, one of whom was John Blanchard. This could very well be John Blanchard of Milford, particularly in light of the fact that one of his sisters would marry one of Ruleff's sons—although at the time he would have been only six months shy of his eighteenth birthday.[44]

It was George Blanchard's daughters who left the strongest imprint in the history of Salem. Sisters Hipsy, Ruth, and Sally, who arrived later than their siblings, were involved in the various mutual aid societies set up to support and protect themselves and their members.[45] Sisters Molly and Betsy never married, but they went from working as laundresses and domestic help to running a dressmaking business. The three younger sisters eventually married—Hipsy to a Cape Verdean sailor who went by the name of Peter Johnson; Ruth to a Salem-born sailor named London Ruleff, Jr., son of the man whose estate was administered by John Blanchard some thirty years before; and Sally to a Virginian named William Colman, or Coleman, who was a "trader"; that is, he sold all sorts of articles from a pushcart or a horse-drawn wagon.[46]

All of these Blanchard descendants were established residents of Salem and intimately involved in the community, yet they are practically hidden from public view. Meanwhile, Sally's spouse, William Colman, was active in the Zion Wesleyan Methodist Church of Salem, one of the leading black churches of Salem.[47] He and his wife would eventually have five children. Their eldest daughters, Cecelia, or "Celia," born in 1826, and her sister Sarah (later Mrs. Gideon T. Turner), born two years later, were contemporaries of Little Hattie (Harriet) Adams. It's possible that Cecelia Coleman was the little girl described in *Our Nig* as a "little colored girl, a favorite playmate," who accompanied Frado on her jaunt into the country, where they promptly got lost.[48]

When their nieces were in need, the sisters organized themselves and took them in. Lizzie Blanchard was formally adopted by her Aunt Hipsy Johnson, and was known as "Elizabeth B. Johnson."[49] Sixteen-year-old Sara Malysa Blanchard appears to have been taken in by the Colmans. At the time of the 1850 census she was working for a "victualer" named William R. Morison, but in future years, after her marriage to a Virginian named John S. Washington — who would later own a "stove store" and a coal yard on Lafayette Street — she would live two doors down from the Colman house on Porter Street for almost fifty years, rearing a family of eight.[50]

It is unknown why the charity of the aunts only extended to the girls and not to their two youngest nephews, both of whom were younger than either Lizzie or Sara Malysa. According to David Edwin Proctor, whose father ran the Milford Poor House, both of the younger brothers, James and Henry, were sent to the town poor house as paupers. By 1850, James Blanchard, aged twelve, was working for Francis Wright, a farmer in nearby Amherst, while Henry Blanchard, aged ten, was still an inmate of the Milford Town Poor House.[51] Though James and Henry Blanchard had been left behind, they were not forgotten by the rest of their relatives. Sometime after 1850, Henry Blanchard was apprenticed to a barber in Springfield, Massachusetts, named William Henry Montague. A native of Washington, D.C., Montague ran a barber shop as well as a Turkish bath and a small restaurant. He was an anti-slavery activist who was also active in the Abolitionist movement and probably served as a conductor on the Underground Railroad.[52]

Although it is possible that Milford abolitionists like Humphrey Moore or Leonard Chase or one of the Singing Hutchinsons could have drawn someone's attention to the plight of Henry Blanchard, the young mulatto boy languishing at the Town Poor Farm, it is more likely that his aunts in Salem contacted their pastor, the Reverend Thomas H. Jones of the Zion Wesleyan Methodist Church. Jones, who had escaped from slavery in North Carolina, wrote a book about his experiences, and lectured in New England towns to raise money for his freedom and that of his family left in slavery. Soon after the Fugitive Slave Law was enacted in September 1850, Jones, still a fugitive, went to Nova Scotia, where he would stay for several years. However, he

Eagle Hall, Union Square (c. 1847). On January 4 and 5, 1843, Eagle Hall hosted an anti-slavery convention attended by famous abolitionists. *Courtesy of the Milford (NH) Historical Society*

Eagle Hall, Union Square, 2006.
Courtesy of JerriAnne Boggis

had lived in New Hampshire before that time, and he could very well have been the "itinerant lecturer" who took Hattie Adams to "W——." It is also possible that he took Henry Blanchard at the same time to be apprenticed to Montague in Springfield. Henry would remain in Montague's household for at least ten years before striking out on his own.[53] For his part, James Blanchard remained in Amherst working on farms until the outbreak of the Civil War. He enlisted in the Union Army on August 16, 1862. On the following September 9, he was mustered into Company H of the 10th New Hampshire Infantry.[54] This enlistment in itself was a feat, as the Union Army was not enlisting African Americans to serve in "white" regiments — or even in segregated units — until after September 1862. However, many light-skinned men of partial African American descent successfully enlisted and served in white regiments. Although no photographs have yet been discovered of any of Tim's children, it's evident that, as they were all light-skinned, George Walter, James, and Lizzie were all able to pass as white, according to legal documents. James was fair enough to pass muster and enlist in the Army, where he served until he fell ill of dysentery and died in a military hospital near Norfolk, Virginia, on August 19, 1863; he was only twenty-five.[55]

It is in the context of her son's death that Dorcas Blanchard Elliott (as she spelled it), now again a widow and virtually destitute, reappears in the written record. After Luther Elliot's death, it seems that his widow was continually on the move, staying by herself or with relatives in Amherst, Milford, or Salem, barely scraping by with odd jobs and primarily dependent on the charity of her relatives. Soon after James's death, she applied for a "mother's pension," for which she was eligible as long as James hadn't married or otherwise left behind any dependents. James had died unmarried and without any offspring, so Dorcas applied to receive a pension of eight dollars a month. It was not much but it was money upon which she could depend. Despite their troubled history together, her family banded together to come to her aid. Dorcas moved from Milford to the house of her daughter Sara Malysa Washington in Salem, claiming that as her home address; her sister Sarah H. Swinington of Amherst, and her sisters-in-law, Hipsy Johnson and Sarah Colman of Salem, signed affidavits swearing that James had been the sole support of his mother, that he had cheerfully and willingly contributed a portion of his earnings for her support, and that without that support she would find herself in dire straits. The pension request was approved on December 12, 1864. The eight dollars a month appears to have aided her in her attempts at self-sufficiency. During the next twelve years or so, Dorcas Elliott bounced from Salem to Amherst and subsequently back to Milford (where she was enumerated in the 1870 Federal Census). Then, for a short time, she moved back again to Salem, subsequently returning to Amherst, and finally back to Milford, where we lose her trail after 1876.[56]

Soon Tim Blanchard, with the majority of his family, was forgotten by Milford. Blanchard's participation in the organization and administration of School District Number Four went unsung and unnoticed in the town histories. After his death his homestead became known as the "Pete Shedd" Farm, even though the Shedds themselves would not live there as long as the Blanchards, since they lost the property when they failed to pay property taxes on it. In 1900, when he compiled his "Register" for the Milford town history, William P. Colburn noted in reference to the descendants of George and Tim Blanchard that none of them had resided within the town "for quite a long time."[57] It is to be hoped that this account of the Blanchards will bring the family back into the notice of history. As important, this reconstruction of a single black family history serves as a case study of the racialized erasure of nineteenth-century African American lives in Northern New England, an immeasurably damaging act of historical forgetting that has only now begun to be rectified.

APPENDIX A
Children of George Blanchard (1740–1824)
of Wilton, N.H., and Milford, N.H.

By first wife Hannah ——— Blanchard (died December 10, 1779)

   a. Hannah Blanchard, b. June 22, 1778, Wilton, N.H., d. September 23, 1868, Wilton, N.H., unmarried; town pauper who lived on Wilton Town Poor Farm for over thirty years before her death.

By second wife Elizabeth "Bettie" Nichols Blanchard (died August 28, 1832)

   a. James Blanchard, b. October 20, 1781, Wilton, N.H., d. November 25, 1781, Wilton, N.H.

   b. Mary "Molly" Blanchard, b. October 11, 1782, Wilton, N.H., d. February 8, 1862, Salem, Mass., unmarried.

   c. Elizabeth "Betsey" Blanchard, b. March 26, 1784, Wilton, N.H., d. September 23, 1864, Salem, Mass., unmarried.

   d. George Washington Blanchard, b. August 25, 1785, Wilton, N.H., d. April 10, 1812, Wilton, N.H., unmarried.

   e. John Blanchard, b. December 25, 1786, Wilton, N.H., d. March 4, 1828, Milford, N.H., unmarried.

   f. Anna Blanchard, b. June 21, 1788, Wilton, N.H., d. September 15, 1862, Francestown, N.H., unmarried.

   g. Hepzibah "Hipsy" Blanchard, b. March 1, 1790, Wilton, N.H., m. Peter Johnson (b. "Bona Vista," Cape Verde Islands; sailor and day laborer of Salem; died July 3, 1872, Salem, Mass., aged about 88 years), April 2, 1828, Salem, Mass., no children, d. February 2, 1867, Salem, Mass.

   h. Timothy Blanchard, b. October 1, 1791, Wilton, N.H., m. Dorcas Hood, February 26, 1824, Milford, N.H., 8 children, died October 3, 1839, Milford, N.H.

APPENDIX A *(continued)*

i.   Ruth Blanchard, b. April 9, 1794, Wilton, N.H., m. London Ruleff, Jr. (sailor and day laborer of Salem; died July 16, 1839, Chelsea, Mass.), after June 28, 1834, no children; died July 16, 1872, Salem, Mass.

j.   Sarah "Sally" Blanchard, b. April 25, 1795, Wilton, N.H., married William Colman (Coleman), trader and peddler of Salem after April 10, 1819, 6 children, died March 18, 1877, Salem, Mass.

Descendants of Timothy Blanchard and Dorcas (Hood) Blanchard

1. George Walter Blanchard, b. November 19, 1824, Milford, New Hampshire; worked as a cooper, farm laborer, and carpenter in Milford and, after 1876, in Mont Vernon, N.H. Married Bedelia "Delia" Finerty (daughter of Michael Finerty and Delia (Linehan) Finerty, b. August 2, 1832, County Galway, Ireland, d. May 26, 1917, Mont Vernon, New Hampshire); d. November 2, 1896, Mont Vernon, leaving issue:

    a.   George D. Blanchard, b. 1862, Milford, N.H.; farm laborer and carpenter of Mont Vernon, N.H., d. February 21, 1933, Mont Vernon, N.H., unmarried.

    b.   James Blanchard, b. March 4, 1865, Milford, N.H., d. December 13, 1891, San Bernardino, California, unmarried.

    c.   Walter James Blanchard, b. July 18, 1869, Milford, N.H., farm laborer and cooper of Mont Vernon, N.H.; ran a sawmill in Coos County, New Hampshire; last listed 1910 Census in Mont Vernon. Married Hannah J. Averill (b. June 29, 1878, Mont Vernon, N.H., third child and only daughter of Granville C. Averill and Nancy Jane [Green] Averill; married (2) George Page, after March 1901, no children; d. July 18, 1901), October 20, 1895, Manchester, N.H., divorced on grounds of "extreme cruelty" February 17, 1901, and had issue:

        i.   Walter James Blanchard, Jr., b. January 23, 1897, Mont Vernon, N.H., d. January 25, 1897, Mont Vernon, N.H.

        ii. Walter Averill Blanchard, b. February 13, 1898, Mont Vernon, N.H.; farm laborer of Mont Vernon, d. 1964, Mont Vernon, N.H., unmarried.

2. Samuel Woodbury Blanchard, b. August 23, 1826, Milford, New Hampshire, d. May 4, 1833, Milford, New Hampshire.

3. Timothy Blanchard, Jr., b. July 20, 1828, Milford, N.H.; cooper and farm laborer in Massachusetts and New Hampshire; date of death unknown. Married ———— and had issue:

    a.   ?Annie L. Blanchard, born 1856, Salem (?), Mass.; lived in household of her aunt Mrs. Sally Colman in Salem from before 1860 to after 1880; enumerated in 1880 Census as a single woman who works in a printing office; living in Philadelphia as a clerk and notary public from before 1914 to after 1920. Unmarried.

    b.   ?George Blanchard, born 1856 in Massachusetts; enumerated in 1880 Federal Census for Holyoke, Mass. (Hampden) as a teamster working for one William Bishop.

4. Sara Malysa [Sarah Melissa] Blanchard, b. July 16, 1830, Milford, N.H.; taken to Salem, Mass., after her father's death and reared by her aunts; lived with her family at 16 Porter Street in Salem; d. July 1, 1910, Salem, Mass.; married John S. Washington (b. Richmond, Va., June 21, 1829, son of John Washington and Julia A. Fountain [married 2nd, Abram Williams]; d. Salem, Mass., January 16, 1913), tinsmith, stove dealer, and coal yard owner of Salem, January 5, 1854, Danvers, Mass., and had issue:

    a.   George A. Washington, b. October 1854, Salem, Mass., d. April 18, 1895, Salem, Mass. Vaudeville performer. Unmarried.

    b.   Walter Washington, b. December 9, 1856, Salem, Mass., d. infancy.

c. Elizabeth Ruth [Lizzie R.] Washington, b. 1857, Salem, Mass.; married William Henry Saunders, September 7, 1885, Salem, Mass., no surviving issue; d. 1914, Medford, Mass.

d. James J. Washington, b. January 8, 1859, Salem, Mass., d. February 9, 1859, Salem, Mass.

e. Emma C. Washington, b. January 1860, Salem, Mass., d. March 26, 1860, Salem, Mass.

f. John William Washington, b. September 23, 1862, Salem, Mass. Clerk in Boston General Post Office as well as teacher of penmanship and elocution; d. 1925, Boston, Mass.; married Lucy Ann Wyllys (b. Savannah, Georgia, 1863), November 29, 1886, Salem; three sons, including Forrester Blanchard Washington (1887–1974), pioneer social work educator and practitioner.

g. Ella Lee Washington, b. December 1, 1865, Salem, Mass., d. December 22, 1865, Salem, Mass.

h. Henry Blanchard Washington, b. April 3, 1867, Salem, Mass., d. June 5, 1885, Salem, Mass. Unmarried.

i. Richard W. Washington, b. May 1, 1869, Salem, Mass. Owned bicycle shop (sales and repairs) on Lafayette Avenue in Salem; married Marion Baltman (b. Capetown, South Africa, 1878), February 9, 1901, Boston, Mass., one daughter died at birth; d. July 29, 1906, Salem, Mass.

5. William Coleman Blanchard, b. August 25, 1832, Milford, N.H., d. February 8, 1835, Milford, N.H.

6. Elizabeth "Lizzie" Blanchard (Johnson), b. September 6, 1834, Milford, N.H.; adopted by Aunt Hipsy Johnson after her father's death and mother's abandonment; married Joseph B. Morris, restauranteur and caterer of Salem (b. 1831, Salem, son of York and Mercy [Thomas] Morris, brother of Robert Morris, pioneer attorney of Boston), March 25, 1852, Salem, Mass., d. June 2, 1878, Salem, Mass., leaving no issue.

7. James Blanchard, b. 1838, Milford, N.H.; sent to Milford Poor Farm after father's death, then boarded out among various families in the neighboring town of Amherst; at the beginning of the Civil War, enlisted in Company H, 10th New Hampshire Infantry; died of illness, Julian's Creek, Virginia, July 17, 1864. Unmarried.

8. Henry Blanchard, b. 1839 or 1840, Milford, N.H., sent to Milford Poor Farm after father's death; apprenticed to William Henry Montague, barber of Springfield, Mass.; lived in his household from approximately 1852 to 1864. when he last appears in the Springfield city directories; no further information, although he may have died before 1866.

APPENDIX B

Inventory of the Estate of Timothy Blanchard, Late of Milford, Deceased

Hillsborough County Will Book 46:241 (1839)

Personal Estate

Ox cart	3.00	2 Axes	.50
Elves & pin [?]	.25	2 do.*	.25
Horse Cart	4.00	Hatchet	.08
Gig	3.00	Pair iron fetters	.10
Single Harness	1.75	Lot measures	.13
Whiffletree and chain	.50	Saw Horse	.12
2 Draft Chains	2.25	Wheelbarrow	.06
Large Chain	1.00	Scythe & swash[?]	.50
Grindstone	.75	2 do. "	.25
3 Hoes	.25	2 Cow Bells	.25
Wood saw	1.00	Cheese Press	.10
2 Iron wedges	.25		———
Kiddle [kettle]	1.50		$22.79

1 prong fork	.06	1 book .50; lot do. .75	1.25
Horse Rope	.25	Keg salt	.10
2 Barrells Ashes	.33	Meal flour	1.00
Lot Baskets	.13	Lot bags (?)	.24
Tin Baker	.06	Tub .75; do. .06	.81
Spinning Wheel	.13	Churn	.13
Small pail and barrel	.13	2 casks Indian wheat	1.25
Pair steelyards	.13	Lot potatoes	3.00
Lot of posts	.50	Single sleigh	5.00
Lot firewood	4.00	Large plough	4.00
Tub	.06	Cast iron plough	3.00
Lot corn	8.00	Cast tires, hoops & boxes	—
Cask oats	3.00	Chest	.06
3 baskets white beans	4.00	2 Boxes	.04
Do.	12.00	Iron Kettle	.50
Meadow of Hay	4.00	Iron Shovel	.25
Straw & Corn Fodder	2.50		———
10 fowls	1.67		38.88
2 Sickles	.10		
1 [illegible] auger	.25	Lot coloured beans	.40
Disks & contents	2.00	Lot old harness	.22
Searing Iron	.10	3 Old Bedsteads	.13

*"Do." = "ditto," or the same.

Pair saddle bags	.06
Handsaws	.25
2 yokes & bars	.25
small chain	.06
Standing stool	.25
Foot Wheel	.06
Lot old iron	1.00
Pair hollow & round Planes	.12
"Fros" [?]	.12
Box of old iron	.50
Horse Blanket	.25
Remainder in shop	.50
String of Bells	.10
Harrow	1.50
Horse Sled	.50
Iron bar, 1.50 Do.Do. .40	1.90
Manure Fork	.80
Shovel	.06
2 Pitchforks	.07
3 Rakes .25	.32
Horse	30.00
Cow	22.50
Do.	22.50
Turkey	17.00
Chest	1.00
Light stand	.50
Looking Glass	.50
Window curtains	.06
	———
	39.76
6 Chairs	1.50
Pair bellows	.06
Pair pincers	.25
	———
	$127.74
sink concern	.25
Cheese Basket	.06
Frying Pan	.30
Lot of iron ware	2.00
Contents of dresser	1.00
6 Silver spoons	1.50
2 Pails, .20—1 Do. .10	.30
Fowling piece	2.00
Reel	.06
Provender Basket	.06
Pot of fat	.30
8 milk pans	.67
2 stone jars	.25
Brown earthen ware	.25

1 table	.07
Basket line and clothes line	.10
Barrel corn xc.	.17
Medicine chest	.25
" & contents	1.00
Valise & contents	.10
Farrier's Instruments	.75
medicine ca[binet?]	1.00
contents	1.50
Iron Mortar	.50
Jug or Bottle	.13
Coffee Mill	.25
Lot books	.06
Bed & Bedding	2.00
Bed, bed & bedding	8.00
4 sheets, $1. 5 Blankets 1.50	2.50
Bedstead and cords	.25
Bed cord, bed & bedding	4.00
trundlebed	.25
8 pillow cases	.40
Quilt .25, coverlet 2.00	2.25
Table Linen	1.67
Table Cloth	1.50
Steel Trap	.50
40 bu. Potatoes	9.00
Two cheese 1. "turned" (?) .06	1.06
Lot sauce	.50
Hay	10.00
Pork Barrel & pork	.40
Contents of cupboard	.25
Pair shovel and tongs	.75
" " "	.25
Pair fire dogs	.40
10 Chairs	1.00
Chest .25 Do. 50	.75
Table	.13
Basket	.06
Chest with Drawers	.15
Lot Books, Bible xc.	.25
Clock .50	.50
Cooking Stove	8.00
Crane, hooks & andirons	.25
Contents of chimney "pire" [?]	.25
Butter Tray	.13
2 Bottles	.10
Contents of cupboard	.25
Pair sad irons	.13
Towel .03 Tooth Drawers .25	.28
2 trace chains	.12
Upper Leather	.28
7 pcs. Sole leather	1.75

APPENDIX B *(Continued)*

3 Sheep skins	3.50	Pocket Book	.13
Dried apples [in] cask	1.60	Comb case [?]	.06
2 cocks .15 pair [candy?] .13	.28	3 Razors	
Shoes	.25	Lancet	.12
Shoe seat xc.	.25		———
Meat Barrel	.25		1.30
Barrel of soap	1.25		
2 soap barrels & soap	.50	Whole Amount	$274.72
Butter Tub	.25		
Tin Kettle	.06	Moses Foster	
	———	Stephen C. Marshall	Appraisers
	42.25	Daniel Lakin	
		Administrators & Appraisers sworn	
Cider Barrels	.56	Rec'd & Accepted Dec. 3rd	
Tub pickles	.13	1839	
Lot old casks	.20		
2 Bottles	.10	L. Woodbury, Judge of Probate	

NOTES

1. Lorenzo Johnston Greene, *The Negro in Colonial New England* (New York: Columbia University Press, 1942), 298–99.

2. For a discussion of the African American inhabitants of Exeter in Rockingham County, see Charles Henry Bell, *History of the Town of Exeter, New Hampshire* (Exeter, N.H., 1883), 396–99; for Amos Fortune (c. 1710–1801), see Elizabeth Yates, *Amos Fortune, Free Man* (New York, 1951), and Peter Lambert, *Amos Fortune: The Man and His Legacy* (Jaffrey, N.H., 2001); for Primas Chandler, a freed slave who died fighting the British during the American Revolution, and his son Primas, Jr. (1775–1853), a longtime farmer of Bedford, as well as a thorough discussion of slavery within the town's borders, see Bedford Historical Society, *History of Bedford, New Hampshire 1737–1971* (Bedford, N.H., 1971) and *History of Bedford, New Hampshire from 1737–1900* (Bedford, N.H., 1903), 573–77.

3. Greene, 311.

4. *Vital Records of the Town of Andover, Massachusetts to the End of the Year 1849* (Topsfield, Mass., 1912), 475. There is also a reference to the baptism of "George, servant to Mr. Isaac Blunt," who was baptized on November 15, 1761, when George Blanchard would be twenty-one.

5. ". . . but no one has resided there for many years, and the buildings have decayed." Kimball Webster, *History of Hudson, New Hampshire*, ed. George Waldo Browne (Manchester, 1914), 164. In 1880, George W. Hazard (Hazzard), a fifty-six-

year-old native of (Norwich?) Vermont and a Civil War veteran, was living there with his wife and family, and had been there for over twenty years. 1880 Federal Census of Population for Hudson, Hillsborough County, N.H. George Hazard may have been the son of Thomas Hazard and Belinda Lewis, who married in Norwich, Vt., in 1824; Belinda, originally from Sutton, N.H., was the daughter of one Caesar Lewis (died 1860 in the Sutton Poor House aged 105) and one Jemima Blanchard; they were married September 2, 1796, in Sutton. Joann Heselton Nichols, "Hazard/Hazzard Family in Vermont" in Rachel L. Duffalo, "People of Colour in Vermont and New England." — www url: http://www.freepages.genealogy.rootsweb.com/~rduffalo/

   6. For a discussion of the legal concept of "warning out," see Josiah Henry Benton, *Warning Out in New England 1656–1817* (Cambridge, Mass., 1911); for a list of some of those folks traveling in Hillsborough County who were chased out of certain towns (including a number of African descent), see Pauline Johnson Oesterlin, *Hillsborough County, New Hampshire Court Records, 1772–1799* (Bowie, Md., 1991). George and Hannah appear on page 370 along with another grouping of Blanchards — Eber, Dolley, Sarah, and Susannah, originally from Andover, who appear to have been warned out of Wilton ten years later. Whether they also are "colored" is not made clear.

   7. Abiel Abbot Livermore and Sewall Putnam, *History of the Town of Wilton, Hillsborough County, New Hampshire* (Boston, 1884), 92–93. For the "Enumeration of Inhabitants in the Town of Wilton" dated October 24, 1775, see p. 87; for Lt. Jonathan Burton's diary entries of the regiment's activities in Winter Hill for the six weeks or so they were camped there, see pp. 238–42.

   8. Nathan Abbot, yeoman of Wilton to George Blanchard, yeoman of Wilton, Hillsborough County Deed Book 4:67, dated July 13, 1776.

   9. James Brown, yeoman of Wilton to George Blanchard, yeoman of Wilton, Hillsborough County Deed Book 7:302, dated May 17, 1780.

   10. William P. Colburn, "Register of Milford Families," in George Allen Ramsdell, *History of Milford, New Hampshire* (Concord, N.H., 1900), 592.

   11. Return of Marriage of George Blanchard and Bettie Nichols by the Reverend Samuel Cotton, Litchfield, N.H., dated November 24, 1810; copy on file at New England Genealogical and Historical Society, Boston.

   12. J[ames] Fred[erick] Smithcors, *Evolution of the Veterinary Art: A Narrative to 1850* (Kansas City, Mo., 1957), ch. 2; Bert W. Bierer, *American Veterinary History* (Fort Dodge, Iowa, 1980), 17–35.

   13. Ramsdell, 40.

   14. James Brown, farmer of Wilton, to George Blanchard, farmer of Wilton, for land in Wilton, Hillsborough County Deed Book 7:302, dated May 17, 1780. This may have been the farm later "owned by Samuel Goldsmith" (Livermore and Putnam, 322–23).

   15. George Blanchard, farmer of Wilton, grantor, to Joseph Gray, farmer of Wilton, grantee, for 40 acres in Wilton, Hillsborough County Deed Book 30:345, dated September 22, 1793; George Blanchard, farmer of Wilton, grantor, to Thomas

Means, Gent., of Amherst, grantee, for land in Wilton, Hillsborough County Deed Book 66:460, dated August 23, 1805.

16. Return of Death of George Washington Blanchard, aged 27, son of George and "Bettey" from Town of Wilton, dated April 12, 1812, from Wilton Town Clerk; copy on file New England Genealogical and Historical Society, Boston.

17. Index to Seamen's Protection Certificates Issued, 1798–1823, Customs District of Salem and Beverly, Massachusetts, Records Group 26, National Archives and Records Administration, Northeast Regional Archives, Frederick C. Murphy Service Center, 390 Trapelo Road, Waltham, Massachusetts 02452–6499.

18. Simeon Gutterson to George Blanchard for land in Milford, Hillsborough County Deed Book 98:41, dated November 22, 1813; George Blanchard to Timothy Blanchard for land in Milford, Hillsborough County Deed Book 102:461, and Timothy Blanchard to George Blanchard, Hillsborough County Deed Book 102:462, both dated November 18, 1814, registered November 23, 1814. This is the same property described as "later occupied by Peter F. Shedd" (Ramsdell, *History of Milford*, 183), since razed.

19. Timothy Blanchard, yeoman, of Milford, to the Directors of the Fourth School District of the Town of Milford, lease of realty for a schoolhouse, Hillsborough County Deed Book 103:504, dated January 26, 1815. There is also extant a receipt for firewood supplied to the school signed by Timothy Blanchard. For the short period that she did attend public school, Harriet Wilson — then Adams (or Green) — appears to have attended District School Number 3.

20. 1820 Federal Census for the Town of Milford, Hillsborough County, New Hampshire, 2.

21. Return of Marriage of Timothy Blanchard and Dorcas Hood by the Reverend Humphrey Moore of Milford, dated February 26, 1824, from Milford Town Clerk; copy on file New England Genealogical and Historical Society, Boston; Colburn, "Register," in Ramsdell, 593, 752.

22. Colburn, "Register," in Ramsdell, 592–93.

23. Ramsdell, 183.

24. Jeremiah Hood (1802–82) married Harriet E. Elkins (1801–82) of Henniker, N.H., in 1830 (Colburn, "Register," in Ramsdell, 752).

25. Charles E. Clark, *The Meetinghouse Tragedy: An Episode in the Life of a New England Town* (Hanover, N.H., 1998), 23. While work continued on the building, one of the support beams broke and the building collapsed. Five people were killed outright or died later from their injuries; almost fifty others were injured.

26. Oesterlin, *Hillsborough County, New Hampshire Court Records, 1772–1799*, 348, 367, 370.

27. Timothy Dodge, *Poor Relief in Durham, Lee, and Madbury, New Hampshire, 1732–1891* (Baltimore, 1985), discusses the local welfare system in small New Hampshire towns like Milford. For an overview of how antebellum America handled "the relief of the poor" see Michael B. Katz, *In The Shadow of the Poorhouse: A Social History of Welfare in America* (New York, 1986).

28. Harriet Wilson noted that her father's name was Joshua Green on two legal documents — the record of her second marriage in 1870 (*Massachusetts Marriages* 228:129) and on her death certificate (*Massachusetts Deaths* 506:95 for 1900). She apparently did not know where Joshua came from, as the space where that information would have gone was blank.

29. John W. Hutchinson, *The Story of the Hutchinson Family Singers* (Boston, 1894), 1:32–33.

30. Ibid.

31. Ibid., 1:33–34.

32. 1830 Federal Census of Population for Milford, Hillsborough County, New Hampshire, 13; the household included one white woman aged between 20 and 30 (unknown), one white woman between 30 and 40 (Dorcas H. Blanchard, aged 32), three free colored males under the age of 10 (George Walter Blanchard, aged 6, Samuel W. Blanchard, 4, Tim Blanchard, Jr., 2) one free colored male aged between 10 and 24 (unknown) and one free colored male aged between 36 and 55 (Timothy Blanchard, aged 39).

33. Timothy Blanchard, yeoman, of Milford, to Mrs. Mary P. Shedd, housekeeper, of Milford, Hillsborough County Deed Book 194:203, dated November 20, 1837. For family information see Colburn, "Register," in Ramsdell, 920.

34. John Gutterson, yeoman, of Milford, to Timothy Blanchard, yeoman, of Milford, Hillsborough County Deed Book 192:610, dated November 11, 1837. This would be the property that in 1900 was "that of Stephen C. Coburn" (Ramsdell, 183).

35. Timothy Blanchard to Robert B. Wallace, three tracts in the town of Milford, Hillsborough County Deed 201:91, dated March 7, 1839; Timothy Blanchard to Timothy Gray, an assignment on property in the town of Milford, Hillsborough County Deed Book 194:568, dated March 14, 1838.

36. Return of death of Timothy Blanchard from Milford Town Clerk, dated October 3, 1839. New England Genealogical and Historical Society, Boston.

37. Letters of Guardianship for Minor Children under Fourteen Years of Timothy Blanchard, late of Milford, deceased, Docket Number 795, December 5, 1839. Hillsborough County Will Book 42:58.

38. See Appendix B.

39. Estate of Timothy Blanchard to Moses Foster, Hillsborough County 210:149, dated March 1, 1841; Estate of Timothy Blanchard to Simeon Smith Stickney, M.D., Hillsborough County Deed Book 217:500, dated November 4, 1842; Estate of Timothy Blanchard to David P. Needham, Hillsborough County Deed Book 221:208, dated October 3, 1843.

40. Luther Hutchinson, Martin W. Hall, and Stephen C. Marshall, as administrators for the Estate of Timothy Blanchard to Dorcas H. Blanchard, Hillsborough County Deed Book 221:207, dated March 3, 1840, recorded October 3, 1843.

41. 1860 Federal Census for Mason, Hillsborough County, N.H., at 25, shows Luther "Elliott," a forty-year-old farm laborer, owning $350 in realty and $50 in personal property and Dorcas "Elliott," aged sixty-one.

42. 1850 Federal Census of Population for Milford, Hillsborough County, New Hampshire, 12.

43. The birth record of George Walter's youngest son Walter J. Blanchard (July 18, 1869, in Milford) lists George's color as "mulatto"; the 1870 Federal Census for Population for Milford lists George W. Blanchard as "Mu" for "mulatto"; however, someone crossed it out and inserted "W" (white). Succeeding census returns and other references in the public record, including his death certificate, list his color as "white." George Walter married an Irish girl from County Galway named Bedelia, or "Delia" Finerty, whose family had been among the first Roman Catholics to move into Milford; George and Delia would have three sons. In 1876, the Blanchards moved to the neighboring town of Mont Vernon, where they lived at a house at what is now 132 Francestown Turnpike; this would remain in the family for the next half century. Freida C. Day, editor, *Historic Mont Vernon: Volume 1 — Households, 1750–1957* (Mont Vernon, N.H., n.d.), 38.

44. Jacob Sanderson, John Blanchard, and John Watson, appraisers of the Estate of London Ruleff, mariner of Salem, filed April 18, 1804; Inventory dated June 26, 1804, Essex County (Massachusetts) Will Book 371:406 and 371:520–21; see also Essex County Deed Books 372:146 for determination of dower rights, and 372:240 for the sale of Ruleff's house. See also Melinde Lutz Sanborn, *Essex County, Massachusetts Probate Index, 1638–1840; transcribed by Melinde Lutz Sanborn from the original docket books transcribed by W[illiam] P[hineas] Upham* (Boston, 1987), 805.

45. Dorothy Sterling, ed., *We Are Your Sisters: Black Women in the Nineteenth Century* (New York, 1997), 114, prints an excerpt from the records of a mutual society where Molly Blanchard is listed as treasurer, Betsy Blanchard as vice president, and Sally Colman as the secretary. Sally may have been the only one of the sisters who learned to read and write.

46. 1850 Federal Census for Third Ward of the City of Salem, Essex County, Massachusetts, 52. Although their children would spell their last name "Coleman," both Sally and William resolutely spelled it "Colman"; however, it appears with the extra "e" in this census return.

47. George Adams, *The Salem Directory, Containing the City Record, Banks, Insurance Companies, Churches and Societies; the Names and Businesses of the Citizens, An Almanac for 1851; With a Variety of Miscellaneous Matter* (Salem, Mass., 1851), 180.

48. Celia Coleman never married; after her mother's death in 1877, she continued to live in her home at 12 Porter Street in Salem; she supported herself as a dressmaker and later took in boarders; she raised her orphaned nephews and nieces as well as two adopted children and lived to be eighty-six (Federal Census Enumeration of Population for the 5th Ward of the City of Salem, Essex County, Massachusetts between 1880 and 1910; *The Naumkeag Directory for Salem, Beverly, Danvers, Marblehead, Peabody, Essex, Ipswich; Containing a List of the Inhabitants and Business Firms of the District and Other Matters of General and Local Interest* [Salem, Mass., 1910], 140; Death Certificate for Celia Coleman, dated January 17, 1913, *Massachusetts Deaths* 86:420 for 1913).

49. Marriage record, Joseph B. Morris and Elizabeth B. Johnson, March 25, 1852, Salem, Mass., by the Reverend Thomas F. Stone, *Massachusetts Marriages* 60:204.

50. 1850 Federal Census of Population for the 5th Ward of the City of Salem, Essex County, Massachusetts; Marriage record, John S. Washington and Sarah M. "Washington," January 5, 1854, by the Reverend Josiah W. Talbot of the Second Universalist Church of Danvers, Mass., *Massachusetts Marriages* 78:142. One of Sara and John's grandsons was pioneer social work practitioner and educator and civil rights activist Forrester Blanchard Washington (1887–1963). The first black graduate of Tufts University (class of 1908), Washington was the founding executive director of the Detroit chapter of the National Urban League; he was involved with developing and implementing the federal government's response to the questions of welfare and relief issues concerning American blacks during the New Deal; and he would close out his career as Dean of the Atlanta University School of Social Work. See Frederica Harrison Barrow, "The Social Welfare Career and Contributions of Forrester Blanchard Washington: A Life Course Analysis," unpublished Ph.D. dissertation, Howard University School of Social Work, Washington, D.C., 2001.

51. D. E. Proctor, in Barbara A. White, "'Our Nig' and the She-Devil: New Information about Harriet Wilson and the 'Bellmont' Family." *American Literature* 65 (March 1993): 38; 1850 Federal Census of Population for Amherst, Hillsborough County, New Hampshire, 122.

52. Joseph Carvalho III, *Black Families in Hampden County, Massachusetts, 1650–1855* (Westfield, Mass., 1985), 95. Montague was the great-grandfather of pioneer African American anthropologist W. Montague Cobb (1903–90) of Howard University in Washington D.C. James G. Spady, "Dr. W. Montague Cobb: Anatomist, Physician, Physical Anthropologist, Editor Emeritus of the *Journal of the National Medical Association*, and the First Black President of NAACP," *Journal of the National Medical Association* 76 (1984): 739–44.

53. Thomas H. Jones, *The Experience of Thomas H. Jones, Who was A Slave for Forty-Three Years, Written by a Friend, as Related to Him by Brother Jones* (Worcester, 1857), for the first edition of his book; Adams, *The Salem Directory . . .*, 150, 180; 1850 Federal Census for the 3rd Ward of Salem, Essex County, Massachusetts, 123; Carvalho, *Black Families in Hampden County, Massachusetts, 1650–1855*, 33.

54. Daniel F. Secomb, *History of the Town of Amherst, Hillsborough County, New Hampshire* (Concord, N.H., 1888), 420–21.

55. Augustus Ayling, *Revised Register of the Soldiers and Sailors of New Hampshire in the War of the Rebellion 1861–1866* (Concord, N.H., 1895), 717.

56. Pension Records for Mrs. Dorcas H. Elliott, mother of Private James Blanchard, deceased, late of Company H, 10th New Hampshire Infantry Regiment, Pension Certificate Number 63,173. National Archives and Records Administration, Washington, D.C. Mrs. Johnson signed her deposition with an "X."

57. Colburn, "Register," in Ramsdell, 592–593.

"As Soon as I Saw My Sable Brother, I Felt More at Home"

Sampson Battis, Harriet Wilson, and New Hampshire Town History

David H. Watters

HARRIET WILSON'S *Our Nig* announces its location on the title page: "Two-Story White House, North. Showing That Slavery's Shadows Fall Even There." Critics argue that the shadows of Southern slavery darken her life as a servant indentured to a white New Hampshire family.[1] However, the shadow of slavery from New Hampshire's past also casts a pall over the lives of slaves who served in the Revolutionary War and over their descendants, such as Harriet Wilson, for whom freedom does not mean full equality and citizenship. The early pages of *Our Nig* provide glimpses of an African American community of laborers and craftsmen, long lost to the historical record, whose economic difficulties and erasure from the official memory of the struggle for freedom underlies Frado's demand for rights as a free, native-born resident of Milford, New Hampshire. The last sentence of the novel avers that slavery will haunt the state's memory: "Frado has passed from their memories, as Joseph from the butler's, but she will never cease to track them till beyond mortal vision" (131). By referencing Genesis 40:14–15, 23, Wilson challenges New Englanders, and particularly its historians, to remember Joseph: "But remember me, when it is well with you, and do me the kindness, I pray you, to make mention of me to Pharoah, and so get me out of this house. . . . Yet the chief butler did not remember Joseph, but forgot him." Historian Joanne Pope Melish argues that the antebellum era in New England was characterized by an "erasure by whites of the historical experience of local enslavement" to make a "region whose history had been re-visioned by whites as a triumphant narrative of free, white labor, a region within which free people of color could be represented as permanent strangers whose presence was unaccountable and whose claims to citizenship were absurd."[2]

In contrast to this erasure, Wilson's novel sketches her origins in an African American community rooted in New England. In Milford as in other New Hampshire towns, generations of African Americans had negotiated their enslaved and free identities as colonials and Americans, in a multinational and multiracial frontier of Native Americans, French, English, Scotch Irish, and Africans. To create a context for understanding Wilson's place in New Hampshire's African American history, this essay will explore the life of Sampson Battis of Canterbury, New Hampshire, a slave who, like Wilson's possible grandfather, Peter Greene, served in the American Revolution.[3] Battis's war service, his long life in Canterbury, and his family's complex racial heritage reveal the shadows of slavery. The shadow of slavery also falls on the means by which Battis's story is made known, since town histories and genealogies elide Anglo-Saxon bloodlines and the struggle for freedom in the creation of frontier New Hampshire towns. An examination of the representation of Battis in historical texts will help us understand Wilson's strategies for writing her history of an African American girl in Milford.

On a hillside in Canterbury, New Hampshire, the village cemetery has the look and feel of an iconic New England place. Surrounded by a well-built stone fence, with white picket gates hanging on hand-forged hinges, it sits at a crossroads bounded by crisp white-clapboarded old town hall, community church, country store, bandstand, small brick library, and a Civil War monument. The eye is drawn to the Morrill family plot, where massive granite monuments and a bronze plaque mark the resting places of a pioneer family whose six sons served in the American Revolution.

Down a steep bank, where the cemetery wall runs out into a swampy swale, one small government-issued marble monument sits accompanied by an American flag and Washington soldier of the Revolution medallion. It is for Sampson Battis, an enslaved man who served in the American Revolution. Clustered around the Battis marker are small fieldstones, blackened with lichen and leaf mold, indicating perhaps a score of kin or other members of an early African American community. When asked, locals don't know who Sampson Battis was.

In many New Hampshire towns, memory, history, and genealogy are tethered to monuments for Revolutionary War soldiers, and the contrasting Morrill and Battis sites signify the racial component in the creation of town and national identity.[4] The Morrill family looms as large in Canterbury's written history as it does in its cemetery. A massive granite monument embraces a bronze plaque:

Morrill family monuments, Center Cemetery, Canterbury, New Hampshire.
Courtesy of David H. Watters

Sampson Battis grave marker, Center Cemetery, Canterbury, New Hampshire. *Courtesy of David H. Watters*

Erected in 1929 by ROBERT SMITH MORRILL, GEORGE PEVERLY MORRILL, descendants of Deacons LABAN and DAVID MORRILL and others of the fifth, sixth, seventh, and eighth generations from EZEKIEL and JEMIMA MORRILL — MORRILL from Salisbury, Mass. And South Hampton, N.H. Whose children numbered fifteen. This couple, pioneers of Canterbury, were great grandchildren of Abraham of England, on Ship "Lion." 1632. They had six sons in our war for Independence and descendants in all our wars since. It is a "Long, long trail" from the Norman French Morel soldiers with William the Conquerer to the Morrells and Morrills the British emigrants to America who now reach the eleventh and twelfth generations in the United States.

The names of the six sons who served in the Revolution are engraved into the side of the stone. A massive granite bench is nearby, facing westward, with the inscription: "OUR KINDRED / ARE ALL OVER THE / U.S.A. / Deacon E. Morrill the 4th Gen. / Erected by 'Geo P.' of the 8th Gen. / in the U.S."

The Morrills proclaim descent from nation builders and warriors.[5] James Otis Lyford's *History of the Town of Canterbury, New Hampshire 1777–1912* inscribes this genetic legacy in the town's soul: "Pride in its past and hope in its future animate the present inhabitants of the town who, though fewer in numbers, are still for the most part of the good New England stock that for nearly three centuries has risen superior to its environments."[6] Town histories customarily join a volume of history to a volume of genealogy, as if narrative and biology speak with one voice to tell the story of New England. By erecting monuments for founding families, locals and their diasporic relatives evoke mythic nation-building to invest a declining rural landscape with the imagery of a flourishing seed of Abraham.[7] "Good New England stock" is presumably European, despite the genealogical and historical evidence of Canterbury's racially mixed heritage.

The story of Sampson Battis reveals town origins in slavery and in the murder of Abenakis. This story begins with a government-issued nineteenth-century marble gravemarker:

Sampson
Battis
Head's Co.
Reynolds N.H.
IIII Rev. War

The gravestone identifies Battis by name and by military service. A descendant of his master, Archelaus Moor, wrote in 1918, "Here sleeps the old slave. There is neither birth nor death record but a prouder one, doubtless nearer to his heart's choice."[8] Surmising what may have been Sampson Battis's choices in terms of a name and the meaning of his military service depends on a patchwork of records and anecdotes. In a deposition in his Revolutionary War pension application filed in 1832, he states he was born in Canterbury in 1752, and it is possible his parents were from the Durham area, from which Archelaus Moor and other families moved in the 1740s to settle Canterbury, or from one of the other seacoast area towns that supplied many slaves to central New Hampshire.[9]

Battis is called Sampson Moor, a slave of Archelaus Moor, in the first record of his Revolutionary War service in a Canterbury company in 1776.[10] Shortly thereafter, he becomes Battis in most documents, and this is the name used by his many descendants in Canterbury over the next century. The adoption of the Battis name declares independence from the Scotch Irish Moors, but Battis and his descendants maintained a familial connection with the Moors. The denial of kinship relations was an essential feature of slavery, so the use of two surnames has profound implications for Sampson Battis/Moor's consciousness of the nature of his freedom.[11] By shucking off a colonial slave name during the Revolution, Battis fractures familial and patriarchal bonds peculiar to African Americans. As we shall see, it is striking that he chose a form of the name "Sabattis," given the history of that name in Canterbury, and it suggests that Sampson Battis's identity is a complex negotiation involving African, European, and Native American histories and genealogies. This name, then, requires us to tease out and conjecture how Sampson Battis established his identity in the transition from colony to nation.

In Canterbury, Battis would have been understood as a form of the common Abenaki name Sabattis, or Is-battis, derived from St. Baptiste. A notation in the manuscript Canterbury town vital records confirms the connection between the names Battis and Sabattis. Canterbury records segregate on a separate page from those of white families the record of births of the children of two of Sampson Battis's sons, Sampson Battis, Jr., and Peter Battis, and those of the children of Sampson's grandchild, Nathaniel H. Battis. The births of Sampson, Jr.'s, children were recorded from 1815 to 1847, those of Peter from 1809 to 1816. The town clerk has crossed out Battis in Peter Battis's list, inserting "Sabattis," and a later clerk has placed an asterisk here and written clearly below "Sabattis," as the original insertion was crowded at the top of the page.[12] This notation indicates that the clerks understood the derivation of the name and its significance in Canterbury history.

Sabattis was the name of an Abenaki whose murder in 1754 put the town at the center of a colonial crisis. The tale of the murders of Sabattis and another Abenaki, Plausawa, for kidnapping Canterbury slaves reveals the role slavery played in continuing conflicts in frontier New Hampshire. New Hampshire colonists depended upon slave labor to establish towns on contested Abenaki lands, and Abenaki resistance focused in part on taking slaves for sale to the French. On May 8, 1752, Sabattis and Plausawa captured two Canterbury slaves, Mr. Linsey's Tom and Mr. Miles's Pier.[13] William Patrick's historical sermon of 1834 tells us, "At the close of the first day's march, they were inquired of, if they could point out the course they came. Tom honestly pointed in the true direction; but Pier more artful, pointed to a different course. This made the Indians less cautious in securing him. — Shortly after, he made his escape and returned to his master. Tom was never heard of afterwards. He probably ended his days in captivity." For Patrick's Canterbury auditors this moment of complex choices and allegiances showed that the "artful" slave prefers slavery to captivity, so the story functioned to establish allegiance of English and enslaved African against Indian and French.[14]

At the conclusion of open hostilities between the French and the English colonies, Sabattis and Plausawa returned to Canterbury in 1754, carrying a large number of furs for trade. Confronted by Mrs. Linsey about the kidnapping of Tom, Sabattis defended the earlier kidnapping as "lawful plunder" and stated that they now were "hunting" for captives in New Hampshire to redeem another Sabattis, a kinsman of Plausawa, "who had at Cape Sable killed an Indian and that they had agreed for his Redemption (being held by them) to pay five hundred pounds or get an English Slave. That Sabattis being his Namesake offered to assist him in the Redemption and said the Hunting was best this way."[15] Peter Bowen and John Morrill decided to take matters into their own hands. On the pretext of trading, they used rum to distract the Indians, removed charges from their guns, and stabbed and bludgeoned them to death. The crime was revealed when animals dug up their bodies.[16] Because these murders had the potential to inflame English-Abenaki relations across the northern frontier, Governor Shirley of Massachusetts insisted that Governor Wentworth of New Hampshire bring the perpetrators to justice, so Bowen and Morrill were arrested. Taken to Portsmouth for trial, they were freed by a mob, including prominent men from Canterbury and Boscawen, and no sheriff would subsequently arrest them as they freely went about their business.[17] This is a significant moment in New England history on the northern frontier, for it excises Abenakis from legal protection and erases recognition of Abenakis as persons with claims on Canterbury land and people, all in the name of preserving African slavery. Historian Margaret Ellen Newell calls towns like Canterbury a "race frontier," where people of color lost "certain rights enjoyed by their white counterparts."[18] The founding mythos of such towns as places of civilization and freedom depends on stories of heroic whites resisting savage Indians, so Battis's name disrupts the town's version of its origins. If both black and red identity were limited by white property rights, then indications of African American allegiance with Abenakis would link the origin of white freedom to slavery and the murder and dispossession of native people. In this context, Sampson Moor's decision to take Battis as his freedom name may indicate his family's mixed racial heritage as well as his desire to embody another version of Canterbury's origins.

In choosing the name "Battis," Sampson Moor must have known its Canterbury history and its Native American origins. He lived in Canterbury and shared military service with Simeon Ames, Jacob Hancock, and Edward Blanchard, who participated in the Bowen and Morrill prison break. He may have known John Morrill, and it's likely he knew Pier, the slave who returned to Canterbury. Battis probably knew another Canterbury slave, Dorset, who was kidnapped by Abenakis in 1757 and redeemed in 1761.[19] Whether the name signified Battis's native heritage is complicated by the presumption of African heritage for individuals enslaved in New England. Town histories often confuse slave racial heritage, as in the case of Battis's wife. Concord's historian Nathaniel Bouton writes, "William Coffin, the grandfather of Samuel Coffin, Esq., owned a Negro woman named 'Lucy.' 'Sampson,' a Negro belonging to Archelaus Moore, of Canterbury, wanted her for his wife; and there was an agreement that Sampson should work for one year for Mr. Coffin to pay for her. A man's wages at that time were about forty dollars a year, or the price of a yoke of oxen." Bouton misidentifies Lucy. The Canterbury genealogy explicitly states that Lucy was a "West India Indian."[20] "Sampson" was a name often associated with Native Americans in New England, most famously the Mohegan minister, Samson Occom. The desire to preserve the name "Sampson" was strong in the Battis family, as evidenced by the fact that a son was named Sampson and a granddaughter was named "Samson" Battis.[21] The name "Sampson Battis," therefore, may encode a complex, interracial history embedded in the early Canterbury, and it alerts us to the possibility of a mixed population of Abenakis and African Americans in Canterbury's "New Guinea." As Margaret Ellen Newell argues, "color became associated with slavery, and slavery with color; in the process the very 'Indianness' of many Native American servants come under attack."[22]

Strategies for preserving complex identities in New Hampshire's "New Guineas" in white-dominated towns exhibit features of Native American acculturation, conversion, or survivance, whereby choices are made to mediate one's visibility as racial other, especially as intermarriage and changing circumstances intervene over the generations.[23] For example, there is the story of Canterbury's Dinah, who was sold as a slave in 1764 to a Concord family, but who later moved to Canterbury, married, and had descendants still seen selling baskets in the streets of Concord in 1855. Basket-making and itinerant basket-selling were common markers of Indian identity. Indeed, as Ruth Phillips, Nan Wolverton, and Laurel Ulrich demonstrate, these crafts preserved identity as well as provided a livelihood for New England Native Americans.[24] Basket-selling in and of itself does not mean that Dinah was of Native American descent or mixed Native American and African descent, but craft and itinerant work, both of which Harriet Wilson practiced, had a distinctive Native American tradition in New England. Whether by kinship or by community, the Battis name allied Sampson's family with Canterbury's red and black history.

The Battis gravestone also locates his identity in the context of Revolutionary War service. The abstract of his Revolutionary War pension application states that he enlisted "at Canterbury in 1775 immediately on hearing of the Lexington Battle . . . under Capt. Benjamin Sias," and was discharged after serving one month, probably camped with other New Hampshire troops on the outskirts of Boston. He enlisted for two months in September 1777, marching to Saratoga and then Fort Edward under Sias and Lieutenant David Morrill of Canterbury. He enlisted again in July 1781 for three months in Capt. Nathaniel Head's company, "marched for West Point, N.Y.; got as far as Danbury, Conn., when they were ordered back to Springfield, Mass., then to Charlestown, N. H., where they were when the news of Cornwallis' defeat was received 'and the troops had a day of rejoicing on the occasion;' served his three months and was verbally discharged[.]" His pension claim was accepted on February 16, 1833, and he is listed as a pensioner in 1840, age 89. He may have lived until 1853.[25]

Nineteenth-century town records show landholdings of Battis descendants, but stories conflict as to whether he was given his freedom and one hundred acres for his service in the Revolutionary War. The Moor family genealogy notes, "In 1802, John Moore, son of Colonel Archelaus, leased to Sampson Battis for $1 for his natural life a lot in Canterbury between No. 51 and the Concord line. This is the only document on the records but tradition has it that his master, Col. Archelaus, gave Sampson a 100-acre farm 'for good fighting in the Revolution.'"[26] Battis is a resident of Dunbarton in the 1790 census, so he may not have owned land in Canterbury before the lease of 1802. The earliest published information on Battis landholdings is by Chandler Potter in 1866, and he seems to draw on lost historical records as well as local memory in his footnote on Benjamin Sias's company:

Sampson Moore was a volunteer under Capt. Sias. He was a slave of Col. Archelaus Moore, of Canterbury, who promised him his freedom, for good fighting in the revolution. Col. Moore not only redeemed his promise, but gave Sampson a 100 acre lot in the south west part of Canterbury, upon which his descendents lived for many years, and which was called "New Guinea." Sampson was a fine specimen of a negro, was in command of a battalion in the early part of the present century, and is well recollected by people in Concord as attending Election and Muster, dressed in his "regimentals," and greatly enjoying his title of Major, which he honorably held from Governor Gilman.[27]

Given the shift of verb tense, Potter draws on personal testimony to confirm Battis's militia title and command. This is a complicated assertion, given the fact that the state militia act of December 12, 1792, states "that all free, able-bodied white male citizens, from eighteen to forty years of age, should be enrolled. . . ."[28] Canterbury's battalion in the eleventh regiment lists Nathaniel Head and other white commanders, but it is possible that Battis served in some capacity. In the Revolutionary War, he served with John Taylor Gilman, who as New Hampshire's governor, 1794–1805 and 1813–15, was Captain General and Commander-in-chief of the militia. If Potter is correct, Battis was the first African American commissioned to lead white troops in United States history.

The militia act of 1808 provided "music-money" and mandated inspections in June and a battalion parade in September or October. "Music-money" paid for the fifes and drums necessary for drills and parades and perhaps for musical entertainment and dances associated with muster days. Bouton provides this glimpse of his fiddling: "Sampson was a famous fiddler, and for many years afforded fine fun for frolicsome fellows in Concord with his fiddle on election days."[29] As William Piersen notes, fiddling and fine dress for African Americans may have blended local military and civic customs with the elements of Negro election ceremonies. These are probably the events at which Battis was remembered in his "regimentals."[30] As Sarah Purcell, David Waldstreicher, and Simon Newman write, white Americans by the early decades of the nineteenth century viewed such military and election celebrations in terms of rites of white citizenship that came to exclude African Americans. Indeed, by the 1820s, as Joanne Pope Melish documents, racist caricatures of blacks in military garb were standard fare in Massachusetts broadsides that ridiculed black pretensions to participate in such rites.[31] Thus Battis's regimentals may express his assertion of citizenship as well as a badge of past military service.

Town histories diminish black participation in the Revolutionary War by presenting it in terms of quaint anecdotes and as a validation of white aspirations for freedom. Emancipation for war service is a personal transaction between benevolent owner and slave ("freedom, for good fighting") rather than an inalienable or constitutional right resulting from that service. The archetypal New Hampshire story involves Prince Whipple of Portsmouth, enslaved by General William Whipple, a signer of the Declaration of Independence. As historian Charles Brewster told the story in 1859, Prince, reluctant to join General Whipple in preparations for war, says, "'Master, you are going to fight for your liberty, but I have none to fight for.' 'Prince,' said the general, 'behave like a man, and do your duty, and from this hour you shall be free.' Prince did his duty, accompanied his master in his expedition, and was a free man." The historical record shows that Prince, in fact, was not manumitted until 1784, but Brewster's version accords with the beliefs of the time in which freedom is granted for faithful service, manhood, and duty, all defined by a white man.[32] By making this a personal, white-centered bargain, the larger question of group rights and identities in the context of the Revolution and their extension beyond the Northern states is not raised, nor is the fact that emancipation in New Hampshire was not secured by legal statute until 1857.[33]

Popular literature, such as Harriet Beecher Stowe's "The Old Meeting House" (1840), depicted black Revolutionary War veterans as curiosities of old times who confirmed enduring New England customs and social structures.

> Prominent there was the stately form of old Boston Foodah, an African prince, who had been stolen from the coast of Guinea in early youth, and sold in Boston. . . . He was servant to General Hull in the Revolutionary war, and at its close was presented by his master with a full suit of his military equipments, including three-cornered hat, with plume, epaulets, and sword. Three times a year, — at the spring training, the fall muster, and on Thanksgiving day, — Boston arrayed himself in full panoply, and walked forth a really striking and magnificent object. In the eyes of us boys, on these days, he was a hero, and he patronized us with a condescension which went to our hearts.[34]

African American historians William Nell and William Wells Brown opposed such images by recasting Revolutionary War service as a fight for freedom that was betrayed. William Nell writes in *The Colored Patriots of the American Revolution*, "It is not very surprising, that in the time of the Revolutionary War, when so much was said of freedom, equality, and the rights of man, the poor African should think that he had some rights, and should seek that freedom others valued so highly. There were slaves then, even in New Hampshire, and their owners, like the Egyptians of old, and the Carolinians now, were unwilling to 'let them go.'" To counter the image of just masters freeing slaves who fight for white liberty, Nell quotes New Hampshire historian Jeremy Belknap's statement in 1795 that owners took enlistment bounty money for their slaves "'as the price of their liberty. . . .'"[35]

Nell and Brown evoke the memory of black veterans to confront Northern racism and Southern slavery. William Wells Brown's "Visit of a Fugitive Slave to the Grave of Wilberforce" points to the ways in which monuments to the Revolution recapitulate inequality. Brown forces us to re-examine the relationship between the Morrill and Battis monuments in the light of his response to English and American sites. Viewing Nelson's column in Trafalgar Square, he at first objects to the carnage of the wars of civilized nations, but then he notices an African figure:

> . . . as soon as I saw my sable brother, I felt more at home, and remained longer than I had intended. Here was the Negro, as black a man as was ever imported from the coast of Africa, represented in his proper place by the side of Lord Nelson, on one of England's proudest monuments. How different, thought I, was the position assigned to the colored man on similar monuments in the United States. Some years since, while standing under the shade of the monument erected to the memory of the brave Americans who fell at the storming of Fort Griswold, Connecticut, I felt a degree of pride as I beheld the name of two Africans who had fallen in the fight, yet I was grieved but not surprised to find their names colonized off, and a line drawn between them and the whites. This was in keeping with American historical injustice to its colored heroes.[36]

Brown criticizes the injustice of historical memory, but he also suggests that black revolutionary consciousness is "colonized off" as a dependency of white liberty. He attacks colonization schemes among abolitionists that would export to Africa people whose ancestors fought for America's freedom. These forms of colonization deprive African Americans of the ability to feel at home, and it is this homelessness that Battis and Wilson resist as they claim their place in Canterbury and Milford.

Battis fights homelessness by establishing a family, asserting his status as a veteran, maintaining connections with the Moors, and finding a place in history. As Melish notes, for the Revolutionary War generation, "The problem facing people of color in the 1780s was the same problem they had had all along: to enact their conception of themselves as heads and members of families, as community leaders, as workers, lovers, parents, and friends within a structure of formal regulation and informal custom and expectation maintained by people who took their status of servitude for granted."[37] Battis's appearance in regimentals decades later at celebrations for elections in which he could not vote raises questions about what freedom really meant to him. By 1790, he had married and established a family, and he eventually acquired land. Paid labor and his fiddle could support a household independent of the Moor family. Around 1790, Archelaus Moor sold his holdings in Canterbury and moved to land held with his son in Loudon, possibly ending employment for Moor on the Canterbury farm. Joanne Pope Melish notes the double-edged issue of African Americans' relationships with previous owners. Formerly enslaved people may have felt entitled to financial support or employment as compensation for enslavement, and they may have expected support from the household kinship network of their former master's family. But such continuing support played into racist assumptions about black dependency and inferiority.[38]

We know Battis valued freedom of movement, since the 1790 census lists him as the head of a household of eight persons in Dunbarton. Dunbarton's town meeting authorized construction of a new meeting house in May, 1789, to be completed by November 1, 1790, and such projects often required labor beyond what townspeople could provide. For Battis and other free persons of color, the project may have offered employment and the opportunity to form a community. Battis may have worked as an ox drover, hauling stone for the granite foundation and timber for the massive frame, and he may have sawn boards, split clapboards and shingles, and then worked on the construction of the building. Battis's wife and children may have plied the local trade of making brush brooms and baskets for sale in Concord. In Dunbarton in 1790, there was a "new Guinea" of some twenty people on Guinea Road, perhaps clustering around the family of Scipio "Sip" Page, formerly a slave of Captain Caleb Page.[39] New Guineas in many towns formed around African American veterans who owned land, so freedom meant free association, mobility, family formation, and employment.

When Battis became a pensioner in the 1830s, the rise of abolitionist sentiments in New Hampshire provoked a local backlash against African Americans. William Patrick's historical sermon of 1834 names Battis as one of the Canterbury veterans still living in town, and he writes, "We review these scenes of peril and suffering and would gratefully cherish in our minds, the memory of those who fought our battles, and under God, achieved our independence."[40] Given the rising debate over the meaning of the Revolution for American slavery, is Battis truly included in the "our" of Patrick's "our independence," or is his status marked by the "Our Nig" construction of Wilson's text? Battis's military record paralleled that of another Canterbury veteran, Col. David Morrill, under whom Battis first served at Fort Edward, but war service for Morrill gained all the fruits of freedom and citizenship, from land grants to public office. The 1835 mob attack on the interracial Noyes Academy in Canaan, N.H., an attack defended by New Hampshire Senator Isaac

Hill in terms suggesting that New Hampshire towns should, by nature, be white, must have troubled Battis and other residents of "New Guinea" in Canterbury. P. Gabrielle Foreman and Reginald H. Pitts argue that this attack may well have inspired Harriet Wilson's depiction of Frado's schooling in Milford.[41] Battis lived just across the Merrimack River from Boscawen, New Hampshire, where in 1837 there was another example of the harassment of black children seeking an education. Town historian Charles Coffin Webster wrote in 1878 that anti-slavery agitation on July 4, 1837, was accompanied by "an intense prejudice against color." When black families living in a house in the Corser Hill school district presented their children at the school, the district quickly convened a meeting to vote to bar their admission. The children were eventually admitted to the North Water Street school. Coffin recounts the local fear that freed slaves would move to the North:

> Thomas Coffin was an emancipationist; his brother-in-law, Dea. Nehemiah Cogswell, was a colonizationist. Their discussions were always friendly, though sometimes warm.
> "The negro is a man, and is entitled to freedom," said the first.
> "Brother, do you want all those niggers to make their appearance on Water Street?" was the reply, often repeated.[42]

This racism must have been a particular affront to New Hampshire black residents whose family roots reached back into the Revolutionary Era. Racism in Boscawen or Milford schools betrayed the common school movement, which claimed to advance equality through public education. As Eve Raimon argues, Miss Marsh's speech criticizing prejudice against Frado in *Our Nig* extends schoolhouse class egalitarianism to race, but in practice educational equality was not a reality for the grandchildren of black Revolutionary War veterans.[43] Given the examples of Battis in his regimentals and Frado in her classroom, we can look to other ways in which Battis and Wilson challenged racial exclusion from the town and family rights secured by the Revolution.

The traditional New England concepts of "family" and "household" extended to servants, slaves, and others who may or may not be biologically related. Towns like Canterbury and Milford recognized the "town" as a physical, political, and psychological nexus of rights and responsibilities based in a genealogical and historical web of people who were born there and thus rooted in its history.[44] People "of the town" became visible in town and church records as they were baptized, schooled, taxed, married, supported in indigence or old age, and buried. Those not of the town could be warned out. However, many people were left in a kind of limbo as a result of their racial status. Battis and his children and grandchildren owned land, but there is no evidence of their participation in civic life through voting or office-holding, and the spouses of two of his children were pointedly noted as transients.[45] Harriet Wilson receives little schooling and she struggles for help from the Bellmonts and the town when ill. Wilson's and Battis's expectations to be treated as family members are harder to trace. We see Frado's search for parental and sibling care and affection from the Bellmonts, and, as we shall see, the Battis and Moor families maintained contact for 150 years. Most difficult to determine are their expectations of visibility in town history, since their lives embody a history that challenges the racial lines that constituted American political life.

The cluster of stones around the Battis monument confirms there were many African Americans whose names, lives, and genealogies are either unrecorded in town history or partially documented in relationship to white families. Sampson's daughter Sophia had twenty-two children, and his son Sampson had seven, but few are named in town records.[46] Records are silent on four of the children in the Battis household in the 1790 census. In a similar case, it is only in the Reverend William Patrick's *Historical Sketches of Canterbury, N.H.* (1834) that we learn that Deborah, enslaved by Joseph Ayres on land near the Battis family, lived to be 102 years of age and had fourteen children.[47]

As intermarriage in Canterbury and Milford blurred the color line, locals probably acknowledged a diverse ancestry, but published histories circumscribed racial visibility.[48] The Colonial Revival movement of the nineteenth century emphasized New England's Anglo-Saxon heritage, and African American lives were relegated to anecdotes, miscellaneous information, and footnotes. It is highly unusual that Lyford's Canterbury genealogy includes a separate though fragmentary Battis family entry, but there is no discrete narrative of the family in the history volume. Footnotes about Moor family lots locate the Battis property in "New Guinea" and state that Sampson Battis worked there for Moor until freed.[49] The Battis family exists in town history only as part of the Moor family. This difference between evidence and narrative represents, in Joanne Pope Melish's formulation, the "campaign to remove former slaves and their descendants from their [whites'] landscape and memory" perhaps through colonization schemes and other physical means, or through the "symbolic removal of people of color from their place in New England history."[50] Harriet Wilson's telling phrase, "two-story white house," alerts us to the alternative histories of her town. Therefore, we must examine town histories closely not only for the scraps of black history they contain but also for the strategies by which they contain or demarcate this history in relation to the narrative of white, freedom-loving pioneer families who founded towns and a nation. We need to consider how evidence is made visible and meaningful for contemporary readers. This examination establishes a context for the intervention of Sampson Battis and Harriet Wilson in white historiography.

Given the uncertainty of early boundaries between Canterbury and Concord and his movement between them, Battis appears in both volumes. These town histories and the appended family histories and genealogies reveal the organizational and representational structures that presumed to make the past knowable. The title of the 1856 Concord history by Nathaniel Bouton is: *The History of Concord, From Its First Grant in 1725, to the Organization of the City Government in 1853, with a History of the Ancient Penacooks. The Whole Interspersed with Numerous Interesting Incidents and Anecdotes, Down to the Present Period, 1855; Embellished with Maps; with Portraits of Distinguished Citizens, and Views of Ancient and Modern Residences.* The book was the largest and most costly original work to date from a New Hampshire press, and Bouton's epigraph evokes biblical authority: "This shall be written for the generation to come."

The title reveals the insufficiency of organic political chronology to encompass Concord history since the "interesting incidents and anecdotes" present competing sources of information, narrative methods, and historical authenticity. Its organizational plan includes Indian history, Penacook before settlement by the whites, then decennial periods, roughly, from 1725 on, and within these, miscellaneous items, anecdotes, and lists of town officers. It also includes topographical description, biographies, ecclesiastical history, genealogical lists, occupational histories, a list of college graduates, miscellaneous matters, and a documentary and statistical chapter. The "interesting incidents and anecdotes," with their folkloric oral sources and creative narrative style, disrupt the developmental political history that structures the book. These features probably reflect the interests of the private and public citizens who contributed information to and paid a subscription for the work, the expectations of presumed readers, and perhaps most important, the wisdom and curiosity of the author upon whom the coherence and authority of the history depend. The New Hampshire town historian often was a minister, whose education, experience as an interpreter of texts, duties as church record keeper, and social status gave him the requisite skills and authority for the task. Bouton tells us he served as minister for thirty years while gaining access to records from earlier times, "recitals of aged citizens," newspapers, original records, archives of town clerks, the secretary of state, the New Hampshire Historical Society, family papers and genealogies, and personal correspondence.[51] In Bouton's scheme, African Americans exist in connection to whites, appear in footnotes and in "Anecdotes" appended to the historical narrative of a period or decade. For example, Battis appears in an anecdote section placed just before a section on "Bears."

Published fifty-six years later, Lyford's *History of Canterbury* provides a similar combination of chronological and topical history, but with a new historiographic emphasis on documentation. Without surviving oral traditions or diaries, he can't include the "spice of personal equation" in early Canterbury history. His aspiration to present "at least the history of what was done, rather than a compilation of what is remembered to have happened . . ." serves to diminish even further the presence of people of color, who are underrepresented in town documents.[52] In Bouton's and Lyford's volumes, Native Americans exist as "ancient Penacooks" eliminated in the frontier crucible, and African Americans are displayed as curiosities.

Town histories share strategies for presenting racial others with the contemporary establishment of state and local historical societies. Their collection plans and taxonomies are derived from European curiosity cabinets (*wunderkammern*) of the sixteenth and seventeenth centuries, in which a privileged collector assembled ethnographic materials, historical items, and exotic natural objects, so-called curiosities, to incite curiosity in the observer.[53] The private, often aristocratic, collector orchestrates the collective curiosity of a select audience through the display of objects, but the American town historian or museum curator appeals to a public that constitutes the town, state, and nation. Museum historian Susan Crane argues that museums contributed to the creation of national identity by presenting "'primitive' peoples and 'exotic' cultures" for the "fascination and consumption" of bourgeois audiences. The display of a primitive past provided viewers with a narrative about the development of their own modern identities.[54] Individual identity has historical meaning as part of a collective identity, be it town, state, or nation, and a museum, like a town history, serves as a storehouse and archive for the collection, preservation, and display of artifacts from individuals whose lives exemplify that collective identity. Michael Fehr proposes that museums are "representation machines that point via the material stored inside them to something outside themselves," thereby creating an illusion that what is outside, such as all the contingency and heterogeneity of the past, should be understood in terms of a museum's set of interpreted artifacts.[55]

It is instructive, then, to think of local histories and genealogies, such as the Bouton, Lyford, Moor, and Morrill books, as *wunderkammern*, or cabinets of curiosity, that present figures like Sampson Battis on display as exotica whose presence is detached from an independent historical agency and subsumed in the classification system of the elite collector or the narrative of the town historian. As in a museum display, documents about Sampson Battis appearing in texts from 1834, 1856, 1866, 1910, 1912, and 1918 resonate both with the surrounding materials and with the reader's historical and racial consciousness to create a representation of Battis's African American identity. As Grimes notes, the cabinet, and I argue the town history, is a "theater of suspended disbelief, where the context of objects is dematerialized to reappear in different forms, dressed in new meaning and altered realities. The objects of the cabinet are therefore embedded in two worlds: one represented by the time, place, and cultural context of their origin: the other represented by the world conjured by the cabinet itself, a world of the collector's mind and the values of his or her culture."[56] Bouton and Lyford serve as guides to the cabinet of curiosity that is Concord's and Canterbury's past, and they presume readers share their privileged position as Anglo-Saxon elites to whom the meaning of the past is entrusted.

Local history identifies recent political constructs, Concord and Canterbury, as a natural development of Anglo-Saxon identity forged in colonial and Revolutionary times. Through local history and genealogy, the towns legitimate origins and a heritage of freedom. Therefore, New Hampshire's displaced Abenakis and enslaved African Americans are exotic curiosities, remnants of uprooted family trees, remembered only to be forgotten.

Sampson Battis and Harriet Wilson must have been aware of their towns' origin stories and anecdotes about slavery. Barbara White and R. J. Ellis have displayed in meticulous detail the abolitionist sentiment and activity in Milford during Wilson's life, but less has been written about Milford's history of slavery. In George Ramsdell's *History of Milford*, the only paragraph on slavery is sandwiched between information on the town poor auction and the establishment of post routes. Ramsdell claims that "slavery was never legalized or established by law," and in a careful circumlocution he writes about the situation after 1789: "after that date, in some instances, servants who had been held as slaves remained in the families in which they had lived, and were sometimes spoken of as slaves. How many persons have at any time been held in servitude upon the soil now the town of Milford cannot be ascertained, but the number is small."[57] The elision of the condition of slavery in a mumbojumbo about "servants," and the disconnection of the name "Milford" from the soil on which slaves were held, suggests that forgetting Joseph was at the root of Milford's origin narrative. It is a mythology perpetuated by one of Milford's most famous residents, Abby Hutchinson, in her "Song of Our Mountain Home": "Among our free hills are true hearts and brave, / The air of our mountains ne'er breathed on a slave."[58] A bizarre footnote depicts slavery as a humorous curiosity in the story of the Crosby family's arrival in 1753:

> Mr. Crosby was one day in Boston, with his wife, making purchases. The mistress of the shop was complaining of the large number of children that from time to time appeared in the family of her negro wench, rendering her of little service as a servant. The shop keeper added that she did what she could to keep the number at home within bounds, by occasionally giving away a negro baby, and offered one to Mr. and Mrs. Crosby. They concluded to accept the gift, and named the boy Jeffrey. They sold him at the age of five years to go to Billerica, Mass. . . .[59]

This display of slavery, to prove, in effect, its absence as a significant part of early Milford history, permits Ramsdell, when the subject turns to abolitionism, to assert, "It can truthfully be said that in no town in New Hampshire were the seeds of opposition to the institution of African slavery earlier planted than in the town of Milford," an opposition he dates to opinions expressed "from the time of the adoption of the constitution. . . ."[60] This assertion about Milford's past, like that of many town histories at the time, requires the allocation of the fragments of the history of slavery into anecdotes and curiosities. The narrative of pioneer families who create "an almost Utopian state of society, in which selfishness and exclusiveness had but small part," is founded on white bloodlines: "The Puritan element in the character of the early settlers of the town had about the right amount of Scotch-Irish blood in combination to make a strong and enduring foundation upon which to build a town, a state, or a nation."[61]

Selective amnesia about servitude and the evocation of white bloodlines effectively erases Battis's life and Wilson's ancestry from town history. The developing consciousness of American freedom after the Revolutionary War as a feature of Anglo-Saxon bloodlines requires an amnesia about the racially mixed origins of the society, so the stories of Sabattis and Plausawa's murder and of slavery in Canterbury become a pretext for the emergence of a free, enlightened, white society. The reader of town history will, like Pharoah's butler, hear Joseph's story, only to forget him.

These historical practices provide a context for Wilson's and Battis's interventions in New Hampshire history. Battis's name and regimentals and Wilson's novel disrupt the images, symbols, and narrative representations of American freedom. Homi Bhaba writes, "Minority discourse . . . contests genealogies of 'origin' that lead to claims for cultural supremacy and historical priority. Minority discourse acknowledges the status of national culture — and the people — as a contentious, performative space of the perplexity of the living in the midst of the pedagogical representations of the fullness of life."[62] If white Americans trace freedom to the founding of families and towns and to the Revolutionary War, both Battis and Wilson demonstrate how their presence complicates and contests this vision of freedom.

For example, Wilson reveals the artificiality of New England's antebellum historical recollections when she assembles her own *wunderkammern* of white folks in the pages of *Our Nig*. In this "two-story white house" museum, artifacts of oppression and Frado's body are put on display in tableaux vivant that subvert the performance of white abolitionist historical narrative and biography.[63] A "rawhide, always at hand in the kitchen," the piece of wood stuck in her mouth, a carving knife, an ancient bonnet, a dessert plate, a tear-stained Bible, and a fifty-cent piece are simple household objects that resonate with curiosity when exhibited as instruments of oppression. Entrance into this curiosity cabinet of racism implicates the reader in a history that belies the public meanings of the community and its idealized homes. Critics read the metaphor of the two-story white house in terms of slavery and oppression North and South. For Eve Raimon, the "structure functions as the national imaginary . . . an architectural metaphor for the regional, racialized systems of labor." Lois Leveen finds the hierarchies of slavery embodied in northern domestic space, so Frado's exclusion from domestic space reveals the whiteness of the cult of domesticity in New England and causes the persistent homelessness of African Americans. In Joanne Pope Melish's analysis of *Our Nig*, Wilson "explodes the notion of the model of white fireside culture" promulgated in sentimental literature.[64]

Wilson's story also disrupts the narrative formulas of New England historiography. The very "sketchiness" of Wilson's narrative signifies the incoherence that racism inflicts on a black authorial voice, as surely as the piece of wood stuck in Frado's mouth, since the book makes explicit the whiteness of the authorial voice of New England history. By putting her own subjectivity on display as "Our Nig," Wilson undermines the pretense that histories and sketches and white houses are stable representations of the North. If *Our Nig* is, in Priscilla Wald's words, a "narrative about autobiography," it is also a narrative about the creation of historical narrative.[65] Frado's struggle to tell her story in the household provokes Mrs. Bellmont to violence: "if she ever exposed her to James, she would 'cut her tongue out'" (72). Mrs. Bellmont attempts to "cure her of tale-bearing" by wedging wood between her teeth. When Frado tells the truth to the supposedly enlightened and sympathetic James, who stands in for the white readers of the book, it won't be heard. Frado does "expose the cruel author of her misery," but "Poor James shut his eyes in silence, as if pained to forgetfulness by the recital" (83–84). A "cruel author" writes misery on Frado's body, but when she authors her own tale, eyes and ears close. Wilson's book includes the kinds of speech that constitute identity — oral history, tales, anecdotes, testimonies, prayers, and religious experiences. Mrs. Bellmont embodies the white community's fears of loss of control over both authorized forms of public and household speech and historical representation itself by which whites construct their identity. She says, "'I found her reading the Bible to-day, just as though she expected to turn pious nigger, and preach to white folks'" (88). Mrs. Bellmont further asserts, "'prayer was for whites, not for blacks,'" who should follow commands rather than make petitions. She is terrified that Frado has an audience when she "'related her experience the other night at the meeting'" (94).

Drawing on her repository of oral reports, Wilson practices the literary craft of town history in *Our Nig*, including genealogy, anecdote, topographic description, family history, religious testimony, and letters. Wilson, speaking late in the book in the first person, contemplates historical authorship as the means to gain visibility "within the compass of my narrative" (126). Frado's impulse to write arises from "useful books" containing "deeds historic and names renowned," and "she felt that this book information supplied an undefined dissatisfaction she had long felt but could not express" (124). However, the representational structure of whiteness in historical writing may have inspired Wilson to escape from autobiographical and historical forms. "Mrs. B. had always represented her ugly" (108), much as white writing presented African Americans as physically ugly or morally degenerate. To see herself outside of such regimes of representation, Frado, like many emancipated slaves a few years later, "felt disposed to flee from any and every one having her [Mrs. B's or Jane Bellmont's] similitude of name or feature" (110). For Wilson, autobiography itself may have been a prison-house of memory. Wilson's attempt to liberate herself from the white generic bondage implied in the "Our Nig" formulation has consequences similar to those experienced by Sampson Battis when he takes a new name and leaves the Moor farm. To move completely beyond the bounds of a hometown resulted in civil and historical erasure, but to remain risks dependency and misrepresentation.

Sampson Battis was aware of the celebration of pioneering white families and their old homesteads. In Howard Moore's *Descendants of Ensign John Moor*, the story of the old homestead of Archelaus Moor's brother William includes a subversive performance by Sampson Battis. Moore reflects that the hallowed building "has heard many strange things. Tragedy and comedy, war and love, romance and drudgery, sickness and reveling. . . ." An old elm cut down in 1905 in the dooryard contains a trace of memory:

Samuel Gilman . . . used to relate that when a boy . . . a very aged negro man
used to visit his father, reclining under the big elm to tell the story of his youth
when as the slave of Col. Archelaus Moore, who lived on the next place, he
once pulled up that very elm 'to see if it was growing' shortly after it was trans-
planted there, and was roundly whipped for it. . . . He is said to have been over
6 feet tall, very erect in carriage and in later years with hair as white as snow.
Samuel Gilman estimated the age of the tree at about 150 years when he cut it
down. It is interesting and convincing that all of these dates, ages and traditions, corroborate each other fully.[66]

Battis's self-fashioning in this story is complex. It recalls a boyhood prank, but
it also suggests his disruption of white notions of origins, since his presence
shows other lineages, Native American and African, that were uprooted when
that elm was planted in the ancestral dooryard, and that are now uprooted
from town history.

In planting this alternate story of a whipping tree at the root of New England's freedom, Battis complicates the mythology of honest George Washington barking his father's tree. His uprooted tree story may also be a wry
comment on the cultural practice of making trees icons of Revolutionary War
history, like the Washington elm in Cambridge or the Whipple horse chestnut in Portsmouth.[67] William Nell criticizes the liberty tree mythology when
he envisions an abolitionist regeneration of "public sentiment in favor of Universal Brotherhood. To this glorious consummation, all, of every complexion,
sect, sex and condition, can add their mite, and so nourish the tree of liberty, that all may be enabled to pluck fruit from its bending branches; and,
in that degree to which colored Americans may labor to hasten the day, they
will prove valid their claim to the title, 'Patriots of the Second Revolution.'"[68]
Sampson Battis, on whose body the marks of slavery remained, and in whose
name persists the history of Canterbury's Native Americans, and whose uniform displays the ambiguous meaning of the American Revolution, lives on in
the Moor family history. Battis's dramatic gesture and his oral tradition requires Howard Moore to cross racial lines to include the Battis family at a
time when Jim Crow racism North and South was sundering such bonds. All
but invisible to town and state historians, the Moor and Battis families testify
to their shared history into the 1920s. Howard Moore calls Battis "famous,"
notes a descendant in the area, Calvin D. Battis of Boscawen, and asserts,
"There was for generations affection and esteem between the two families and
it is testified to this day by living descendants of Archelaus Moor in the far
West."[69] With this anecdote, Battis, in Wilson's phrase, passed from human
memory and from New Hampshire history.

The Bible tells us that the butler finally did remember Joseph. Remembering Sampson Battis reconnects Wilson's life to a complex, interracial community with roots in the colonial era, but it also forces recognition that New Hampshire cannot pass as a state with only white roots. New England historians must pull up the tree by the roots to reveal New Hampshire's multiracial origins and to learn that the kindred of Sampson Battis are also "ALL OVER THE USA."[70]

NOTES

1. Harriet E. Wilson, *Our Nig, or, Sketches from the Life of a Free Black*, ed. Henry Louis Gates, Jr. (New York: Vintage, 2002). Subsequent quotations are from this edition. The P. Gabrielle Foreman and Reginald H. Pitts edition (New York: Penguin, 2005) and R. J. Ellis, *Harriet Wilson's Our Nig: A Cultural Biography of a "Two-Story" African American Novel* (Amsterdam–New York: Rodopi, 2003), document in extraordinary detail the cultural and biographical contexts of Wilson's book. Ellis argues persuasively that the "two-story" motif critiques southern sentiments among northern abolitionists. See also Barbara A. White, "'Our Nig' and the She-Devil: New Information about Harriet Wilson and the 'Bellmont' Family," *American Literature* 65.1 (1993): 19–52; John Ernest, "Economies of Identity: Harriet E. Wilson's *Our Nig*," *PMLA* 109 (1994): 424–38; Julia Stern, "Excavating Genre in *Our Nig*," *American Literature* 67 (1995): 439–66; and Lois Leveen, "Dwelling in the House of Oppression: The Spatial, Race, and Textual Dynamics of Harriet Wilson's *Our Nig*," *African American Review* 35.4 (2001): 561–80.

2. Joanne Pope Melish's *Disowning Slavery: Gradual Emancipation and "Race" In New England, 1780–1860* (Ithaca: Cornell University Press, 1998), 3.

3. Foreman and Pitts, 84–85. Ellis also discusses Wilson's ancestor's war service, 34–35. For a comprehensive survey of New Hampshire's veterans, see Glenn A. Knoblock, *"Strong and Brave Fellows": New Hampshire's Black Soldiers and Sailors of the American Revolution, 1775–1784* (Jefferson, N.C.: McFarland & Company, Inc., 2003).

4. Benedict Anderson, *Imagined Communities: Reflections on the Origin and Spread of Nationalism*, rev. ed. (New York: Verso, 1991), 9, and see especially chapter 11, "Memory and Forgetting." Sarah J. Purcell, *Sealed with Blood: War, Sacrifice, and Memory in Revolutionary America* (Philadelphia: University of Pennsylvania Press, 2002), 1. For the forms of celebration and commemoration of the Revolutionary War, see also David Waldstreicher, *In the Midst of Perpetual Fetes: The Making of American Nationalism, 1776–1783* (Chapel Hill: University of North Carolina Press, 1997).

5. Annie Morrill Smith, *Morrill Kindred in America*, 2 vols. (New York: Grafton Press, 1914, 1931). See also James Otis Lyford, *History of the Town of Canterbury, New Hampshire 1777–1912*, 2 vols. (Concord, N.H.: Rumford Press, 1912), II: 253–66, for the Morrill family's first settlement in Canterbury and Revolutionary War service.

6. Lyford, I: 94.

7. For the development of the New England vernacular landscape and commemoration of early settlers, see Joseph S. Wood, *The New England Village* (Baltimore: Johns Hopkins University Press, 1997); John Brinckerhoff Jackson, *Discovering the Vernacular Landscape* (New Haven: Yale University Press, 1984); and John R. Stilgoe, *Common Landscape of America, 1580 to 1845* (New Haven: Yale University Press, 1982). An especially perceptive study of the vernacular landscape of New England is Kent C. Ryden, *Landscape with Figures: Nature and Culture in New England* (Iowa City: University of Iowa Press, 2001). For studies of the racial implications of the creation of images of New England, see Dona Brown, *Inventing New England: Regional Tourism in the Nineteenth Century* (Washington: Smithsonian Institution Press, 1995); Joseph A. Conforti, *Imagining New England: Explorations of Regional Identity From the Pilgrims to the Mid-Twentieth Century* (Chapel Hill: University of North Carolina Press, 2001); David H. Watters, "Revising New England: Self-Portraits of a Region," *Colby Quarterly*, 39.1 (March 2003): 10–33, and David H. Watters, "Introduction," Images and Ideas, *Encyclopedia of New England*, ed. Burt Feintuch and David H. Watters (New Haven: Yale University Press, 2005), 723–38.

8. Howard P. Moore, *The Descendants of Ensign John Moor of Canterbury, N.H. Born 1696 — Died 1786* (Rutland, Vt.: Tuttle Company, 1918), 95. For the life of Archelaus Moore, and references to Sampson Moor (Battis), see Moore, 83–84, 89–97, 94–97. For the published Battis genealogy, see Lyford, II: 21–22.

9. Pension Record S13961, abstract recorded in "New Hampshire Revolutionary Pension Records" (New Hampshire Historical Society): 30: 178–80. Glenn Knoblock speculates that Sampson Battis's father was John Battis, one of three persons enslaved by Robert Thompson of Durham, as noted in Thompson's probated estate after his death in 1753. Knoblock's entry on Sampson Moore repeats several errors in earlier published sources.

10. Lyford, *History of the Town of Canterbury*, II: 143, pieces together the service of Canterbury men, including Battis, from the Chandler E. Potter's *Report of the Adjutant-General of the State of New Hampshire, for the Year Ending June 1, 1866. Vol. II* (Concorde: George E. Jenks, 1866) and various state documents. Battis (listed in this document as "Moor") served in Capt. Benjamin Sias's company, 10/4–26/77 at Fort Edward. Lyford (II: 144) notes he was a volunteer at Saratoga when Burgoyne surrendered, and he was listed as "Sampson Battis, servant of Archelaus Moor." His next service was in Capt. Nath'l Head's Company, Col. Reynold's Regiment, 1781, and he was listed as Sampson Battas, serving 8/20–11/25/1780 (when others mustered out), marked "'Deserted November 22" (Lyford, II: 152, 156–57). This information is also present in Pension Bureau record, the *New Hampshire State Papers*, XVII: 430.; the document for his service as a volunteer, signed on 7/24/1781, "Samson Battis his mark," indicates he was not literate at this time (*New Hampshire State Papers*, XVI: 264.

11. See Melish, 23–26.

12. Canterbury, N.H., Town Records, FV Deposit Shelf, New Hampshire State Library, n.p.

13. For captivity incidents involving Sabattis and Plausawa, see Colin G. Calloway, *North Country Captives: Selected Narratives of Indian Captivity from Vermont and New Hampshire* (Hanover: University Press of New England, 1992), 17–21, and Nathaniel Bouton, comp., *Provincial Papers. Documents and Records*, vol. VI (Manchester, N.H.: James M. Campbell, 1872), 262–66. The complex archival record of the kidnapping of Tom and Pier and the murder of Sabattis and Plausawa can be found in several sources: *Provincial Papers*, VI: 306–308; Jeremy Belknap, *The History of New Hampshire*, 2 vols. (New York: Johnson Reprint Corp., 1970): I: 305–308. The fullest early narrative account is by Chandler E. Potter, "The Last of the Pennacooks," *The Farmer's Monthly Visitor*, ed. C. E. Potter, XIII: 9 (Sept. 1853), 257–67; XIII: 11 (Nov. 1853), 321–25. The best analysis of the incident in terms of colonial politics is in Colin G. Calloway, *The Western Abenakis of Vermont, 1600–1800: War, Migration, and the Survival of an Indian People* (Norman: University of Oklahoma Press, 1990), chap. 9, "The English, French, and Indian War, 1754–1760," 160–82.

14. William Patrick, *Historical Sketches of Canterbury, N.H.* (1834). Lyford, *History of the Town of Canterbury*, 37. Elizabeth Miles's deposition tells a different version, "That the said Peer about three days after return'd pinion'd & Bound with Indian Lines and said that Sabbattis and Christo had taken them and that by accident he made his Escape." *Provincial Papers*, VI: 304. See also Potter, "The Last of the Pennacooks," 262–63.

15. *Provincial Papers*, VI: 304–305.

16. Belknap, 308; *Provincial Papers*, VI. Charles Coffin Webster, *The History of Boscawen and Webster, from 1733 to 1878* (Concord, N.H.: The Republican Press Association, 1878), 56, states that Sabattis and Plausawa were buried near Stirrup Iron brook, near the Northern Railroad bridge.

17. Lyford, *History of the Town of Canterbury*, 38–39; *Provincial Papers*, VI: 262; Letter of February 4, 1754, and Governor's message of March 26, 1754. The *Provincial Papers* editor notes people thought the murders were meritorious (VI: 308), a view reflected in Smith, *Morrill Kindred*, 113.

18. Margaret Ellen Newell, "The Changing Nature of Indian Slavery in New England, 1670–1720," in *Reinterpreting New England Indians and the Colonial Experience*, ed. Colin G. Calloway and Neal Salisbury (Boston: Colonial Society of Massachusetts, 2003), LXXI: 108.

19. Ebenezer Price, *A Chronological Register of Boscawen, in the County of Merrimack, and State of New-Hampshire, from the first settlement of the town to 1820* (Concord: Jacob B. Moore, 1823); Patrick, *Historical Sketches*, 9.

20. Nathaniel Bouton, *The History of Concord, From Its First Grant in 1725, to the Organization of the City Government in 1853, with a History of the Ancient Penacooks. The Whole Interspersed with Numerous Interesting Incidents and Anecdotes, Down to the Present Period, 1855; Embellished with Maps; with Portraits of Distinguished Citizens, and Views of Ancient and Modern Residences* (Concord: Benning W. Sanborn,

1856), 252; Lyford, *History of the Town of Canterbury*, II: 21. Margaret Ellen Newell writes, "New Englanders evaded the new barriers to enslaving local Indians by importing natives from outside the region" ("The Changing Nature of Indian Slavery in New England, 1670–1720," 116). This practice meant there was an export of New England natives into slavery in the Caribbean while "West Indian Indians" were imported as slaves.

21. See n. 45 below.

22. The "New Guinea" designation may refer to the southwestern area of town near the Moor grants where Sampson Battis lived while enslaved and perhaps until about 1790 when Archelaus Moor removed to what is now Loudon. Near the river in this area lived Peter Sampson, an African American whose property became known as "Peter's Crossing" when the railroad was constructed. According to Canterbury church records, William Robinson, "a Transient man," married Sophia Battis, Sampson's daughter, on May 24, 1820 (Canterbury Church Records, ms. New Hampshire Historical Society, 314; Lyford, *History of the Town of Canterbury*, "Genealogies," 21). There may be a connection here to the family of Peter Sampson, who lived to the west of the Moor holdings, and whose "colored" daughter Laura A. Robinson lived there (Lyford, *History of the Town of Canterbury*, 404). The next residence to the east was that of John B. Glover, who may be related to the Jane Glover who was married to Nathaniel Battis, January 6, 1843 (Canterbury Church Records, 321). On the other hand, "New Guinea" may refer to the Battis/Ayres properties in the northwestern corner of the town. In either case, a number of African American, Native American, European, and mixed-race families may have comprised the population of this "New Guinea." Newell, "The Changing Nature of Indian Slavery in New England, 1670–1720," 127, suggests that shifting attitudes about color and slavery on the "racial frontier" set white against red and black; but I complicate this story here by showing that in New Hampshire, whites set black against red as a result of captivities.

23. Ulrich, *The Age of Homespun: Objects and Stories in the Creation of an American Myth* (New York: Alfred A. Knopf, 2001), 360. For "conversion," Ulrich cites the work of Ann McMullen, "What's Wrong with This Picture? Context, Conversion, Survival, and the Development of Regional Native Cultures and Pan-Indianism in Southeastern New England," in *Enduring Traditions: The Native Peoples of New England*, ed. Laruie Weinstein (Westport, Conn: Bergin and Garvey, 1994), 123–50. Laurel Ulrich notes that, "Intermarrying with non-Indians, white or black, many of the descendants of New England's earliest people gradually ceased to register in their neighbors' consciousness as 'Indian.'"

24. Bouton, *History of Concord*, 250–51. For an Abenaki perspective on basketmaking and survivance, see Frederick Matthew Wiseman, *The Voice of the Dawn: An Autohistory of the Abenaki Nation* (Hanover: University Press of New England, 2001), 136–38; Ruth B. Phillips, *Trading Identities: The Souvenir in Native North American Art From the Northeast, 1700–1900* (Seattle: University of Washington Press, 1998); Ulrich, *Age of Homespun*, 347, 360. For a similar story in southern New

England, see Nan Wolverton, "'A Precarious Living': Basket Making and Related Crafts Among New England Indians," in *Reinterpreting New England Indians and the Colonial Experience*, 341–68.

25. Pension S13961 Abstract; "Miscellaneous Revolutionary Documents of New Hampshire Including the Association Test, the Pension Rolls, and Other Important Papers," State Papers, vol. 30 (Manchester, John B. Clarke Co., 1910). Here Battis is recorded as 89 years old in the 1840 pension report, although the source from which this is taken erroneously listed him as 80 years of age ("A Census of Pensioners for Revolutionary Military Service; With Their Names, Ages, and Places of Residence, As Returned By The Marshals Of The Several Judicial Districts, Under The Act For Taking The Sixth Census" [Washington: Blair and Rives, 1841], 19). Battis is listed as Sampson Moore, age 82, in the "Pension List, Act of Congress, Passed June 7, 1832," placed on the roll on Feb. 16, 1833, as a Private due $20.00 annual pension, commencing on March 4, 1831, an entry that seems to confirm a birth date c. 1750 (397, 348–49). See also n. 36. Howard Moore, in *The Descendants*, gives the age of 103 for his age at death, in about 1853.

26. Moore, *The Descendants*, 95; Lyford, *History of the Town of Canterbury*, II: 133.

27. Chandler E. Potter, *Report of the Adjutant-General of the State of New Hampshire, for the Year Ending June 1, 1866* (Concord: George E. Jenks, 1866), II: xx. This commission may have occurred in 1800, for this is a date inserted by Lyford in a quotation from Potter about Sampson's title.

28. Potter, *Report*, 379.

29. Bouton, *History of Concord*, 252. Archelaus Moor played violoncello in the Canterbury church, so it is likely that Battis learned to play in the Moor household. Thus the musical traditions of church and dance in this early Canterbury household may have been an interracial mix. Moore, *The Descendants*, 97.

30. Potter, *Report*, 379. See also *Collections of the New Hampshire Historical Society*, vol. 9 (1889), 193, for a description of the earlier 15th regiment militia uniform of 1774.

31. For these celebrations, see William D. Piersen, *Black Yankees: The Development of an Afro-American Subculture in Eighteenth-Century New England* (Amherst: University of Massachusetts Press, 1988); Mark J. Sammons and Valerie Cunningham, *Black Portsmouth: Three Centuries of African-American Heritage* (Durham: University of New Hampshire Press, 2004); Robert Blair St. George, ed., *Material Life in America, 1600–1860* (Boston: Northeastern University Press, 1988); and Charles W. Brewster, *Rambles About Portsmouth* (Portsmouth, 1859), 210–11. For the use of parades and other festivities in the creation of national culture, see Purcell, *Sealed with Blood*, and Waldstreicher, *In the Midst of Perpetual Fetes*, n. 4, and Simon P. Newman, *Parades and the Politics of the Street: Festive Culture in the Early Republic* (Philadelphia: University of Pennsylvania Press, 1997). For training day and muster activities, see H. Telfer Mook, "Training Day in New England," *New England Quarterly* 11 (December 1938): 675–97, and Melish, *Disowning Slavery*, 179.

32. Charles W. Brewster, *Rambles About Portsmouth*, I: 154–55. This story ap-

pears in various forms in several antebellum New Hampshire publications. For Prince Whipple and the Whipple family, see Sammons and Cunningham, *Black Portsmouth*, 67–69. For New England African American service in the Revolutionary War, see William C. Nell, *Colored Patriots*; and Sidney Kaplan and Emma Nogrady Kaplan, *The Black Presence in the Era of the American Revolution*, rev. ed. (Amherst: University of Massachusetts Press, 1989). Glenn Knoblock, in "Strong and Brave Fellows," provides additional examples of African Americans who were freed for service in the war (17)

33. For the history of emancipation in New Hampshire, see Melish, *Disowning Slavery*, 66.

34. Harriet Beecher Stowe, "The Old Meeting House," in *Oldtown Folks* (Boston: Fields, Osgood, 1869). This sketch was first published in 1840.

35. William C. Nell, *Colored Patriots of the American Revolution: The Colored Patriots of the American Revolution, With Sketches of Several Distinguished Colored Persons: To Which Is Added a Brief Survey of the Condition And Prospects of Colored Americans* (Boston: Robert F. Wallcut, 1855).

36. William Wells Brown, "Visit of a Fugitive Slave to the Grave of Wilberforce," in Julia Griffiths, ed., *Autographs for Freedom* (Auburn: Alden, Beardsley, 1854), 70. For a discussion of this battle and monument, see Kaplan and Kaplan, *The Black Presence*, 55–57.

37. Melish, *Disowning Slavery*, 79–80.

38. Ibid., 240.

39. Caleb Stark, *History of the Town of Dunbarton, Merrimack County, New Hampshire, From The Grant By Mason's Assigns, In 1751, To The Year 1860* (Concord: G. Parker Lyon, 1860), 83–84. In an unusual decision, the Proprietors of Dunbarton included "Sippes" Page in the division of common lands on November 2, 1788. Stark writes in a footnote, "Sippes, or Scipio, was a favorite negro man, who lived and died in the service of Capt. Caleb Page and his family. The lot assigned to Scipio was in the vicinity of what is now called 'One Stack Brook.' He remained there for a time, but was glad to come back to the hospitable shelter of Capt. Page's roof, and bring his colored wife with him" (85). Alice M. Hadley, *Where the Winds Blow Free* (Canaan, N.H.: Phoenix Publishing, 1976); p. 169 refers to Guinea Rd.

40. Patrick, *Historical Sketches*, 33.

41. Foreman and Pitts, xxxiv–xxxv. Melish, *Disowning Slavery*, discusses the exclusion of African Americans from schools throughout New England in this period (188).

42. Charles Coffin Webster, *The History of Boscawen and Webster, From 1733 to 1878* (Concord, N.H.: Republican Press Association, 1878), 201. Wilson writes about such "abolitionists who didn't want slaves at the South, nor niggers in their own houses, North."

43. Eve Allegra Raimon, *The "Tragic Mulatta" Revisited: Race and Nationalism in Nineteenth-Century Antislavery Fiction* (New Brunswick: Rutgers University Press, 2004), 135.

44. See Michael Zuckerman, *Peaceable Kingdoms: New England Towns in the Eighteenth Century* (New York: Knopf, 1970).

45. Neither Battis nor his children are listed as members of the Canterbury Church, but the children's marriages are listed in the church records. "Canterbury Church Records" (New Hampshire Historical Society ms. 285.877b C229re 1803–91), 311, January 23, 1809, "Peter Battis of Canterbury to Lydia Harvey a transient woman"; 312, November 19, 1815, "Sampson Battis to Elizabeth Lusters [Lester] both of Canterbury"; 313, October 9, 1819, "Silas Battis of Loudon to Sally Peters of Meredith"; 314, May 24, 1820, "William Robinson a transient man to Sophia Battis of Cant"; August 22, 1820, "John Francis to Samson Battis both of Canterbury" (Samson appears to be a case of naming a daughter to preserve a family name); 321, January 6, 1843, "Nathaniel Battis and Jane Glover both of Canterbury."

46. Lyford, *History of the Town of Canterbury*, II: 261–62. The New Hampshire vital records list Phillis Battis, a single black female who died November 24, 1858, at the age of 83, possibly a daughter of Sampson Battis and Lucy Carey. Jack Battis, a "colored" male "Froze. Found dead in the morning" in Keene, New Hampshire, on March 18, 1816. Sampson Battis is listed as Sampson Moor in Canterbury in the 1800 census as a head of household with 8 other free persons. In the 1810 census, he is listed in Canterbury as Sampson Moore, with all household members called free white, one male under 10, two females under 10, one female 10 through 15, two females 16 through 25, with one male and one female 45 and over, Sampson and his wife Lucy. There is no record for Battis in Canterbury for 1820, but this may be because of a missing page or an oversight by the enumerator, since the general enumeration includes 18 "colored persons" who do not appear as individuals. In 1830, he is listed as Sampson Battus, head of a household with one male and one female, age 65 to 100. In 1840, he is listed in Canterbury with an employment in agriculture, head of a household with one male, age 55 to 100, and two females aged 55 to 100, one possibly being his unmarried daughter, Phillis. There is no listing for 1850.

47. William Patrick, *Historical Sketches*, and Lyford, *History of the Town of Canteruby*, II: 9, 412. Deborah died in 1816 at the age of 102. For a map of holdings in this area, see "Map of Canterbury, 1858, also showing location of original proprietor's lots," manuscript, New Hampshire Historical Society 912.778b C229. The three Battis lots (here written as "Battes" but corrected to "Battis" in the printed version included in Lyford's *History*, II: 417) are near Oak Hill, in the northwest corner of Canterbury. Lot # 66 is S. Battes and lot # 60 is D. Battes and N. Battes. These lots together probably make up Sampson Battis's original 100-acre lot. These lots are just west of the Ayres family lots.

48. In New Hampshire vital records submitted by the town clerk of Canterbury, it appears that at some point in time Battis family members were considered white. For example, Sampson Battis, Jr.'s, son, John Franklin Lester Battis, is listed as white when he marries, at age 35 in 1864, a Lydia A. Bennett, age 16, whom the clerk describes as *"Dark"* without giving the customary "W" or "B" for race.

49. Lyford, *History of the Town of Canterbury*, I: 417, 405–407.

50. Melish, *Disowning Slavery*, 208, 213.

51. Bouton, *History of Concord*, 1. For a useful history of the writing of local history, see Carol Kammen, *On Doing Local History: Reflections on What Local Historians Do, Why, and What It Means* (Walnut Creek: AltaMira Press, 1995), chap. 1; David D. Hall and Alan Taylor, "Reassessing the Local History of New England," in *New England, A Bibliography of Its History*, ed. Roger Parks (Hanover: University Press of New England, 1989), xix–xlviii; and the essays in "Part II: Nineteenth-Century Views of Local History," in *The Pursuit of Local History: Readings on Theory and Practice*, ed. Carol Kammen (Walnut Creek: AltaMira Press, 1996). For a discussion of the status and practice of the minister/historian, see George B. Kirsch, *Jeremy Belknap: A Biography* (New York: Arno Press, 1982), and Russell M. Lawson, *The American Plutarch: Jeremy Belknap and the Historian's Dialogue with the Past* (Westport, Conn.: Praeger, 1998). Bouton's extraordinary record as a historian includes his editorship of the volumes of the New Hampshire provincial and state papers as well as many other historical, biographical, and religious works.

52. Lyford, *History of the Town of Canterbury*, 1: xi, xi, xiv.

53. Susan A. Crane, "Curious Cabinets and Imaginary Museums," in Susan Crane, ed. *Museums and Memory* (Stanford: Stanford University Press, 2000), 69

54. Crane, *Museums and Memory*, 3.

55. Michael Fehr, "A Museum and Its Memory," 59

56. John R. Grimes, "Introduction: Curiosity, Cabinets, and Knowledge—A Perspective on the Native American Collection of the Peabody Essex Museum," in John R. Grimes, Christian Feest, and Mary Lou Curran, *Uncommon Legacies: Native American Art From The Peabody Essex Museum* (Seattle: University of Washington Press, 2002), 21.

57. George A. Ramsdell, *The History of Milford*, and William P. Colburn, *Family Registers* (Concord, N.H.: Rumford Press, 1901). For commentary on Wilson's *Our Nig*, abolitionism, and African American citizenship, see Ellis, *Harriet Wilson's Our Nig*, 62–63 and 135–49; White, "Our Nig and the She-Devil"; and Gretchen Short, "Harriet Wilson, *Our Nig* and the Labor of Citizenship," *Arizona Quarterly* 57.3 (Autumn 2001): 1–27.

58. Quoted in Ellis, *Harriet Wilson's Our Nig*, 55.

59. Ramsdell, *History of Milford*, 75.

60. Ibid., 106.

61. Ibid., 38.

62. Homi K. Bhaba, *The Location of Culture* (New York: Routledge, 1994), 157.

63. For a perceptive discussion of the physical spaces of the Bellmont house, see Leveen, "Dwelling in the House of Oppression."

64. Raimon, "Tragic Mulatta," 142; Leveen, "Dwelling in the House of Oppression"; Melish, *Disowning Slavery*, 280.

65. Priscilla Wald, *Constituting Americans: Cultural Anxiety and Narrative Form* (Durham, N.C.: Duke University Press, 1995).

66. Moore, *The Descendants*, 84. For information about the Gilman residence,

see Lyford, *History of the Town of Canterbury*, I: 406. The home was on lot No. 16, across from Moore house on lot No. 18.

67. For a discussion of the significance of trees in New England familial and historical mythology, see Howard Mansfield, "The Washington Elm Reassembled," *The Bones of the Earth* (Washington, D.C.: Shoemaker Hoard, 2004), 19–34. He notes on p. 23 that, "The Washington Elm was the center of the Revolution, the axis mundi." This notion connects to a "belief in marking time and the land with trees" (26). The Whipple horse chestnut was planted by William Whipple on his return from Philadelphia in 1776 after signing the Declaration of Independence. The tree still stands on the grounds of the Moffatt-Ladd House in Portsmouth. From my own observation, and as the case of the Gilman household shows, trees were often planted at the time of the building of a house, and if such a construction was marked by a wedding, a pair of marriage trees was planted flanking the path to the front entrance. The ceremony marking the cutting of the Berry Elm in Northwood, New Hampshire, including the distribution of hundreds of pieces and the creation of a sculpture from its trunk in 1983, shows the staying power of such associations in the state.

68. Nell, *Colored Patriots*, 380.

69. Moore, *The Descendants*, 95

70. The Battis family's complex interracial legacy was noted in a Public Broadcasting website, for a Frontline broadcast, "The Buried Racial Lines of Famous Families." The "Battis" page was written and researched by Mario de Valdes y Cocom: *http://www.pbs.org/wgbh/pages/frontline/shows/secret/famous/battis.html*, 1998, viewed 11/3/03. The information on this page may not be entirely accurate. Genealogical postings from Louisiana and Martha's Vineyard seek information concerning this ancestor. *http://genforum.genealogy.com/nh/merrimack/messages/5.html*, July 7, 1999, viewed 11/3/03.

New Hampshire Forgot

African Americans in a Community by the Sea

Valerie Cunningham

ON THE MORNING of Tuesday, October 7, 2003, during construction for a Portsmouth, New Hampshire, water and sewer project, workers unearthed a coffin under Chestnut Street a few feet from its intersection with Court Street. The backhoe operator immediately notified the consulting archaeologists for the project. Given the relatively small size of this old town by the sea, word of the discovery spread quickly. Within minutes, all interested parties were there: members of the city's black community, staff from the city's numerous historical institutions, newspaper reporters, television crews, office workers, teachers, their students, and passersby all gathered at the site. Some professed their ignorance of this ancient burial ground, which they had unknowingly traversed for years, although its location is clearly marked on old maps of the city and described in the text of a bronze marker a few yards away from where the construction occurred.[1]

This literal unearthing of New Hampshire's black history not only provided concrete proof of a black history in the state, it highlighted a corresponding history of white indifference to black life and death, an indifference that once allowed real estate development to proceed over sacred burial ground. Likewise, community interest in and scholarship on Harriet Wilson and her novel, *Our Nig*, are forcing us to revisit the history of slavery and black subjugation in New Hampshire—a state that prides itself on its anti-slavery past.

Recent studies have shown that from the time of its earliest settlement, New Hampshire merchants, shipbuilders, and seamen were active participants in the Atlantic slave trade and the slave-based economy that helped build this country. Yet, these memories quickly faded as the New England states removed legalized slavery from the region. As scholarly attention turned to the South and the new western territories, the small but significant role once played by New Hampshire in the early history of American slavery was all but forgotten.

True, New Hampshire's involvement with the "peculiar institution" of slavery seems small when compared to almost any place else. Even during the Colonial Era, when the affluent mercantile center of Portsmouth was a trend-setting social center comparable to Boston and Philadelphia, the number of slaveholders and their chattel was relatively small. After the Revolution, Portsmouth's economic and social position was diminishing even as slavery as an institution was growing less popular across the Northeast. Meanwhile, the invention of the cotton gin motivated Southern planters to demand more cheap labor. The product of that labor supplied international textile markets, a system that intensified the debate over abolition. By mid-nineteenth century, there was virtually no comparison of a few formerly enslaved blacks scattered among the white population of New Hampshire with the expansion of slavery throughout the South and West. By that time, the subject of slavery in New Hampshire had been reduced to anecdotes in town histories and popular publications of the day.

In terms of population, a majority of blacks in New Hampshire have been concentrated within a twenty-mile radius of Portsmouth since 1645. In 1760, enslaved black workers accounted for 4 percent of Portsmouth's population, about 160 people out of 4,000. By comparison, ten times as many blacks lived in Massachusetts at the time of the Revolution; by 1860, the ratio was twenty-to-one.[2] As Portsmouth's African American population grew older its numbers became smaller and, as the people disappeared, stories of "slavery days" seemed to vanish with them. Of course, it is precisely this very "forgetting" in town histories and records that resulted in the loss to history of Harriet Wilson's *Our Nig* until Henry Louis Gates's 1983 discovery.

Slavery gradually ended in New Hampshire around the turn of the nineteenth century, not by law but by practice. It was a time of great hope and great disappointment. In 1779, twenty enslaved African men petitioned the State for their freedom and for an end to the practice of slaveholding in New Hampshire. Their petition was read by the legislators and tabled without further action.[3] Regardless, most slaves were manumitted by their owners one by one, perhaps because the declining postwar economy could no longer provide enough business to offset the financial burden of maintaining unpaid laborers in the household. As slavery was ending throughout New England, especially in the adjacent states of Vermont and Massachusetts (which then included Maine), it seemed inevitable that bondpersons would free themselves by simply running away.

As slave labor was routinely replaced by low-wage white workers, former slaves and their descendants in New Hampshire were perceived by non-blacks to be part of the social and economic servant class that would eventually include all black Americans. White America defined servants as Negroes and Negroes as servants. This attitude continued for at least a century after Harriet Wilson wrote *Our Nig*. African Americans were competing with the newest wave of immigrants for the most menial jobs, or they were reinventing themselves as entrepreneurs, working as day laborers or laundresses; cooks or caterers; mariners or landlords; footmen or truckers; maids or seamstresses. Many, including Wilson, made their living as peddlers of various household goods.[4] Men and women who were disabled or too old to work became residents of the towns' poor farms, as did children who were not yet hired out as family domestics or farm laborers.

Among the black leaders to emerge during this period was Thomas Paul, a teenaged "exhorter" from Exeter who later would be ordained and lead his congregation in Boston to build the African Meetinghouse on Beacon Hill.[5] As well, Wentworth Cheswell was elected to hold every public office in his hometown of Newmarket.[6] The president of Portsmouth's African Society, Pomp Spring, was a self-employed baker whose home and grog shop were located just a short walk from the expanding business center of this seaport town.[7] Just two blocks away stood the home of Prince Whipple's widow, Dinah, who taught African American children for the Ladies' Charitable African Society School.[8]

This was the world into which Harriet Adams was born. Whether or not she ever visited Exeter, Newmarket, or Portsmouth would not have mattered much. She would have heard stories about these figures, for such oral history was part of the cultural patterns of the region. At nightfall, when most work stopped, people had time to sit and talk. It was a deep tradition for those of African descent to carry volumes of information in their heads and to pass these storehouses on, creating a vast communications network between places that linked generations. This was also the time when traveling entertainers and preachers served as major news carriers in the black community. It is possible that Wilson received reports of events in her state from Richard Potter, an itinerant ventriloquist and magician who lived in Andover, New Hampshire.[9] Potter may have performed in Milford on one of his many journeys across the country. No matter how she got the news, Harriet E. Adams Wilson certainly knew the stories of African American life in the North.

In 1857, New Hampshire officially declared itself to be a "free state."[10] By 1859, when Wilson published *Our Nig*, Portsmouth's role in the Atlantic slave trade and slaveholding was being erased from public memory. Slaves and their owners were no longer mentioned in the publications of the day. The emphasis had shifted from ownership of slaves to their representation in more stereotypical, childlike guise. Non-blacks in New Hampshire seemed only too willing to forget the complicity of the founding fathers and their own economic dependence on the slave-based economy. References to the presence of slaves were typically modified by declaring that there never had been very many, or that a black "servant" complemented the elegant lifestyle of the "master."

Between 1840 and 1860, the editor of the *Portsmouth Herald*, Charles W. Brewster, used oral histories gathered from the city's elders to inform himself about many of the seaport's past events and people. He blended those recollections with his own research of public documents to publish a series of newspaper columns called "Rambles," which he later republished as a two-volume collection entitled *Rambles About Portsmouth*. In Ramble XXX, Brewster provides an accounting of an Inventory of the Polls and Estates of the Town of Portsmouth in 1727: ". . . oxen 121, cows 407, horses 154, hogs 108, slaves 52, houses 298 . . . ," revealing that enslaved people were taxable property, no different from farm animals and houses. He continues by identifying who owned the slaves and the houses (since slaves generally also worked in the houses): "Of the slaves, Capt. Walker had 4, William Vaughan 4, Col. Walden 2, Richard Wibird 3, R. Waterhouse 2, George Jeffries 2; the remaining 35 were owned singly in families. Richard Wibird owned 5 houses, William Vaughan 4. . . ."[11] Ramble XXXII lists "the principal tax payers in Portsmouth in 1770." That list can be compared to a list of slave owners to show that at least eight of the top ten tax payers, and more than half of the thirty-two Brewster men paying the highest taxes, were known to have owned slaves (165). Brewster's writings offer valuable insights into the role enslaved blacks played in this colonial New Hampshire city. Slaves in Portsmouth were often used as status symbols. The higher the master's social standing the more well-dressed were his slaves. These records also highlight the hypocrisy of the church, a theme that is featured prominently in Wilson's narrative. Brewster reveals that while it was very important for colonial whites to baptize their servants, those same servants were made to sit in segregated pews in the church.

Brewster's anecdotes also provide colorful accounts of daily life in old Portsmouth. His language, describing a wide range of activities and personalities, reflects the mid-nineteenth-century political and social attitudes. While Brewster acknowledges that "Portsmouth had a large proportion of the slaves held in the State," he demonstrates that the process of forgetting the realities of slavery and its consequences was well underway in his day. For instance, in Ramble XLIII, Brewster writes nostalgically that, "There were negroes of distinction then" and refers to individuals as being among "the top of the negro

Esther Whipple Mullinaux, daughter of Prince and Dinah Whipple of Portsmouth, New Hampshire. *Courtesy of Valerie Cunningham*

quality" (210). Some of those individuals belonged to the Negro Court, a self-governing body with limited authority over the local black community. Officials were elected by blacks, an occasion that was deemed a holiday. The eighteenth-century Negro Court and elections in Portsmouth were typical of slave societies throughout the Americas. Because Brewster reported this, we not only know that the court existed, but we have the names of at least one slate of officers, the locations of the ceremonies, and a description of the activities included in the celebrations (212–13).

Indeed, Brewster's vignettes reveal a lot about the patronizing attitude of whites toward bondpeople just before the start of the Civil War (210). One such tale concerned Peter, a slave who was challenged to create a rhyme for his owner, Jonathan Warner, in return for replacement of his worn-out hat. According to Brewster, Peter could not generate a rhyme but was rewarded nonetheless for making the attempt. That story was followed by one about an enslaved woman in Samuel Ham's household who did not count by five when planting corn kernels, but by three, which Brewster explained was an indication of her having an "intellect somewhat inferior to Peter's" (211–12). Here, Brewster pandered to his subscribers' perceptions of blacks as primitive and childlike creatures unable to adapt to Anglo American ways.

One exception to these stereotypical anecdotes in Brewster's *Rambles* is the respectful and detailed description of the black Whipple family. Some members of the family were still living and active in the community during the writer's lifetime. He wrote about them rationally, and in much more detail than he did about other blacks, indicating that they were highly regarded by both black and white people in the community. Building upon his generous descriptions, further research has provided rare insight into this family's life and the emerging African American community as slavery was ending in New Hampshire.

Dinah Whipple was a young widow when she started teaching African children in her home. She shared the house with Cuffee and Rebecca Whipple. Dinah's husband, Prince, had been a Revolutionary War veteran and one of the twenty African men who unsuccessfully petitioned the New Hampshire Legislature in 1779 to end slavery in the state. Prince, along with Cuffee, had been enslaved since childhood by William Whipple, who would later become one of George Washington's generals in the Revolutionary War and a signer of the Declaration of Independence. Prince was still enslaved in 1781 when he married Dinah Chase. Dinah had been manumitted on her twenty-first birthday by the widow of the Congregationalist minister who had enslaved her. Both Dinah and Prince were well respected in the community. They were educated and faithfully attended church. At the time of Prince's death in 1797, the couple had five children. Dinah conducted classes of the Ladies Charitable African School in her home on High Street from around 1806 until she moved in 1832.[12] Recent documents discovered from the lending library at the North Church list the books the Whipples borrowed.

The school was just two blocks away from the home of Pomp Spring, the baker, and his wife, Candace. As Pomp was the president of Portsmouth's African Society, Candace was very likely a member of the Ladies Charitable African Society that sponsored Dinah Whipple's school. The Society would have offered other services to needy black people, especially those just released from slavery. As owner of a baking business and grog shop in their home, the Springs were well-positioned to know the political climate of the town and beyond. The strict requirements for membership in the African Society are testimony to Pomp's high moral standards. His good character was confirmed by a newspaper obituary upon his death in 1807 asserting that Pomp would be missed by all in the town, "especially the poor." The dates of Pomp and Candace's manumission are unknown, but her former enslavement is documented and his is implied by his "slave" name. Following Candace's death just four months after Pomp's, their two household inventories revealed a well-appointed home that could have comfortably accommodated meetings of the Ladies Charitable African Society and the men's African Society. The executor of their estate had also been enslaved. He was Cesar Whidden, a laborer and a landlord.[13] All were part of Portsmouth's established black community in the early years of the nineteenth century.

An item in the *Portsmouth Journal*, dated August 27, 1836, addressed the question of admitting twenty black children (boys) to the public schools. The editorial was emphatically supportive, maintaining that, "The town of Portsmouth ought not to have in it one child of twelve years old, who cannot read and write. We want no ignorance near us." The writer continues, "The difference of color and condition creates a strong repugnance to it on both sides. They will not go together, as experience shows. Yet they ought to be taught, for the safety and good of the public, if not for their own. . . . Would it not be a good plan for the town to open a school for them." Portsmouth, unlike Boston, never did have a separate public school for its black students. The numbers were never large enough to make it feasible. Clearly, however, white taxpayers would have favored a separate school for its children, which would have been in keeping with other existing forms of racial separation.

With only the most menial jobs available to African Americans, regardless of their skills or willingness to work, there were few incentives for able-bodied people to remain in the hostile climate of New Hampshire. Freed men and women left in search of loved ones from whom they had been separated in slavery. Young people born free were attracted, then as they have been ever since, to the social and economic opportunities available in the more dynamic black communities around Boston and Providence or even in Portland, Maine. The aging black population of Portsmouth was not replacing itself. In the thirty-year period from 1760 until 1790 the percentage of blacks to whites had dropped from 4 percent (160 of 4,000) to 2.2 percent (100 of 4720) as, apparently, some formerly enslaved people left Portsmouth upon gaining freedom. For the next thirty years, from 1790 until 1820, while the real numbers increased, there was no significant change in the ratio of blacks to whites. Then, during the thirty-year period that followed, those figures changed dramatically, going from 160 blacks in 1820 to 50 blacks in 1850, or from 1 percent to 0.5 percent of the total population of the city.[14]

Changing economic conditions probably were the primary factor in population shifts along coastal New Hampshire and the development of interior cities during the nineteenth century. However, for black people other issues would have been important considerations, too. There was safety in numbers during a time of increasingly hostile activities against abolitionists and heated public debates over expanding slavery into the western territories. The actual number of black people in Portsmouth reached all-time lows of only about 50 blacks among 9,500 whites.[15] By 1851, after passage of the second Fugitive Slave Act, African Americans could risk their freedom by moving into New Hampshire. Milford was one of a few towns in the state reputed to have conductors helping escapees to seek refuge in Canada.

When slavery ended after the Civil War, the black population slowly began to grow as part of the great black migrations following train routes from the Mid-Atlantic States into the Northeast. Once again, the black community began to establish its own institutions. The state's first black church, People's Mission, which became People's Baptist Church in 1892, signaled that this community was stable. A series of social and civic organizations appeared, filling the needs of a city still divided by color. Employment opportunities did not change significantly from a century earlier. There were menial jobs, such as footmen and housekeepers for affluent white professionals and businessmen — and for the bourgeoning tourist industry along the coast. Some people undertook entrepreneurial ventures, which produced such figures as the ragman, the caterer, and the laundress. These self-directed individuals were often leaders in the black community.

At the turn of the twentieth century, while the South romanticized its pre-Civil War relationship with slavery, most of New England denied ever having such a past. Until recently New Hampshire may not have remembered its own history, but as the stinging reality of the coffins under the Portsmouth street shows, that history is surfacing more forcefully all the time. Wilson's landmark work not only helps to expose such realities, but it disrupts the lingering notion of a state free from "slavery's shadows."

NOTES

1. For more on the "coffins under the street," see the afterword in Mark J. Sammons and Valerie Cunningham, *Black Portsmouth: Three Centuries of African-American Heritage* (Durham: University of New Hampshire Press, 2004), 210–12.

2. Nathaniel Bouton, comp., *New Hampshire Provincial and State Papers*, 1727, 1767, Vol. X: 636–638; *Encyclopedia of African-American Culture and History*. ed. Jack Salzman, David Lionel Smith and Cornell West (New York: Macmillan Library, 1996), 3026, 3028.

3. Bouton, *Provincial Papers*, Vol. XVIII: 705–707.

4. See Harriet E. Wilson, *Our Nig; or, Sketches from the Life of a Free Black*, ed. P. Gabrielle Foreman and Reginald H. Pitts (New York: Penguin, 2005), ix

5. James Oliver Horton and Lois E. Horton, *Black Bostonians: Family Life and Community Struggle in the Antebellum North* (New York: Holmes and Meier, 1979), 40.

6. See Rich Alperin and Erik Tuveson, www.seacoastonline.com/2002news/exeter/12222002/news/4447.htm.

7. Sammons and Cunningham, *Black Portsmouth*, 98–105.

8. Ibid., 91.

9. See Sammons and Cunningham for more information on Potter, 106–109.

10. Joanne Pope Melish, *Disowning Slavery: Gradual Emancipation and "Race" in New England, 1780–1860* (Ithaca, N.Y.: Cornell University Press, 1998), 35.

11. Charles W. Brewster, *Rambles About Portsmouth* (Somersworth: New Hampshire Publishing Co., reprint 1971), 159. Further references are noted in the text.

12. Sammons and Cunningham, 87, 91–94.

13. Sammons and Cunningham, 98–99.

14. All census information is taken from *Table 30, New Hampshire — Race and Hispanic Origin for Selected Large Cities and Other Places: Earliest Census to 1990,* available at www.census.gov.

15. Ibid.

PART II

Reading "Sketches From the Life of a Free Black": Genre and Gender

Slavery's Shadows

Narrative Chiaroscuro and *Our Nig*

Mary Louise Kete

IN 1837, ALVIN GOULD, a white man living in a hill town of southern Vermont, wrote the following verse in his sister's keepsake book:

> New England's fruitful soil
> Requires no culture from servile toil
> No master's torturing lash offends the ear,
> No slave is now or ever shall be here;
> Whene'er he treads upon our sacred fields,
> Their guardian genius an asylum yields;
> His chains drop from him; and on Reason's plan
> He claims the gift of God — the rights of man — [1]

Gould's verse expressed the way many New Englanders wanted to understand their relationship to slavery: New England's "fruitful soil" as an "asylum" where the particular contingencies of "chains" are replaced by the universal "gift of God — the rights of man." New England's "sacred fields" reverse the process by which tyrannical force, the "master's torturing lash," drives "servile toil" from those who "on Reason's plan" are men, not slaves. This vision of New England as antithetical to slavery was not unique to Alvin Gould, but was shared by many New England abolitionists during the antebellum era.[2] It became consolidated during the years after the Civil War and continues to have currency in the stories New Englanders tell to help them make sense of themselves in a nation still shadowed by the unresolved legacies of slavery.

While Gould's poem clearly repudiates slavery, it is conspicuously silent on the issue of race, much less racism.[3] In the pages that follow I will examine two other evocations of New England and New England identity from the same years and from an environment very similar to Gould's. These two stories

THE MISSIONARY SHIP.

MEMOIR

OF

REV. JAMES C. BRYANT,

LATE MISSIONARY OF AM. B. C. F. MISSIONS TO SOUTH AFRICA.

BY REV. THOMAS SAVAGE,
BEDFORD, N. H.

Written for the Massachusetts Sabbath School Society, and approved by the Committee of Publication.

BOSTON:
MASSACHUSETTS SABBATH SCHOOL SOCIETY,
Depository, No. 13 Cornhill.

Title page, *Memoir of Rev. James C. Bryant.*

shadow each other as much as they shadow, and are shadowed by, Gould's poem. Together, they throw the nature of racial difference in antebellum New England into a new and singular relief. One is Harriet Wilson's *Our Nig; or, Sketches from the Life of a Free Black, In a Two-Story White House, North. Showing That Slavery's Shadows Fall Even There. By "Our Nig"* (1859), which has attained canonical status since its republication in 1983.[4] The other, much more obscure story, is told in a Massachusetts Sabbath School Society publication entitled, *Memoir of Rev. James C. Bryant, late Missionary of AM.B.C.F. Missions to South Africa* by the Reverend Thomas Savage of Bedford, New Hampshire (1854).[5] Both stories begin in the same New Hampshire county of Hillsborough during the years 1825–1835. The protagonists of both tales start as servants in families other than their own after economic misfortunes befall their parents. Both go on to recount the lives the protagonists make for themselves. While there are many more parallels, the protagonist of the first story is a black girl at the mercy of a cruel, white family, while the hero of the second is a white boy taken in by a kind, black family. The quality of the mercy each character experiences is clearly shaded by that slavery which is supposed (if we listen to Alvin Gould) to be outside of the New England home. Wilson's *Our Nig* and Savage's *Memoir of Rev. James C. Bryant* tell variations of the story of race in New England that compete with and complement each other as much as they compete with and complement the more familiar and dominant story celebrated by Gould of a New England beyond race and outside the reach of slavery's shadows. I want to suggest that the differences in the setting, content, and plot of these New England tales produce a sense of narrative chiaroscuro — a shadowing that adds a new perspective to what another black New Englander famously called the problem of the color line.[6]

Thomas Savage begins his *Memoir of Rev. James C. Bryant* by explaining his impetus for writing:

> Examples of successful perseverance amid obstacles and discouragements are worthy of special notice. When from obscure beginnings and humble poverty a youth, rising above every disadvantage, consecrates himself to God, and with much effort and self-denial, becomes qualified for extensive usefulness, some brief record of such a career may be beneficial to the living, as a stimulus to Christian enterprise and moral heroism. (5)

Written for the Massachusetts Sabbath School Society, Savage's *Memoir* seeks to instruct and delight by weaving information drawn from his own personal acquaintance with Bryant and from Bryant's letters. Working from the testimony of Bryant's colleagues, the work follows a familiar narrative framework meant to highlight Christian and American virtues. Self-reliant, hard working, and modest, Bryant joins the ranks of historical and fictional American boys — witness Benjamin Franklin and Horatio Alger — who start out poor and "make good." Like them, Bryant joins the ranks of Christian heroes whose lives are patterned upon the life of Christ, even to the extent of sacrificing his health in the service of God. Bryant's biographer, Thomas Savage, was a prolific chronicler of New England life, who also wrote and compiled an extensive town history of Bedford, one of the towns in Hillsborough County.[7] As with such histories, there is much that is conventional about this missionary tract. However, James Bryant's story is not only a "stimulus to Christian enterprise and moral heroism." It is also an unusual story about life on the color line in antebellum New England. Savage's subject, a white boy named

James Bryant, becomes a Christian in a household of black New Englanders
and dies ministering to a black congregation in South Africa.[8] While Gould's
poem is clearly antislavery yet also silent upon issues of race, Savage's biography acknowledges both race and racism yet is silent upon the issue of slavery.

Racial difference figures prominently throughout Savage's *Memoir*, but
most dramatically at both the opening and the close of his story. "Such was
the course of Rev. James C. Bryant," Savage explains, to die "among the sable
descendents of Ham, for whose instruction and salvation he left a beloved pastoral charge, and with his companion, bid adieu to home, country, and friends"
(6). More remarkable is the way Bryant's odyssey begins. To indenture or bind
out — either legally or informally — impoverished children to more affluent
families was standard procedure in early nineteenth-century New England.[9]
Yet for a white boy to serve a black man is so unexpected as to call into question many of the critical commonplaces scholars and non-scholars alike have
about race relations in antebellum New England.[10] In chapter 1, devoted to recounting Bryant's "Birth. — Early Hardships. — Conversion," Savage depicts
Bryant's "obscure beginnings and humble poverty" in a New England that is
both the same and yet vastly different than Gould's. If Gould's New England needed no "servile toil," it did need laborers to till its "sacred fields." People like the Bryants provided the boys, girls, and men who made such fields
fertile. Though born in Easton, Massachusetts, in 1812, Bryant and his family
soon moved to "New Boston, Hillsborough Co., where they lived in a state of
indigence, but were respected for their habits of industry and probity. Finding it difficult to maintain a young and rising family, some of the children were
taken by neighbors as soon as they could be of any use in the household" (7).
As in Gould's New England, there are no "masters" and no slaves, but the
New Englanders who live and toil in these hills are distinguished in other
ways: by religion, by class, and by race. New Englanders in Savage's story are
marked by and cognizant of racial differences: there are "white neighbors" and
"colored families" in a community where most people are white and whites are
assumed to be prejudiced toward blacks (7–9). The drama of Savage's hagiog-
raphy is not only set in this racialized landscape but depends upon it.

"It so happened," Bryant's biographer explains, "that not far from them [the
Bryants], within the limits of Goffstown, there lived a colored family, con-
sisting of a man and his wife, who owned a small farm, and were thrifty and
estimable people, the wife being an honored and consistent member of the
Congregational Church" (7). This "man and his wife" are Cato and Catherine
Walker. According to the *History of Goffstown, NH*, Cato Walker (1766–1839)
had been the manservant of one of the early settlers of the area, Captain James
Walker, and had attended him during the Revolutionary War even though

he was then a young boy.[11] Although the Goffstown *History* is not clear regarding when exactly Cato's legal status changed, it seems he was a bondslave at least until 1786, when his master, Capt. James Walker, died. Cato bought the original homestead of James Walker in an unusual deal that included caring for James Walker's daughter, Charlotte, for the duration of her life.[12] Catherine Walker (née Owen), a black woman from Amherst, New Hampshire, had married Cato in 1818, and it appears they had no children of their own. Perhaps their childless status accounts for the "interest" they took in the "poor boy"—James Bryant—even before "he became a member of the family of Cato Walker" (7). Like other neighboring farmers in the Hillsborough area, Cato and Catherine informally adopted one of the apparently numerous children of the Bryant family as soon he was able to "be of any use in the household" (7). At twelve, "the lonely lad labored with Cato on the farm, and assisted his wife in domestic duties," along with other "boys," or farm workers, who worked for Cato and Catherine Walker (8).

Although in many ways Savage's depiction of the Walkers and of Bryant's relationship with them is normalized as consistent with local practices, Savage also insists on the critical difference made by race in the development of Bryant's character. Savage points out that the Walkers "fed and clothed him, and felt for him a tenderness which could hardly be exceeded by parents, and had not been equaled by their white neighbors" (7). In fact, Bryant's own parents are depicted quite negatively relative to the Walkers. Having initially relinquished James to the Walkers, they later took him back, presumably after he had had more training and was of more use as a farm laborer. Savage goes on to recount that, "He was soon hired out to a farmer; the profits of his labor being received by his father" (9–10). In contrast to Bryant's own father, who uses James as a commodity, Cato Walker serves as the boy's spiritual father. In 1826, while James is still with the Walkers, "there occurred in Goffstown a revival of religion" (8). While Savage notes that Catherine Walker "was an honored and consistent member of the Congregational church," his memoir depicts Cato Walker as being even more instrumental in James's conversion. Savage remarks that it was "providence" that "brought James Bryant to the Sabbath School" (7–8). Savage quotes the minister who had led the revival as remembering that every Sunday "'the lad might be seen by the side of Cato, wending his way to the Sanctuary'" (7–8). The minister goes on to remark that when "public worship was over, without mingling with the frivolous of his own age, or manifesting mortified pride at associating with his colored protectors, he started with elastic step on his homeward way" (8). James Bryant's uniqueness was marked by a lack of the racial prejudice that both narrators (the revivalist minister and Savage) would have considered as normal as "mingling with the frivolous of his own age." Although Savage uses the word "lonely" to describe James Bryant, he often depicts him alongside Cato Walker, whose "color" Savage does not let his readers forget. Savage presents Bryant laboring with Cato in his fields or "wending his way" to and from church on the "long and mountainous road." Far from being alone, James is described as under the watchful eye of "his colored protectors" who are clearly his masters (9).

Having attracted the attention of local ministers, Bryant is able to build on the Christian foundations that Cato and Catherine Walker helped to establish by studying to become a minister himself. While Savage gives much attention to the process by which Bryant decides to join a church mission, as well as to Bryant's time as a missionary to the Zulu of South Africa, he omits an explanation of how Bryant came to decide on Africa — or the Zulu — as the beneficiaries of his missionary zeal. Savage quotes a letter from Bryant recounting his first day at the missionary station of Umlazi:

> The Sabbath morning was as beautiful and quiet as any that ever dawned in New England. Soon after breakfast, the natives were seen coming from the various directions to attend the Sabbath schools; their dark forms moving in silent procession, one after another, over the neighboring hills and valleys toward the sanctuary. (45)

Savage's initial image of Bryant as one of a biracial pair walking across the New Hampshire countryside is replaced here by Bryant's own image of a line of "dark forms moving" over "the neighboring hills and valleys" of a land that is not New England but nonetheless recalls New England. In these words, Bryant's difference and distance from the "dark forms" is clearer than when he had attracted the "interested" gazes of Savage or the revivalist minister or the Walkers. Once again, Savage draws the reader's attention to a landscape that frames a dramatic relationship between blacks and whites. In this scene, however, the provocative image of a white boy subservient to a black man is replaced by a more conventional image of white dominance and black subservience. Bryant is now the minister, waiting and watching to see which of these "dark forms" will be responsive to his preaching.

As is typical in accounts of brief, though sanctified lives, Savage devotes much attention to recounting the details of Bryant's death in Ifafa, South Africa, in 1850. Savage presents this "good death" from several different perspectives, including Bryant's own. Aware that he was dying, Bryant wrote in a letter home that he counted his mission to Africa as his singular contribution to humanity: "'O, blessed privilege! To labor for the poor benighted Africans, and be the means of their salvation!'" (65). The main form Bryant's labor took was his efforts to learn Zulu in order to translate key texts — including psalms and an arithmetic primer — into that language. But Bryant himself becomes a kind of testament to the power of Christianity when he succumbs to a chronic illness. Savage quotes a letter from one of Bryant's colleagues who witnessed Bryant's death. In this interpolated narrative, the dying man is surrounded by fellow missionaries, his own family, and "seventy of our church members," who had "seen gloomy, dejected heathen die in sullen silence, but had never before witnessed the decease of a joyful Christian. It will do them good. Some of them helped to shroud him; and they all went in a body and dug his grave" (73–74). Once again, Savage offers his readers a scene of blacks and whites in a setting of dramatic intimacy.

Savage seems less concerned with the good this vision of Bryant's Christian death will do for the Zulu than with the good it will do for his American readers. He concludes the text of his biography by exhorting his readers to emulate Bryant's "singleness of purpose" (84). After all, Savage's *Memoir* is not explicitly about race or New England identity but about Christian virtue. Yet his depictions of New England and New Englanders are the most fascinating aspect of his book because they are aspects hidden by the more familiar view summarized by Gould in his panegyric. Alvin Gould and Thomas Savage were contemporaries living in areas they would have recognized as being part of the same New England region and culture. Gould is from southern Vermont, in a hill town close to the Massachusetts border; Savage is from southern New Hampshire, in a hill town close to the Massachusetts border. The juxtaposition of the two textual visions — one lyric, one narrative, both produced by white men — offers a stereoscopic image of New England where details that are impossible to see by looking at only one view are revealed through the effect of a special lens that allows the images to overlap. Seen together, the images provide what visual artists call chiaroscuro, or revealing shadows. In this combined image of New England, Gould's political opposition to slavery seems linked to his blindness toward race and racism within the New England he celebrates; Savage's ability to see race and racism on a personal level seems linked to a blindness to the political dimension of his New England. The vision of New England produced by forcefully overlaying the two is a New England that repudiates slavery without repudiating racism. It is a New England in which New Englanders are hard put to see the relationship between racism and slavery.

To be sure, Alvin Gould made no claim to being a political philosopher or even a good poet; he was merely adorning his sister-in-law's keepsake book. Yet he might stand in for those "in a two-story white house, North," whom Harriet Wilson felt needed to be shown that "slavery's shadows fall even there."[13] Thomas Savage might stand in as well, as resident, pastor, and local historian in Bedford, New Hampshire, during the years Harriet Wilson was likely serving out her indenture with the Haywards of Milford, New Hampshire.[14] Bedford, Goffstown, Milford, New Boston, and Amherst—these are all towns crowded onto the hilly terrain of Hillsborough County and all towns that figure in the lives of Thomas Savage, James Bryant, and Harriet Wilson. If the chronologies developed so painstakingly for Harriet Wilson are correct, young James Bryant would have been living with the Walkers and participating in an evangelical revival during the same years Wilson's mixed-race birth family was struggling and failing to make a living in Milford and Bedford. During the 1830s, when the Reverend Thomas Savage is following Bryant's career so closely, the mixed-race child who grows up to be Harriet Wilson was living in Milford in a situation of abusive servitude to the white Hayward family. While Bryant drew the sympathetic interest of black and white New Englanders, Wilson's situation was apparently not remarkable enough to draw comment or interest from either her black or her white neighbors. It remained to Wilson herself to comment upon her experiences in the *Sketches* she published in 1859. Wilson's narrative, like Savage's, delineates the color line created by the shadows of slavery within New England. Read together, these two narratives also reveal a dimension to the New England landscape that is not readily available when looking at either one alone. This stereoptic view depicts a culture that suffers under the shadow of harsh economic realities, where class differences are crucial to the way individuals understand themselves and are understood by others.

Harriet Wilson's *Our Nig* uses a combination of novelistic devices, including the fictionalization of the names of her characters and a third-person narrative voice, to convey a story that in other ways signals it is a form of personal memoir or autobiography.[15] Like Savage, Wilson's didactic intent governs the inclusion and exclusion of elements in the storyline. The protagonist is a young child who is abandoned by her white mother and her black stepfather at the home of a white family when—not unlike the situation of the Bryants—the family's marginal social and economic position becomes untenable. The child, Frado, becomes a virtual slave to the Bellmonts: she has no home, no family, no name, no religion. Frado is left to be exploited by the family, who use her as both domestic and field labor.[16] The Bellmonts deny her the perquisites of the indentured "boys" and "girls" conventional in that time and place—she is barely fed, barely educated, and unchurched. Her health is seriously compromised by her early hardships but, like James Bryant, Frado overcomes the disadvantages of such "obscure beginnings and humble poverty." Wilson concludes her story by offering an image of the heroine "busily employed" in pursuing "her steadfast purpose of elevating herself" (130).

The most important shadows thrown by slavery, those *Our Nig* is intent on showing, are the effects of racism in New England. Both narratives foreground the importance of race to New England identity and on the prevalence of racism. As in Savage's tale of Christian conversion in a biracial context, race is an important attribute of both protagonists. All the New Englanders in Wilson's *Our Nig* are either "[b]lack, white" or "yeller" (21). In Savage's *Memoir*, the racist assumption of white supremacy is the norm for most characters, black and white. Likewise, Frado's father, Jim, expresses his understanding of the relative status of the races in his New England when he proposes marriage to the woman he loves: "'She'd be as much a prize to me as she'd fall short of coming up to the mark with white folks.'" (11). At the nadir of her indenture, Wilson has Frado herself express a desire to be white because she understands that the abuse she endures is generated and excused by the color of her skin (11). After all, to the family she works for she isn't a motherless girl with a name of her own. She is, for all intents and purposes, their "Nig," a possession that both bestows status and makes life easier for its putative owners.[17]

Racism in Wilson's narrative is much more virulent than in Savage's. Her narrative, after all, is focalized through the eyes of the child who endures it, rather than through the eyes of a white observer who shares the values of the community he is depicting. Savage commends his subject for an apparent and surprising lack of mortification at being seen with the black Walkers. Unlike Wilson, Savage doesn't name the source of such mortification in a community where it seems normal for school children to cast racist taunts at their non-white neighbors. By contrast, in her fictional town of Singleton, Wilson shows both children and adults expressing overt racism. No one other than the schoolteacher, Miss Marsh, offers to intervene on Frado's part when she appears at school "with scanty clothing and bared feet" (31). No one comes to Frado's rescue when her "winter over-dress was a cast-off overcoat once worn by Jack," despite the fact that the family who had assumed responsibility for her seems to have no lack of money (37). In fact, the racism in Wilson's story is not expressed merely in words or by passive neglect, but rather by active violence that is hard to distinguish from the "master's torturing lash" that Gould, like many New Englanders, associated with the regimes south of the Mason-Dixon line. Not only does Mrs. Bellmont wield a rawhide whip with impunity, Frado is beaten, locked up, and silenced with a chunk of wood—a New England version of the kind of "biting" slave masters used to treat slaves the same as they treated cattle (33–44). Thus, *Our Nig* intensifies the connection between the racism that both Wilson and Savage assert is characteristic of their New England and the slave system that many antebellum New Englanders might otherwise want to disavow.

The plot of Wilson's novel, like Savage's *Memoir*, turns upon moments of what might be called interracial intimacies. For example, the beginning of the story explains how Frado's parents came to marry despite community sanctions against "the evils of amalgamation" (13). Wilson's narrator imagines the aesthetic pleasure felt by Frado's father, Jim, at the prospect of the "pleasing contrast between her [Mag Smith's] fair face and his own dark skin" (11). Like the Reverend Savage, Wilson's narrator seems to share Jim's pleasure at the contemplation of the "pleasing contrast" produced by different skin tones. Throughout *Our Nig*, Wilson heightens the reader's sense of Frado's darkness by juxtaposing her dark body with the white bodies of the Bellmonts. Mrs. Bellmont is "determined the sun should have full power to darken the shade which nature had first bestowed upon [Frado]." The malevolent matriarch wants to emphasize the blackness of her main character, whose skin, she acknowledges, is otherwise nearly the same color as her own daughter's (39).

At each critical moment in the story of Frado's advance toward self-reliance, the color line between black and white is crossed. Before being left at the Bellmonts', Frado "had never learned to read, never heard of a school" (30). By the end of the story, despite the best efforts of her antagonists, Frado has learned to read, become "serious" about spiritual matters, and internalized the New England virtue of independence. She accomplishes her freedom under the intimate guidance of Jack, James, and Abby, who risk the wrath of Mrs. Bellmont in a community in which casual racism was normative and violent racism not exceptional. Mrs. Bellmont "did not feel responsible for [Frado's] spiritual culture, and hardly believed she had a soul" (86). Still, Mrs. Bellmont's son, James, and her sister-in-law, Abby, help Frado become "a believer in a future existence" (84). Frado's conversion hinges on the affection she feels for James for his kindness to her and because of the grief she feels at the thought of his impending death: "As James approached that blessed world, she felt a strong desire to follow, and be with one who was such a dear, kind friend to her" (85). Wilson depicts Frado as having so internalized the racism of her environment that she doubts whether there is "a heaven for the black." Frado is surprised and relieved to learn from her white minister that "all, young or old, white or black, bond or free" may come "to Christ for pardon" (85). Toward the end of the story, Frado finds a mentor in a Massachusetts woman, "a plain, poor, simple woman, who could see merit beneath a dark skin," who agrees to teach her the trade of sewing "straw bonnets" (124). Frado's mentor "sought also to teach her the value of useful books." Wilson concludes this chapter with a vision of women reading aloud "to the other" while they both pursued a course of economic and intellectual "elevation" (124–25).

Wilson's final chapter, "The Winding Up of the Matter," underscores the rarity of such affectionate intimacies. In Wilson's New England, which by the end of her story encompasses Massachusetts as well as New Hampshire, racist antagonism remains the norm: "Watched by kidnappers, maltreated by professed abolitionists, who didn't want slaves at the South, nor niggers in their own houses, North" (129). "Faugh!" Frado imagines such abolitionists to think, "to lodge one; to eat with one; to admit one through the front door; to sit next to one; awful!" (129). If racism was such a prominent feature of their New England, as both Savage's *Memoir* and Wilson's *Our Nig* agree, what accounts for the moments of interracial intimacies that are so critical to the development of both protagonists? The shaded portrait of New England produced by reading both texts together suggests that these intimacies depend upon an economic landscape characterized by wide discrepancies of wealth and status. In Savage's text, for example, the remarkable intimacy of the white boy, James Bryant, and the black family of Cato Walker occurs only because of the indigence of the boy's birth family. The poverty of the Bryants doesn't elide or cancel out the race of their child, nor does the relative wealth of the Walkers cancel their race, but it does trump it. Similarly, in Wilson's narrative it is the poverty of Mag Smith and the relative financial security of Jim that vitiates the taboo against what Wilson calls the "amalgamation" of the races. Likewise, it is poverty, not race, that subjects Wilson's protagonist to abandonment and "servile toil" in the household of the Bellmonts. The chiaroscuro produced by the two texts reveals the importance to both texts of the plotline of social and class mobility through which both protagonists move. Though both texts critique the endemic racism of New Englanders, neither offers an explicit critique of the economic givens of the culture that exact such costs from those who cut the wood, launder the clothes, wash the dishes, and till the fields.

The play of light and shadow in these two stories of poor New England children deepens the chiaroscuro — the contrasts that reveal depth, perspective, and complexity — to otherwise bright but flat representations of New England that banish both race and class identity. The white house at which the poor black girl was abandoned and in which she suffers the full range of racist abuse was not far from the clapboard farm house in which the poor white boy found refuge from poverty and ignorance in an economically secure and socially respectable black family.[18] Like Wilson's *Our Nig*, Savage's *Memoir* complicates the familiar image of New England's "fruitful soil." In this multi-dimensional vision of New England the problem of the color line is as inextricable from the problems of economic disparity as it is from the institution of slavery.

NOTES

My thanks go to Laura Korobkin for the compassion and patience she showed during this project. I would also like to thank the National Endowment for the Humanities whose generous support facilitated the initial research into *The Memoir of the Rev. J. C. Bryant.*

1. Alvin Gould's poem is transcribed in Appendix 1 of Mary Louise Kete's *Sentimental Collaborations: Mourning and Middle-class Identity in Nineteenth-Century America* (Durham, N.C.: Duke University Press, 2000).

2. John Greenleaf Whittier's poem of 1846, "New Hampshire," is perhaps one of the best examples. This paean concludes, "Courage, then, Northern hearts! Be firm, be true; / What one brave State hath done, can ye not also do?" *The Complete Poetical Works of John Greenleaf Whittier* (Boston: Houghton, Mifflin, 1881), 51. Whittier's class position was more similar than not to that of Bryant's. Like James Bryant's father, Whittier moved several times as he attempted to make a living as a farmer in New Hampshire and Massachusetts.

3. See Toni Morrison, *Playing in the Dark: Whiteness and the Literary Imagination* (New York: Vintage Books, 1993), who reminds us that conceptions of racial difference are integral, even if invisible, to American identity. For Morrison, the "literature of the United States, like its history, represents commentary on the transformations of biological, ideological, and metaphysical concepts of racial difference" (65).

4. First published in 1859, *Our Nig; or, Sketches from the Life of a Free Black, In a Two-Story White House, North. Showing That Slavery's Shadows Fall Even There. By "Our Nig"* languished until republication by Henry Louis Gates, Jr., in 1983. This republication caused significant shifts in the related fields of American literature and history, African American literature and history, and women's literature and history. The edition I refer to in this essay is the 2002 Vintage edition edited by Gates. All further references to the novel will be in parentheses from this edition. The introduction by P. Gabrielle Foreman and Reginald H. Pitts in their edition (New York: Penguin, 2005) provides a comprehensive handling of the extensive scholarship on *Our Nig* and summarizes the work Foreman and Pitts have done uncovering the traces of Harriet Wilson's life after the publication of the work.

5. Thomas Savage, *Memoir of Rev. James C. Bryant, late Missionary of AM.B.C.F. Missions to South Africa by the Reverend Thomas Savage of Bedford New Hampshire* (Boston: Massachusetts Sabbath School Society, 1854). Further page references will be in parentheses.

6. See the first chapter of W. E. B DuBois's *Souls of Black Folk* (Chicago: A. C. McClurg & Co., 1903).

7. Thomas Savage (1793–1866) was one of three men commissioned in 1850 to compile a *History of Bedford, New Hampshire* in time to celebrate the town's centennial in 1850. The copy I am working from is a revision published in 1903 to commemorate Bedford's 150th anniversary: *History of Bedford, New Hampshire from 1737,*

Being Statistics Compiled on the Occasion of the One Hundred Fiftieth Anniversary of the Incorporation of the Town, May 15, 1900 (Concord, N.H.: Rumford Printing Company, 1903).

8. The story told by Rev. Savage turns out to be verifiable. The American Antiquarian Society has copies of Bryant's publications in Zulu. Futhermore, the story of Cato Walker and Bryant's relationship is summarized in *The History of the Town of Goffstown, 1733–1920*, by George Plummer Hadley (Concord, N.H.: Rumford Press, 1924). The elaborately carved grave markers of Cato and his wife Catherine may be seen in the Goffstown Cemetery.

9. While the state constitution of Vermont had abolished both slavery and indenture, informal indenture or "binding-out" of the indigent continued to be common in Vermont through the 1830s, when many towns established poor farms. New Hampshire's original constitution was as vague on indenture as on slavery. As in Vermont, New Hampshire continued the British common law tradition of the indenture of the poor until it also joined in the poor farm experiment. In both cases, indigent residents were considered to be the responsibility of the town, which sought to pay the least amount to either a private family or the managers of the poor farm to keep the poor in a condition of minimal comfort and dignity. Towns tended to contest the residency claims of people like the Bryants (who had come from Massachusetts) or Harriet Wilson's birth family (who seemed to have moved around the various towns of Hillsborough). This might account for the absence of any formal records of indenture for either Harriet Wilson or James Bryant.

10. The oddness of this relationship is remarked on in various places in both Savage's *History of Bedford* and *The History of the Town of Goffstown*, in which it figures as a notable anecdote. Hadley's summary of the story is contained in the genealogical entry of Charlotte Walker: "After the decease of her father, Capt. James Walker, the colored servant Cato eventually came in possession of the farm upon which he lived until his decease which occurred Dec. 1, 1839, aged 73 years. He m. Jan. 27, 1818, a colored woman, Catherine Owen of Amherst, who d. 1854, at an advanced age. They were both members of the Congregational Church in G., and respected citizens. In his boyhood days James Bryant, the missionary, first to translate the Bible into the Zulu language, was a resident in their family, and here by a pitch pine knot, first began his studies, and in after years he tenderly alluded to and exercised kind care and paternal oversight over this colored couple" (537).

11. See *History of Goffstown*, 2: 537. Note that neither the *History of Goffstown* nor the *History of Bedford* has separate entries for black heads of households even if, like Cato Walker, they were early settlers and taxpayers. Lois Leveen has a helpful overview of this system in her 2001 article, "Dwelling in the House of Oppression: The Spatial, Racial and Textual Dynamics of Harriet Wilson's *Our Nig*," published in the *African American Review*. John van der Zee offers a good general introduction to the topic in *Bound Over: Indentured Servitude and American Conscience*, published by Simon and Schuster in 1985.

12. I've been unable to find corroboration of this element of Cato Walker's story,

which, according to Eleanor Porrit of the Goffstown Historical Society, is part of the lore surrounding Cato Walker. Phone conversation with Eleanor Porrit, January 2006.

13. Wilson, *Our Nig*, t.p.

14. Scholars have pursued the mysteries about authorship posed by *Our Nig* since its re-publication by Henry Louis Gates, Jr. Extending the work on Wilson's life begun by Gates, Barbara A. White, and others, Gabrielle Foreman and Reginald Pitts offer new information about the author's life after the publication of *Our Nig*. See Gates, introduction to *Our Nig* (New York: Vintage, 2002); R. J. Ellis's *Harriet Wilson's "Our Nig": A Cultural Biography of a "Two-Story" African American Novel* (Amsterdam: Rodopi, 2003); and Barbara A. White, "'Our Nig' and the She-Devil: New Information about Harriet Wilson and the 'Bellmont' Family," *American Literature* 65.1 (1993).

15. The question of genre and *Our Nig* has been extensively treated because of the hybrid nature of her narrative. The debate begins, of course, with Gates's initial introductory description, which designates the work a novel. See Ellis, *Harriet Wilson's "Our Nig,"* for the best summary of the debate. I prefer to follow Wilson's lead and think of it within the tradition of Washington Irving's "Crayons" or Hawthorne's "Tales."

16. Like Bryant, Frado works in both the fields and the home. This would not have been considered abusive in itself. Rather, it is the kind, extent, and manner of the labor exacted from Frado as well as the extraordinary use of physical discipline that Wilson condemns as torture. Two studies from the 1980s provide insight into the life of laboring women in midnineteenth-century New England: Faye E. Dudden, *Serving Women: Household Service in Nineteenth-century America* (Middletown, Conn.: Wesleyan University Press, 1983), and Joan M. Jensen, *With These Hands: Women Working the Land* (New York: Talman, 1980).

17. See Wilson's depiction of the scene in chapter 3 among the Bellmonts when they are debating what to do with the child, Frado, who has been left in their hands. Jack Bellmont, who becomes one of Frado's advocates, teases his sister Mary by saying, "Poh! Miss Mary; if she should stay, it wouldn't be two days before you would be telling the girls about *our nig, our nig!*" (25–26).

18. If nothing else, Savage's *Memoir* throws many aspects of Wilson's now canonical text into relief. The isolation of Frado, in particular, seems even more tragic since it was clearly not inevitable—there were blacks with resources and less cruelly racist whites in the area—but Frado's plight did not attract the kind of interest that helped James Bryant. In contrast to Bryant, who is aided by the black family he serves and by various white ministers, Frado achieves the "elevation" she had so "steadfast[ly] pursued" with little assistance.

Recovered Autobiographies and the Marketplace

Our Nig's Generic Genealogies and Harriet Wilson's Entrepreneurial Enterprise

P. Gabrielle Foreman

On September 5, 1859, "Mrs. H. E. Wilson" published *Our Nig, or Sketches from the Life of a Free Black in a Two-Story White House, North, Showing that Slavery's Shadows Fall Even There*, an act that went virtually unnoticed in her own time but one that would make her a woman of historical consequence in subsequent centuries. After its 1983 republication nearly a hundred and twenty-five years later, *Our Nig* became known as a novel because it is told in the third person, because it begins by narrating not the author's, but the author's mother's, life, and because Wilson uses pseudonyms for people earlier thought to be fictional characters. Careful readers of the nineteenth century will note that these narrative attributes appear in other autobiographical works, though not often in concert. William Wells Brown narrated a major sketch about his own life in the third person; the opening of Juan Manzano's autobiography (the only extant slave narrative in the Spanish-speaking Americas) describes his mistresses' household and his mother's place in it in artfully novelistic language; and Harriet Jacobs rechristens almost every single person in *Incidents in the Life of a Slave Girl*. Indeed, not Jacobs's name, but the character Linda's, was first embossed in gold on the volume's spine.[1]

In this essay, I re-examine the generic questions that frame *Our Nig's* twentieth-century classification in order to explain how it became characterized as a fiction classic and not as one of the most important and novel African American autobiographies of its time. Examining this case helps to illuminate the marketplace dynamics that inform the politics of literary and historical recovery work. I then go on to revisit some of the historically and conceptually

rich autobiographical correspondences between Wilson's text and her life, including Margaret Smith's death announcement and evidence provided from
the very hair bottles Wilson used when a friend "kindly provided her with a
valuable recipe" to restore "gray hair to its former color."[2] By examining Wilson's antebellum hair tonic business — and by discussing her bottles and the
only known existing (partial) bottle labels for the first time[3] — in this piece, I
also raise questions about social networks that may further illuminate the un-
derexamined issues of labor and class structure within the porous and mobile
black communities of antebellum New England.[4]

IN THE HEADY DAYS of the early 1980s when novelists Toni Morrison,
Alice Walker, and Gloria Naylor strode side by side onto the *New York Times*
bestseller lists and were also being recognized with Pulitzer Prizes and National Book Awards, an Ivy League scholar's discovery of the first black maternal novel-writing ancestor ensured the reception that *Our Nig*, and Harriet
Wilson, needed to be noticed.[5] When it first debuted, Henry Louis Gates, Jr.'s
find was featured in *People Magazine*; stories about its rediscovery appeared in
The New York Times and *The Washington Post*.[6] As a result, the book found a
broader readership than it had enjoyed in its own time.

Savvy about the juncture where the politics of recovery intersect with the
cultural marketplace of race and letters, Gates situated *Our Nig* in relation to
other literary genres to claim its status as a *first*, the *first* black novel to be published in the United States, the *first* novel to be published by a black woman
in any language.[7] He became *Our Nig's* "sponsoring agent," to borrow a concept from theorist Walter Stephens; without such a sponsor, "a text has no
imaginable future, for it cannot 'discover' itself to an audience."[8] Gates recognized that if a newly reintroduced text, "fits in, or can be made to fit in with
the hierarchy of the receiving culture-audience," as André Lefevere asserts, "it
will be greeted as a major contribution."[9] According to Lefevere, textual success can be measured in relation to the "hierarchies of the original culture-
audience and of the one for which the refracted text" (or a work "produced
to replace an original text for a given audience") is intended.[10] As *Our Nig's*
twentieth-century sponsor, to extend Stephen's theory, attending to ushering
this important rediscovery into the world of letters and anticipating the book's
audiences' doubts about its origin and authenticity, this sponsoring agent, like
others of refracted texts, focused on providing a coherent narrative of discovery and literary genealogy and on producing a popular and critical reception
that would help the text gain canonical status. Gates launched a "polemical es-
pousal, a mediation 'for' the text. In rhetorical terms [sponsorship] is a *capta-
tio benevolentiae* aimed at capturing an audience for the text, and determining

their acceptance of its authenticity" to again adapt Stephen's ideas to *Our Nig*'s republication history.[11] Gates performed that role not only with flair but with *savoir faire*; in large part as a result of Gates's effort and expertise, *Our Nig* became a contemporary African American classic in literature, though not in the aligned field of history.[12]

The critical discussion about *Our Nig*'s generic and historical place and placement is tied to the dynamics of contemporary reception. Yet, Wilson herself refers to *Our Nig* as "sketches" or "narrations," while the author of the closing testimonial urges others to buy the "autobiography" (76). Historian Barbara White's discoveries of the identities of the family members who held "their nig" in indentured servitude establish that Wilson's work is based on direct historical and textual correspondences; as White puts it, these "remind us that Henry Louis Gates, Jr., not Harriet Wilson, classifies *Our Nig* as fiction."[13] Indeed, now that we have situated *Our Nig* in the even deeper critical and historical context that has emerged since its rediscovery, readers must acknowledge that the text functions as an autobiography characterized by its complex novelistic qualities just as surely as it can be considered a brilliant novel that makes substantive autobiographical claims.[14]

Our Nig's complex narrative achievements would be diminished were they dependent on its claim to truth, as shifting, situated, and ultimately unrecoverable as such narrative claims are. Still, as we have established, evidence both broadens and bolsters earlier findings that from beginning to end and with very few exceptions, "Wilson's narrative corresponds to the historical record."[15] As we point out, if Wilson's mother Margaret is "Margaret Ann Smith," she moved west from Portsmouth, N.H., to Milford leaving "the few friends she possessed," to "seek asylum among strangers," as *Our Nig* claims (6). In the book, "Jim" "boards cheap" with the cooper who employs him; and the 1820 and 1830 censuses show that Timothy Blanchard ("Pete Green"), a cooperage owner, and one of Milford's two black heads of household, boarded other "free men of color," one of whom was almost certainly Joshua Green, whom the records of death and second marriage that we discovered name as Wilson's father.[16] And, as Barbara White has established, the portrayal of the "county farm" Wilson tried so hard to avoid corresponds almost exactly to descriptions and town records for the institutional support dedicated to the poor.[17]

Wilson claims this story, *Our Nig* by "our Nig," as her own. Born on March 15, 1825, in Milford, according to the record of death we have located, Wilson is the daughter of Joshua Green and, other records reveal, a woman named Margaret.[18] According to *Our Nig*, Wilson's father died of consumption when she was five or six years old; his death marked the family's waning economic

An original building from the Hayward homestead in Milford, possibly the home in which Wilson was indentured. *maplehavenfarm as owned by David M. and Liisa V. Palance*

health as well. Like other nineteenth-century mothers with few resources, Mag, as nineteenth-century Margarets were often called, relieved herself of a child she could not support. The Hayward home where Wilson spent a tortured childhood in service was located just miles from the Hutchinson Family Homestead, which served as a central hub for visiting reform and anti-slavery activists. The Hayward family was connected by blood, marriage, and geography to the Hutchinson Family Singers. One of the most famous nineteenth-century singing groups, they were known in their time "not as performers, but as abolitionists," as the leading anti-slavery paper the *Liberator* proclaimed.[19]

In *Our Nig*'s first chapter title, the author calls Mag Smith "my Mother" in a text otherwise told almost entirely in the third person. Evidence we first introduced supports the possibility that this statement may be literal. If "Margaret Ann Smith," a twenty-seven-year-old New Hampshire woman who died in Boston, is "lonely Mag Smith," a death announcement in Milford's local paper may provide evidence that adds additional insight into the conditions that motivated her actions.[20] In addition to Mag's poverty, drunkenness may explain her stark departure from the rhetorical codes of conventional maternity. Instead of the familiar nineteenth-century cultural tropes of gentle manners and conversation that characterize a properly domestic maternal demeanor, *Our Nig* casts Mag as lowly and animalistic. She snarls and growls, is subject to bursts of anger, and "utters curses too fearful to repeat" (11). After her husband's death, Mag descends into a "darkness," casually taking on one of his business partners as a lover and engaging in tense domestic scenes that became "familiar and trying" (11). Before the new couple decides to disencumber themselves of Mag's child so they can leave town to find work, Mag is "morose and revengeful" (6) and yields "to fits of desperation" (11).

Our Nig's depiction of Mag Smith's volatile behavior and language may anticipate her violent and drunken death. As we report, on March 27, 1830, the *Farmer's Cabinet*—the paper that covered the area in which Wilson grew up—reports a Margaret Smith's death in detail:

> Margaret Ann Smith, black, late of Portsmouth, N.H. about 27 years was found dead in the room of a black man with whom she lived in Southack [sic] Street, Boston, last week. The verdict of the Coroner's jury was that she came to her death from habitual intoxication. It appears that she and the man had quarreled, both being intoxicated, and he had beaten her severely, but that the immediate cause of her death was drinking half a pint of raw rum.—*Patriot*

The *Cabinet's* coverage is much more detailed than the almost careless, corroborating notices that appear in city papers such as the *Boston Patriot*, presumably the *Patriot* listed as the *Cabinet's* source. It leads one to ask why a small southern New Hampshire paper would cover the death of a woman from Portsmouth who died in Boston unless she had recent local connections.[21] The announcement corresponds to *Our Nig's* narration: Mag's age correlates to the story *Our Nig* tells and the book confirms that she was not born in "Singleton," as Milford is renamed, but relocates there. Moreover, in the text she has just left town with her former husband's black partner to seek employment. The *Cabinet's* announcement underscores these connections. Why else, again, would such a detailed notice of Margaret Smith's death—a passing deemed so socially inconsequential that it is not featured in the city papers where she died—appear in the local Milford paper, except to convey news about a Mag Smith about whom the community had some knowledge and interest?

While the *Cabinet* account offers potentially illuminating information, its racial attribution—Margaret Smith as "black"—also raises intriguing questions.[22] Was this simply a mistake, one of the many erroneous racial classifications in the public records that document Harriet, or "Hattie," E. Wilson's life?[23] Or was it punitive, a final way to register outrage at the illicit "Black, white, and yeller" amalgamation against which townspeople had preached dozens of sermons, to borrow from *Our Nig?*[24] In other words, did Smith's being labeled black function as racial commentary rather than racial classification, a way to further underscore, for whites, her socially and sexually compromised status? Was this a dig meant to further blacken her reputation as it were? And how do readers interpret *Our Nig*'s own challenging play with its audience's racialized expectations, as Mag's racial designation isn't definitively identified—she could very well be a prototypical light-skinned black protagonist—until the very last paragraph of the long introductory chapter that tells her story?[25]

Finally, scholars have yet to explain why Harriet Wilson used Adams as her maiden name if her mother's name was, indeed, Smith and her father's name was most certainly Green. Even if they were not married—and no evidence has been found to confirm or deny *Our Nig*'s assertion that they were—their daughter Harriet would presumably carry one of their names. Yet, the 1850 federal census places a black Harriet *Adams* born in New Hampshire boarding with the family of Samuel Boyles in Milford. Moreover, Wilson's June 1851 first marriage to Thomas Wilson lists her as Harriet Adams.[26] "Hattie E. Wilson" from Milford whose father was Joshua Green is the same Harriet Adams who married Thomas Wilson; and there is only one free woman of color in the 1840 and 1850 censuses in Milford—Wilson, who is certainly the "Mrs. H. E. Wilson" who registered the copyright to *Our Nig*, went on to sell Mrs. H. E. Wilson's Hair Regenerator, and then become Boston's colored medium.[27] As scholars spotlight Wilson's own glaringly ironic use of naming in *Our Nig*, questions about the author's own surname still linger. How and why did Wilson come to use Adams? What chapter of Wilson's life do we have we yet to recover and what aspects of and assumptions about her now known life will new revelations complicate?

While some of the discoveries about *Our Nig*'s opening and Wilson's parentage raise almost as many questions as they answer, as it draws to a close, *Our Nig*'s story dovetails with the appended testimonials that authenticate its claims. As we know, after Wilson was freed from her indenture, an acquaintance provided her with "a valuable recipe" that "restored gray hair to its former color" (76). By examining newly emerging material objects, one can argue that Wilson became one of the first African American women to successfully launch a hair product business with regionally wide geographic reach.[28] When Geneva Arrington, one of the officers of the newly formed Progressive Hairdressers of Massachusetts, affirmed in 1938 that "much of the work of bringing [the business] to this point has been contributed by those who have made it possible for so many of the women of our race to make independent livings through the improvement of the appearances of colored men and women of this country" she no doubt had in mind the black beauty magnate Madame C. J. Walker but not her predecessor, "Mrs. H. E. Wilson."[29] Yet before Madame C. J. Walker (née Sarah Breedlove) was born, Wilson almost certainly

Bottle marked "Mrs. H. E. Wilson's Hair Dressing" in the collection of Reginald H. Pitts. *Courtesy of JerriAnne Boggis*

marketed her products door to door, as Walker would as well.[30] Availing "herself of this great help [Wilson] has been quite successful" (76), one of the writers of *Our Nig*'s appended testimonials reports; "but her health is again failing, and she has felt herself obliged to resort to another method of procuring her bread — that of writing an Autobiography" (76).

Wilson's bottles and bottle-selling offer additional insight into her life as a Northern free black and as an itinerant peddler in the Massachusetts and New Hampshire towns to which first editions have been traced.[31] We have established that sometime between 1856 and 1860, "Mrs. H. E. Wilson's Hair Dressing" and "Mrs. H. E. Wilson's Hair Regenerator" bottles were made in Manchester, N.H.[32] One of the hair dressing bottles was manufactured "solely by Henry P. Wilson" (no relation), whom city directories list as a clerk; in 1858, he joined forces with neighboring physician G. J. Tewksbury, and their names appeared together on her now rarer "regenerator" bottles. From the number of "Mrs. H. E. Wilson's Hair Dressing" bottles that have found their way into twenty-first-century collections, it is highly likely that hundreds and hundreds were sold. And a later, noncatalogued, Tewksbury and Wilson "Mrs. H. E. Wilson's Hair Regenerator" bottle also exists. The discovery of this smooth based version with a hand tooled lip allows us to interpret the existence of an 1871 advertisement in a Chicago catalog with more confidence. In addition to selling hundreds of bottles during the middle and late 1850s, Wilson may have continued in this business into the 1870s as she expanded into an even wider geographic area.[33]

The material objects themselves provide evidence that in Wilson's professional life as an itinerant businesswoman, she sincerely appealed, as she had in *Our Nig*'s preface, to her "colored brethren" and sistren "universally for patronage." On surviving label fragments on the inset of Mrs. H. E. Wilson's "Hair Dressing" bottles appears the pledge:

> It will cleanse the ha[ir] . . .
> skin, will cause the h[air?] . . .
> curl, and make it, how[ever?]
> harsh and coarse, to rem[ain in]?
> any desired position or . . .
> and it will not stain . . . the . . .
> linen.

"Directions" follow:

> Apply. . .
> the hand or brush daily . . .
> often as is necessary, rubb[ing] . . .
> To prevent baldness, or stop
> hair from falling off, or to re-
> store gray hair to its nat[ural]
> color, use
> Mrs. Wilson's Hair Regener[ator]

Darker and larger arching type frames the missing face of a dark- and long-haired woman. The incomplete and bold print asks the question "Should the

Cocoa-n- . . . [?]" and also announces ". . . it will readily become soft."[34] The partial image seems to match *Our Nig*'s description of her own "long, curly black hair" (11); these labels could very well be the only extant "correct likeness" of Wilson herself, to borrow a phrase from that era.

Wilson's panacean product promises to cure all hirsutial ailments, those faced by men and women, young and old, black and non-black. Gardner points out that "Wilson would have been well aware that antebellum white American culture was fascinated with hair."[35] He links her bottle selling to his groundbreaking research about Wilson's probable itinerant book peddling and presumes that because the owners of the first editions he has found were white, that her hair customer base was mostly, if not solely, white as well. Wilson surely sold to the predominantly white populations in the southern New Hampshire and west and central Massachusetts region through which she traveled in the late 1850s; yet, the specificity of her labels' language suggests that cocoa customers, those who "brush" their "harsh and coarse hair" with the aim of making it "readily soft," were almost certainly among the "friends and purchasers" in Wilson's circle. Indeed, these newly discovered labeled bottles imply that they were her intended, preferred, or implied customers, even if they did not make up her actual ones.

Hovering between poverty and subsistence when she launched this business, Wilson sallied forth to earn an "easier way of sustenance" (72) without the local and familial connections and capital that her contemporaries, the Remond sisters of Salem, Massachusetts, for example, enjoyed in their hair businesses. Abolitionist authors and activists Sarah Parker Remond and Charles Lenox Remond's three sisters, Cecilia Remond Babcock, Maritcha Remond, and Caroline Remond Putnam of Salem, Massachusetts, were proprietors of the fashionable "Ladies Hair Work Salon"; their wig factory, as Dorothy Sterling points out, was the biggest in Massachusetts. The sisters and their spouses had a large mail order distribution for products — mostly wigs, one can assume — throughout New England. Caroline Remond Putnam also manufactured "Mrs. Putnam's Medicated Hair Tonic" for local sale. The 1851 Salem Directory advertisement page lists Miss M. J. Remond and Mrs. C. Babcock and their "Ladies' and Gentlemen's HAIR MANUFACTORY" at No. 18 Washington Street. In a separate advertisement for a business next door at No. 16 Washington Street is James Babcock's shaving and hair dressing room. Directly below readers find advertisement for J. H. Putnam, hair cutter and wig maker, and Mrs. Putnam, Ladies' Hair Dresser both at No. 175½ Essex Street.

Mrs. Caroline Remond Putnam — the only one of the sisters who seemed to produce hair tonics for sale as Wilson did — continued in the hairdressing business (and in anti-slavery work) over a span of decades. The 1864 Salem Directory announces her election as vice-president of the Salem Female Anti-Slavery Society. Yet her hair bottles evidently did not do anywhere as well as Wilson's did. A leading bottle expert had never heard of "Mrs. Putnam's Medicated Hair Tonic" and knows of no such bottles in current circulation. In contrast, if their survival into the twenty-first century says something about their original sales and circulation, Mrs. H. E. Wilson was much more successful in the hair tonic business.[36]

Wilson's bottle selling may modestly augment our understanding of antebellum black labor and working-class consumption in the North. As an itinerant merchant, even as a rare black female in this expanding business, Wilson probably hoped to enjoy some of the geographic, occupational, and social mobility that David Jaffee argues characterized peddling of that period for whites. Yet, as a disenfranchised laborer in terms of her race, family status, class, and economic access, her lack of a centralized way to establish and maintain a market base suggests she wouldn't have access to as stable a set of customers. Without this home base, in her search for clients Wilson encountered "many frowns" as she put it, as well as "some kind friends and purchasers" (72). These purchasers were likely to have included working-class consumers who sought to share in the "self-fashioning of new identities through the exchange of goods," as Jaffee points out, even though such commodities did not necessarily facilitate "the democratization of gentility and the fluidity of social identity" for African Americans as they did for middle-class and aspiring white Americans.[37] Nevertheless, Wilson's products may provide further indication that black consumers partook in commodity culture to an extent well beyond the economy of material necessities generally attributed to aspiring black workers of the period.

As an orphaned indentured servant and as the only female "free colored person," according to the 1840 federal census, in Milford, New Hampshire—where, as in some of "our New England villages," she writes, "people of color were rare" (70)—young Harriet was isolated from blacks who could have offered support and community. Yet, in some context and in relation to some social networks, Wilson clearly developed the trenchant racial and social analysis she expresses in Our Nig and in later speeches.[38] She went to Massachusetts in 1850, for example, "through the instrumentality of an itinerant colored lecturer" (73). And beyond her short-lived marriage to a "fake fugitive," as she later found out, who died at sea, Wilson may have forged sustaining if not substantive relations with African Americans as well as with Anglo Americans whose common interests and geographies overlapped with her own. Considering her bottles' labels and the presence of black barbers in Nashua and

Manchester, New Hampshire, the person who generously offered Wilson the "valuable recipe" she used to "prepare her [own] merchandise" (72) could have belonged to the black community of southern New Hampshire, men such as abolitionist William Cooper Nell's father-in-law Phillip O. Ames and Zimri Johnson of Nashua, or George Bundy, William Cole, John C. Dunlop, Robert Gibson, and Abraham Roper of Manchester.[39] Indeed, blacks dominated barbering into the 1850s. As Frederick Douglass put it in 1853, "a few years ago, and a *white* barber would have been a curiosity.[40] Historian James Horton examines social networks and interior relations to help flesh out the depth of cooperation and mutual support" Northern blacks exhibited even in the face of disagreements and, one might add, radically different experiences.[41] Considering the case evidence and the broader contexts of black New England life, this community may well have served as key brokers between Wilson and her potential clients.

Placing Wilson's business relationships in the context of black independent struggle in the 1840s and 1850s helps to illuminate the reason she may have importuned, in *Our Nig*, her colored brethren for patronage. Contemporary critics have puzzled over why — considering her explicit appeal for support and the book's Boston publisher — Wilson received no notice from the anti-slavery establishment or from such important periodicals as *The Anglo African*, which launched in 1859, the very year in which *Our Nig* appeared. Yet, beginning a decade earlier, as historian Leslie Harris attests, a "new activism among blacks, independent of white abolitionists [emerged] to address the problems of racism, under- and unemployment, and poverty in the black community."[42] Considering her economic circumstances and her experiences in service and in the domestic labor force, these issues would resonate. Indeed, Wilson would no doubt have agreed with the short-lived American League of Colored Laborers' 1850 pronouncement that "one very great evil now suffered by the free colored people of the United States, is the want of money."[43] In the 1840s and 1850s, larger numbers of free blacks in the North became more vocally critical of white abolitionists' almost myopic focus on Southern slavery, one that seemed to blind them to the glaringly harsh economic and political conditions that free and fugitive blacks faced in their midst.

In her *Sketches from the Life of a Free Black in a Two-Story White House, North, Showing that Slavery's Shadows Fall Even There*, to recall *Our Nig*'s subtitle, Wilson's critiques of Northern power relations mirrored others who forthrightly challenged white hypocrisy and neglect. Writing in the third person, Wilson described her recent travels: "she passed into various towns of the State she lived in, then into Massachusetts. Strange were some of her adventures. Watched by kidnappers, maltreated by professed abolitionists, who didn't want slaves at the South, nor niggers in their own houses, North. Faugh! To lodge one; to eat with one, to admit one through the front door, to sit next to one; awful!" (71). Facing poverty and the increasingly discriminatory laws and codes meant to impoverish and disenfranchise them and their families, free African Americans "largely had to rely on the limited resources of blacks themselves," Harris affirms; in some cases, blacks "also turned to nonabolitionist whites."[44] Perhaps, then, Wilson had in mind these specific communities of independent black and white business owners and their customers as the "kind friends as purchasers" of both her "Mrs. H. E. Wilson's Hair Dressing" and of *Our Nig*.[45]

The questions that emerge from this essay augment, complicate, and unsettle current categories of analysis used to frame our discussion of Wilson and *Our Nig or, Sketches from the Life of a Free Black in a Two-Story White House, North, Showing that Slavery's Shadows Fall Even There*. James Horton's assertion that "we know very little about the interior of free black life in the shadowy world of the antebellum North" still resonates.[46] Revisiting *Our Nig*'s autobiographical dimensions allows readers to fill in that sketchiness and to reframe Wilson's deliberate discussions about the ways in which slavery's shadows — that is, again, white racism — influenced the lives of free blacks in the North. Placing discussions of Wilson's work in the context of black protest and identity and at the intersections of labor and gender helps to illuminate her life and work. Delving deeper into the social networks of African Americans who existed outside the central institutional and personal hub of black leadership also illuminates our understanding of the heterogeneity and complexity of antebellum African American community formation in the North. In this essay, I also seek to link these inquiries to generic questions and marketplace concerns that underwrite how we think of texts' relation to (inter)disciplinary community formation in the Academy and beyond.

NOTES

Thanks to Eric Gardner and Reginald Pitts for their collaborative spirits and fine feedback, to Rhondda Thomas for her early research assistance as we found Wilson's first bottles, and Donald Fadley for sharing his expertise.

1. Jean Fagan Yellin, *Harriet Jacobs, A Life* (New York: Basic Books, 2005), 144.

2. See Harriet E. Wilson, *Our Nig; or Sketches from the Life of a Free Black*, ed. P. Gabrielle Foreman and Reginald H. Pitts (New York: Penguin Classics, 2005), 72, 76, and xlviii, n. 23. Further references to *Our Nig* are taken from this edition and appear in parentheses within the text.

3. All bottles mentioned in this essay are in the author's collection. Leading hair bottle expert Don Fadley does not know of any other labeled H. E. Wilson bottles. Email from Fadley to the author, November 29, 2005.

4. See James Oliver Horton, *Free People of Color: Inside the African American Community* (Washington, D.C.: Smithsonian Institution Press, 1993), 11. I paraphrase directly from his language here.

5. Morrison's *Tar Baby* was published in 1981; Walker's *The Color Purple* and Naylor's *The Women of Brewster Place*, in 1982. Naylor won the National Book Award in 1983, the same year in which Walker was recognized with the Pulitzer Prize. It is in this context—and in the same year—that Gates republished *Our Nig*: Harriet E. Wilson, *Our Nig; or Sketches from the Life of a Free Black*, ed. Henry Louis Gates, Jr. (New York: Vintage Books, 1983).

6. See "An 1859 Black Literary Landmark Is Uncovered," Cultural Desk, by Leslie Bennetts, *New York Times*, November 8, 1982, Sec. C; and Book World, by Ira Berlin, *Washington Post*, July 2, 1983. Also see coverage in the *Washington Post*, April 12, May 8, and August 10, 1983.

7. For an important consideration of the politics of firsts in this era, see Deborah McDowell, "In the First Place: Making Frederick Douglass and the African-American Narrative Tradition," in *Critical Essays on Frederick Douglass*, ed. William Andrews (1991).

8. E. Stephens, "Mimesis, Mediation and Counterfeit," in *Mimesis in Contemporary Theory: An Interdisciplinary Approach*, ed. Mihai Spariosu (Philadelphia: John Benjamins, 1984), 246.

9. Lefevere, "On the Refraction of Texts," in *Mimesis in Contemporary Theory*, 223–24.

10. Ibid.

11. Stephens, 245.

12. Of course these are interrelated and often interdisciplinary fields. Yet because it has been marketed as a novel, *Our Nig* is rarely taught in history classrooms and is rarely addressed by scholars of African American, anti-slavery, New England, or women's antebellum history.

13. Barbara A. White, "'Our Nig' and the She-Devil: New Information about Harriet Wilson and the 'Bellmont' Family," *American Literature* 65.1 (1993): 23. White further suggests that Wilson needed to change the names of her characters, like Harriet Jacobs, out of delicacy and consideration—or in Wilson's case—fear of the people her book exposes. "*Incidents* is classified autobiography and *Our Nig* as fiction, but the only clear difference in form lies in the point of view, *Incidents* being told in the first person" and *Our Nig* mostly in the third. White, "'Our Nig' and the She-Devil," 40.

14. See Foreman and Pitts, "Introduction," xxx.

15. Foreman and Pitts, "Introduction," xxix.

16. The 1820 census shows that, in addition to Blanchard, two other free colored males lived with Blanchard. The 1830 census indicates that one black man, between

10 and 24 was housed there. Blanchard had brothers, but they were all older than he. He was 39 in 1830, the year, presumably, in which Joshua Green succumbed to consumption. "Hattie E. Wilson's" death certificate reads that she was 75 years, 3 months, 13 days on June 28th, 1900, the day of her death, and that she was born in Milford, New Hampshire, to Joshua Green. Her race is listed here as "African." See Foreman and Pitts, xi and xiv, n. 1. I quote directly from Foreman and Pitts, xxix, in this paragraph.

17. See White, "'Our Nig' and the She-Devil," 24.

18. See Foreman and Pitts, xiii and xvi, n. 25. The record of death lists Joshua Green as Wilson's father; there is no birthplace recorded. Both her husband's name and the maiden name and birthplace of mother lines are left blank. The Massachusetts records of her second marriage, September 29, 1870, say she was born in Milford, New Hampshire, the child of "Joshua and Margaret Green." *Massachusetts Marriages* 228:129.

19. *The Liberator*, January 20, 1843, 10. For the Hutchinson Family's relation to the branch of the family that abused Wilson as a servant see White, "'Our Nig' and the She-Devil."

20. See Foreman and Pitts, xxvii and xxviii.

21. See Foreman and Pitts, xxviii and xlvi, n. 14. We have not been able to locate the *Patriot* article the *Cabinet* lists as its source. The *Boston Patriot* only notes an anonymous death from intemperance and the *New Hampshire Patriot* takes no notice at all of Smith's demise.

22. Frado would have just turned five if both her death certificate and this account are correct. *Our Nig* suggests that she is abandoned when she is six. Although we know she was born on March 15 because of several notices of birthday parties she throws for herself on that date, Wilson's birth year is not exact, even taking into account the exactness of the death certificate. Census records and her own accounting, on her second marriage certificate, for example, complicate a definitive answer to that question.

23. Wilson herself is sometimes considered white in census records, for example. She is "white" in the 1870 census and her second marriage certificate. She appears in the 1880 census as white (W), which is then crossed out with "Mu" for mulatto scribbled over it. But she is the same Hattie E. Wilson, colored, who appears, with the same address, in monthly listings in the *Banner of Light*. See Foreman and Pitts, l, n. 46.

24. See Foreman and Pitts, 13 and 9. I paraphrase from *Our Nig*.

25. See P. Gabrielle Foreman, *Dark Sentiment: Reading Black Women in the Nineteenth Century*, forthcoming from University of Illinois Press, for a fuller reading of Mag's simultaneously black and white narrative straddling the first chapters of *Our Nig*.

26. See Gates, "Introduction," xiv–xvi. On Wilson's second marriage, see Foreman and Pitts, xi, xvi, n. 18, and xli. For more on her marriage, see Foreman's "Harriet Wilson's Sketches of the Life of a Free Black and Eloquent Colored Spiritualist," forthcoming.

27. See "Introduction," Foreman and Pitts, and Foreman's forthcoming "Harriet Wilson's Sketches" for more on Wilson's 33-year career as a popular New England Spiritualist.

28. See Foreman and Pitts, xxx. Wilson may have marketed products beyond the New Hampshire and Massachusetts areas she knew well. An advertisement for her bottles was published in the Annual Price Current and Illustrated Catalogue, *Drugs, Chemicals and Medicines*, Van Schaack, Stevenson and Reid Druggists, 92 Lake Street, Chicago, 1871. There is no evidence that she visits Chicago until 1873 when she is a delegate to the American Association of Spiritualists. No mention of her hair tonic business emerges in the public records that describe her work as a Spiritualist lecturer.

29. Sarah Deutsch, *Women and the City: Gender, Space and Power in Boston, 1870–1940* (New York: Oxford University Press, 2000), 273–74.

30. Born in the Louisiana Delta in 1867, Breedlove remarried and rechristened herself "Madame" C. J. Walker. After selling products door to door, she mastered manufacturing and marketing techniques that would make her a philanthropist and the first black woman millionaire. She claimed that her formula was revealed to her in a dream, which provides another interesting link to her Spiritualist forebear in the hair product business, Mrs. H. E. Wilson. See A'Lelia Bundles, *On Her Own Ground: The Life and Times of Madame C. J. Walker* (New York: Simon and Schuster, 2001).

31. See Eric Gardner, "'This Attempt of Their Sister': Harriet Wilson's *Our Nig* from Printer to Readers," *New England Quarterly* 66.2 (June 1993): 226–46, and "On Books and Bottles," in this volume.

32. The bottles were produced by Henry Wilson and Co. and Tewksbury and Wilson of Manchester. In 1856, Henry Wilson was a clerk at 22 Elm St., Manchester. The same year, Monroe G. J. Tewksbury was a physician at 37 Elm. By 1858, the two were together as Tewksbury and Wilson, Apothecaries, 45 Elm Street, and were again listed together in 1860. From 1861 on, Tewksbury continued to be listed as a physician at 233 Elm. See Donald V. Fadely, "Mrs. Wilson's Hair Preparations," in *Hair Raising Stories* (self-published), 164. Also see Manchester City Directory (Boston: Sampson and Murdock, 1871). Foreman and Pitts, xlviii, n. 23.

33. The Tewksbury and Wilson / Mrs. H. E. Wilson's Hair Regenerator / Manchester N.H. bottle stands 7¾" high with an applied square collar and is very rare. It seems clear that she sold many more of the smaller "Mrs. H. E. Wilson's / Hair Dressing / Manchester N.H." bottles which stand at 6¾", with a double-ring top. A third H. E. Wilson Regenerator bottle was also manufactured by Henry Wilson and Co. For bottle descriptions see Fadely, "Mrs. Wilson's Hair Preparations," 164. Another Tewksbury and Wilson Hair Regenerator bottle, without an open pontil mark, leads me to conclude that she continued selling hair tonic beyond the initial period mentioned in *Our Nig.*

34. Bottles with partial labels are in the author's collection. Donald Fadely, a leading expert in nineteenth-century hair bottles, says he currently knows of no other "Mrs. H. E. Wilson" labeled bottles. Information supplied by Donald Fadely to Gabrielle Foreman, November 29, 2005.

35. See Eric Gardner, "On Bottles and Books" in this volume.

36. *The Encyclopedia of African American Business History*, ed. Juliet E. K. Walker (New York: Greenwood Press, 1999), 601–602, reports that the hair tonics to stop hair loss the Remond sisters manufactured were "sold locally." The entry is not clear about whether or not the hair tonics were included in the sisters' larger manufacturing distribution. Also see Gardner's "On Bottles and Books," in this volume. He notes the Remond sisters' business and offers a less sanguine reading of Wilson's success. Also see Dorothy Sterling, ed., *We Are Your Sisters: Black Women in the Nineteenth Century* (New York: W. W. Norton, 1984), 96. Though no precise years are included in the Walker or Sterling volumes, Salem directories provide useful information. See the 1851 directory, "Salem Advertisements," 227, though there is no mention of hair tonic. Caroline Putnam is also listed as Caroline E. Putnam with her husband Joseph in Salem's 1851 City Directory. One finds her there in the 1861–1882 directories as a "hair dresser," "hair worker," or "hair work manufactorer." See the 1864 Salem Directory, 238, for the announcement of her election as vice-president of the Salem Female Anti-Slavery Society. A leading hair bottle expert has not been able to date these bottles, and indeed, has never seen one. Correspondence with Don Fadely, December 2005.

37. David Jaffee, "Peddlers of Progress and the Transformation of the Rural North, 1760–1860, *Journal of American History* 78.2 (September 1991), 513 and 516.

38. See Introduction, Foreman and Pitts, and, especially, Foreman's forthcoming "Harriet Wilson's Sketches" for an examination of the social commentary in her later speeches.

39. In a June 1867 letter Nell wrote to well-known reformer Amy Post, an ardent Spiritualist, that he had "found but little opportunity to attend the New England Convention or the Spiritualists Meetings" and "knew nothing of the Colored Medium Mrs. Wilson. It may be some one of my acquaintances." See Foreman and Pitts, xlii. Foreman and Pitts note Ames's presence and possible connection as well as that of other black barbers. The others named here are identified by Eric Gardner, "On Bottles and Books," in this volume.

40. "Learn Trades or Starve," *Frederick Douglass' Paper*, March 4, 1853. As quoted in Leslie M. Harris, *In the Shadow of Slavery: African Americans in New York City, 1626–1863* (Chicago: University of Chicago Press, 2003). Patrick Rael, *Black Identity and Black Protest in the Antebellum North* (Chapel Hill: University of North Carolina, 2002), 241.

41. Horton, *Free People of Color*, 16.

42. Harris, *In the Shadow of Slavery*, 217–18.

43. As quoted in ibid., 239.

44. Ibid., 218.

45. See Eric Gardner, "Of Books and Bottles," in this volume. My analysis here builds on and is in conversation with his work.

46. Horton, *Free People of Color*, 18.

The Disorderly Girl in Harriet E. Wilson's *Our Nig*

Lisa E. Green

IN 1983, HARRIET E. WILSON'S fictionalized autobiography *Our Nig* (1859) was rescued from oblivion and authenticated as the first novel published by an African American in the United States. Since that time, critics have remarked on the skill with which Wilson borrowed from one of the most popular fictional genres of the nineteenth century—the sentimental novel. According to Henry Louis Gates, Jr., who first rediscovered *Our Nig*, Wilson's innovative use of sentimental conventions was central to her project because it allowed her to transform the abusive members of the white family for whom she worked as an indentured servant "into objects, the stock, stereotypical objects of the sentimental novel."[1] Like many other nineteenth-century women writers, Wilson was also driven to write sentimental fiction out of financial need, calling her work an "experiment which shall aid me in maintaining myself and child without extinguishing this feeble life" (Preface). Indeed, Wilson's imperative to write a financially viable work would itself have justified her choice of the sentimental mode, whose nineteenth-century practitioners, such as Susan Warner, Maria Cummins, and Harriet Beecher Stowe, were among the nation's first best-selling authors.

Following Gates's lead, many critical studies of *Our Nig* have focused on Wilson's use of the sentimental tradition, which includes such genres as domestic fiction and the gothic novel. Many of these studies have centered on Wilson's revision of the tradition's idealistic portrayal of white motherhood and on her interrogation of its moral concern with female sexual vulnerability. Elizabeth Ammons, for example, argues that Wilson draws upon Harriet Beecher Stowe's "myth of the mother-savior" in *Uncle Tom's Cabin* only to absent this figure from her own text and thus to mock it as an impossible ideal. Similarly, Julia Stern focuses upon the ways in which Wilson appropriates Stowe's use of the gothic to represent rage and social protest, while questioning Stowe's "deification" of white motherhood as culturally redemptive. And in an essay comparing *Our Nig* and Harriet Jacobs's *Incidents in the Life of a Slave Girl* (1861), Beth Doriani Maclay argues that these black women's texts "defy the understandings of sexual morality found in white women's genres, challenging readers to think about the complexity of morality and virtue."[2]

Critical approaches such as these have provided crucial insights into Wilson's innovations as a black woman writer. Yet by emphasizing Wilson's construction of black womanhood in *Our Nig*, critics have neglected the young girl whose voice resonates throughout much of the book. While Gates writes at length of *Our Nig*'s connections to "woman's fiction," a category of nineteenth-century sentimental fiction that focuses explicitly upon girlhood development, critics have not yet explored Wilson's portrayal of female childhood. In their discussions of connections between *Our Nig* and *Uncle Tom's Cabin*, for example, neither Ammons nor Stern mentions Stowe's unruly slave girl, Topsy. Yet Topsy, an outspoken and rebellious young girl whose education transforms her into a self-reliant Christian woman, has much in common with Wilson's heroine Frado, as well as with the typical girl heroine of woman's fiction.

In this essay, I will argue that Wilson appropriates the prototypical young heroine of woman's fiction who, in nineteenth-century parlance, may be called "the disorderly girl" as a means to narrate another midnineteenth-century story, the unsanctioned story of racial abuse in the antebellum North. As Barbara A. White observes, Wilson faced a "crucial dilemma" in narrating her true story: "[H]ow to tell the truth about the racism she experienced in the North without harming the cause of slaves in the South. How could she tell the truth, even slant, about the racism and hypocrisy of abolitionists themselves?"[3] One way Wilson addresses this dilemma is through her use of the disorderly girl, a figure already known for her disruptive antics and outspoken, often angry, voice. And because novels of the day that featured the disorderly girl were bestsellers, Wilson had reason to hope that by recasting her true story of suffering and abuse into a fictionalized tale of girlhood she could also earn enough money to rescue herself and her son from destitution.

Certainly, a number of white women of the period turned to fiction writing for monetary reasons. As numerous midnineteenth-century conduct books reveal, middle- and even upper-class status provided no guarantee of financial security during this economically unstable period, and girls and young women were urged to be prepared to rely on their own resources if circumstances necessitated it. In a period when few occupations were available even to well-educated women, writing was a logical option; it not only drew upon women's literacy but proved more attractive in terms of financial reward and influence than millinery work and teaching.[4]

Harriet Wilson also turned to writing out of financial need, but her relationship to what Elizabeth Fox-Genovese calls her "probable" and "imagined" readers was more problematic than were the relationships that Warner and Cummins had with their largely white middle-class audience.[5] Despite her direct appeal to her "colored brethren" for patronage, for example, scholars such as Claudia Tate have noted that Wilson also betrays an awareness of, and need for, sympathetic white readers who "had the financial means to assist her with her project by purchasing the book.[6] As John Ernest explains, this awareness of a white audience is suggested by the novel's subtitle, which includes a phrase referring to the presence of "slavery's shadows" in the North, a fact of which black readers would not need to be reminded.[7] Wilson also faced risks in presenting her book to those one might assume would have had the most sympathy for a story of racial oppression: white abolitionists. While these prospective white readers opposed slavery in the South, they were often reluctant to admit that racism even existed in the "free" North. As Eric Gardner notes, despite their sympathy to the plight of black slaves, many white abolitionists would have been "frightened or offended" by Wilson's graphic portrayal of racism in the North.[8]

Our Nig may also have alienated the black audience that Wilson directly targeted in her preface. Though they were already painfully aware of the presence of racism in the North, black abolitionists would not have approved of Wilson's negative portrayal of a "fake" fugitive slave who lectures to "hungry abolitionists."[9] Furthermore, as Tate writes, Wilson's use of the epithet "nig" in her title might have offended black readers who, not recognizing its intended irony, might have "erroneously concluded that *Our Nig* was a masked white story about black inferiority."[10]

Finally, Wilson also faced personal risks in publishing her true story. Barbara White's research on the real-life family upon whom the fictional Bellmont family was based has shown that "Wilson had much to fear" from the surviving members of this family, who had abolitionist ties and who would have been embarrassed by her exposure of the family's ill treatment of their black servant.[11] Thus, as Gates writes: "It is clear that Wilson's anxieties about offending her Northern readers were not the idle uneasiness most authors feel about their ideal constituencies."[12] Indeed, the project of writing and publishing *Our Nig* was fraught with risks — risks that Wilson would probably not have ventured to take had it not been for the urgency of her need to support herself and her young son.

Wilson's awareness of the risks she would face in publishing *Our Nig* is revealed both in the preface and in alterations she made to the autobiography itself. For instance, Wilson begins by noting that she would not want her work to "palliate" Southern slavery "by disclosures of its appurtenances North" and that she had deliberately edited her true story for this reason (Preface). Indeed, the need to guard against public censure and personal risk was perhaps the primary reason Wilson decided to fictionalize her actual experience by changing the names of the white family members with whom she lived and by making other narrative alterations. Principal among these alterations, according to White, may have been Wilson's omission of the fact that the real-life Bellmonts were abolitionists. White notes that Wilson not only resists including this fact in her description of the Bellmonts, but also deliberately withholds her angry critique against "professed abolitionists" until the conclusion of her text, where it is safely distanced from her descriptions of her mistreatment at the hands of this family.[13] In addition, as Gates has noted, the appended authenticating letters by three of Wilson's personal friends echo the preface not only in their appeals for patronage, but also as "a polemical gesture aimed at diffusing the intensity of her critics."[14]

A close reading of Our Nig reveals that Wilson seeks both to represent and to lessen this authorial risk, which was implicit in the very nature of her project, through her characterization of her alter-ego Frado as a disorderly girl. By appropriating as her heroine this central character from woman's fiction and by inscribing her personal story of abuse into this genre's standard plot, Wilson surreptitiously reveals the truth about the racism and brutality she experienced in ways that a straightforward autobiography would not allow. While for white middle-class authors of the period the speech and antics of the disorderly girl were symptomatic of a kind of moral illness, for Wilson this outspoken girl character represented a freedom of expression that a black woman writer, especially one seeking to expose racism, could not claim for herself. In Wilson's autobiography, Frado as disorderly girl is thus a self-reflexive and, at times, subversive character: a stand-in for the author herself.

Before looking more closely at Wilson's use of the figure of the disorderly girl, it is helpful to define this figure as she appears in white women's novels of the period. According to Nina Baym, the girl featured in these novels is "not loved or valued [and] those who should love and nurture her instead exploit or neglect her."[15] While the girl heroine would thus seem to be a sympathetic figure, in fact her willfulness and uncontrolled anger are always construed as flaws that need correction, usually through an internalization of Christian values. As White writes, this "child heroine" must learn the virtues of self-control: "[I]n novel after novel young heroines must learn to conquer their pride and become humble, docile, and obedient. Any spirit or resistance against injustice is considered a 'sickness' that must be cured by strong doses of religion."[16]

The process of "curing" a young heroine of her girlhood spirit is featured in two best-selling novels from the period, Susan Warner's *The Wide, Wide World* (1850) and Maria Cummins's *The Lamplighter* (1854). In both novels, "girlhood spirit" takes the form of anger. When Ellen Montgomery, the ten-year-old heroine of *The Wide, Wide World*, learns of her father's decision to take her ailing mother away for an extended stay in Europe (where she will eventually die), the girl's response is rage "sharpened by a sense of wrong and a feeling of indignation."[17] Left under the care of her aunt Fortune, an angular spinster who rules her farming household with an iron hand, Ellen is continually roused to anger by her aunt's relentless taunting and ridicule.[18] Meanwhile, Gerty, the eight-year-old heroine of *The Lamplighter*, is filled with fury when Nan Grant, the cruel guardian who neglects and starves her, deliberately drowns her beloved kitten. Gerty responds to this act by striking Nan so hard with a stick that she draws blood.[19] Clearly in both novels the heroine's fury is justified by the mistreatment that provokes it. But for both Warner and Cummins the girl's anger, however justified, is a destructive and dangerous force that must be suppressed. Like the ubiquitous conduct manuals of the period that linked character formation to social reform, novels such as *The Wide, Wide World* and *The Lamplighter* sought to do no less than to impose a sense of order on a changing and unstable society by instilling self control and religious faith in "disorderly" young girls.[20]

Fictional portrayals of the disorderly girl are not limited to novels by women authors. Among the male authors of the period whose work features the figure of the disorderly girl, the most notable is perhaps Nathanial Hawthorne, whose romance *The Scarlet Letter* shares many of the key elements of woman's fiction. Like Gerty Flint and Ellen Montgomery, Hawthorne's Pearl, the young daughter of the adulterous lovers, Hester Prynne and Arthur Dimmesdale, is introduced as so willful a young girl that she seems demonic at times. Described as a "wild and flighty little elf," Pearl is heedless of discipline and insists on following her own impulses, which often include fits of rage during which she shrieks and throws objects at her opponents.[21] Yet in her very lack of regard for discipline and social constraints, Pearl takes on a kind of freedom that allows her to speak and act in ways that the adults in the novel cannot. Like Wilson's Frado, Pearl thus functions as a kind of truth teller. When Dimmesdale, who refuses to acknowledge publicly that Pearl is his child, takes the hands of his young daughter and her mother on the scaffold at night, Pearl demands that he do so again in the daytime so that others may see them and know the truth about their relationship. And in another scene, Pearl refuses to accept Hester's lies about the scarlet letter that Hester must wear on her breast, demanding that her mother tell her the letter's true meaning.[22]

Pearl's transformation from disorderly girl to conforming woman is allegorical rather than sentimental; her character symbolizes the transgression and later penitence of her sinning parents. But this transformation nevertheless enacts the same sort of girlhood metamorphosis dramatized by heroines such as Gerty and Ellen. As Hawthorne writes, by the novel's conclusion Pearl has been "softened and subdued" and "made capable of a woman's gentle happiness."[23] For Hawthorne the disorderly girl's transformation is a containment of female power, while for Warner and Cummins it is a necessary prescription for individual women's success in the world. But for all of these white middle-class writers, the outspoken voice and disruptive antics of the young girl must be suppressed so that, in the words of Hawthorne's narrator, she will "not forever do battle with the world, but be a woman in it."[24]

Wilson's portrait of six-year-old Frado, whose eyes convey an "exuberance of spirit almost beyond restraint" (27) is clearly meant to evoke these earlier fictionalized portrayals of the disorderly girl as literary type. Moreover, Frado shares with these other fictional girls the gumption to "do battle" with an unjust and hypocritical adult world. But while Ellen and Gerty are portrayed as angry victims and Pearl as a demonic wild child, Wilson sees a playful quality in her disorderly girl, using words like "roguish" and "frolicky" to describe her appearance and personality (17–18). Indeed, Frado's antics are often deemed so entertaining that other characters in the novel "shield and countenance" her as she ventures "far beyond propriety" (38).

Frado's story begins similarly to that of these other fictional girls; she too is rejected by her family. But Frado's response to this rejection indicates a resourceful and fearless nature, rather than one that is irate or manipulative. After her black father dies of consumption, Frado's white mother, a pariah in white society because of her interracial marriage, becomes involved with another black man named Seth Shipley. Unlike Frado's kind-hearted father, Seth takes little interest in Frado and her sibling and insists that Frado be given away to Mrs. Bellmont, a white woman known as a "she-devil" (17). After screaming "No!" when Seth informs her that she is to be given away, Frado and her best friend run away, getting lost amid the thickets and marshes at night. When the two girls are later discovered several miles from home, the self-possessed Frado remains calm as she "chats" of her "prospects," while her friend exhibits "childish fears" that Frado attempts to "banish." After the incident Frado's mother is "inclined to think severe restraint would be healthful" and follows through with her plan to send Frado to work for the cruel Mrs. Bellmont as an indentured servant (19–20).

Enraged by Frado's willfulness and free expression, Mrs. Bellmont continually attempts to thwart her servant's attempts to speak out, especially when this speech threatens to expose Mrs. Bellmont's misdeeds. In the series of episodes that take place in the Bellmont household, Wilson presents an allegory of the dangers implicit in her own endeavor at truth telling. This allegory is evident in Frado's attempts to oppose Mrs. Bellmont and her other oppressors and tell the truth about her mistreatment. Despite her risk-taking antics, this brazen young girl is always supported by an audience of sympathetic listeners and watchers who are able to bear witness to her suffering and who help to validate her voice. Wilson clearly hoped that she would have a similarly sympathetic readership for her potentially controversial book.

The episode that initiates the theme of truth telling in *Our Nig* begins in the classroom. On her first day of school, Frado incurs the wrath of Mrs. Bellmont's adolescent daughter Mary, who shares her mother's cruel disposition and who is angered by the fact that she must attend school with the black servant whom her family refers to as "Nig." When Mary is made jealous by Frado's growing popularity with the other school children, her anger escalates to the point that she wishes "to use physical force 'to subdue her,' to 'keep her down'" (33). On their way home from school one day, Mary acts on these angry impulses by attempting to force Frado across a dangerously narrow plank, a plan that results in Mary's own fall into the stream. It is only because of the intervention of "some of the larger scholars" that Mary is saved from drowning and that Frado, who had "hesitated, resisted" Mary's command to cross, is prevented from falling (33).

When the two girls return home, they tell different stories of the incident. While a tearful Mary exclaims that "Nig pushed me into the stream," Frado proclaims her innocence and "relat[es] the occurrence truthfully." Mr. Bellmont is inclined to give Frado the benefit of the doubt, but he refuses to get involved and leaves the house "as he usually did when a tempest was threatening to envelop him" (34). The withdrawal of Mr. Bellmont leaves Frado without protection from Mary and Mrs. Bellmont, who punish their black servant because she "came home with a lie; it made Mary's story false" (35).

Possessing the power to undermine the authority of Mary and Mrs. Bellmont through words, Frado is, throughout the novel, reprimanded by methods of punishment that serve literally to block her ability to speak. In this episode, Mrs. Bellmont punishes Frado for "lying" by propping her mouth open with a piece of wood so that Frado cannot talk. Wilson underscores her point that Mrs. Bellmont's object is to silence Frado by repeating the phrase "shut up" until its first meaning—"to confine"—is overshadowed by its second—"to compel silence."[25] Thus when Mrs. Bellmont's son Jack searches for

Frado, who, the narrator explains, has been "shut up in a dark room, without any supper," Mary tells him that "Mother gave her a good whipping and shut her up." And when Mr. Bellmont enters, he asks if "Frado was shut up yet" (35–36).

Frado is indeed silenced, but her story is finally heard. Jack comes to Frado's aid not only by removing the wood from her mouth and comforting her until she falls asleep, but also by proving the veracity of her story. Countering Mrs. Bellmont's accusation that Frado is a liar, Jack presents an audience of supporters to validate her honesty, telling his mother that "the school-children happened to see it all, and they tell the same story Nig does. Which is most likely to be true, what a dozen agree they saw, or the contrary?" (35). When Jack imparts this tale of unjust suffering to his father, who had been previously indifferent to Frado's plight, Mr. Bellmont is moved to tears. As Wilson writes, Mr. Bellmont "seemed untouched, till a glance at Jack exposed a tearful eye" (36). If this response strikes us as out of proportion to the incident, it becomes appropriate when read allegorically. Like Frado's true version of the stream incident, Wilson suggests, the larger "true story" that contains it — the novel *Our Nig* itself — possesses as much power as the sentimental fiction that was prompting the tears of droves of nineteenth-century readers. But Wilson further suggests that her story would demand more of its audience than sentimental tears; it would require readers, such as Jack and the school children, who were attentive and interested enough to attest to the story's integrity in the face of those who might be inclined toward indifference, skepticism, or even a willful desire to suppress it.

Wilson further explores her concern with audience responses to her literary "performance" through Frado's playful performance on the roof of a barn. In this episode, Frado decides to climb to the top of the Bellmont barn, where the remnants of some recent repair work have provided "a staging." Mounting the roof in "high glee," Frado receives different reactions from the members of the diverse audience watching her. While Mary and Mrs. Bellmont proclaim that they do not care if she breaks her neck, Mr. Bellmont calls "sternly for her to come down," and his invalid daughter Jane "nearly faint[s] from fear." Jack and the hired men who work on the farm appreciate Frado's antics and laugh "at her fearlessness" (53). While the other audience members seem to recoil from these antics out of disdain or worry, the hired men find Frado's performance entertaining and applaud the girl's risk taking. This last response, which nurtures Frado's "mirthful inclination" (53), is clearly the kind of engaged reception Wilson hoped she would have for her novel, a similarly performative endeavor that involved risk taking of a different sort.

The positive response of Jack and the hired men also encourages Frado to attempt even bolder pranks, such as one she performs on a "willful" sheep. As Wilson explains: "Among the sheep was a willful leader, who always persisted in being first served, and many times in his fury had thrown down Nig, till, provoked, she resolved to punish him." Echoing the earlier incident with Mary on the plank, Frado's prank involves standing on "the highest point of land nearest the stream" and tricking the sheep away from his pasture and into the water. Although Frado does not realize it, Mr. Bellmont and the hired men are watching her performance with much anxiety: "Should she by any mishap lose her footing, she must roll into the stream, and without aid, must drown. . . . They watched in breathless silence." Yet when the sheep leaps towards the "mock repast" that Frado holds out and ends up rolling into the water, only the hired men understand the "object" of her trick (54). While Mr. Bellmont "talked seriously to the child for exposing herself to such danger," the men lay "convulsed with laughter" (55) as they applauded Frado's successful act of revenge against the sheep that had tormented her. Again, the hired men are portrayed as Wilson's ideal audience because they are able to understand the "object" of the entertainment.

What the reader further understands in this episode is the implicit connection between this tormenting sheep and Frado's human tormenter Mary. Indeed, Mary's own act of "fury" had earlier resulted in Frado being "thrown down." As Frado later tells Aunt Abby, Mary "is our cross sheep just as much, that I ducked in the river; I'd like to try my hand at curing *her* too" (80). While Aunt Abby reproves Frado for these words, and for celebrating Mary's imminent plans to leave home, Frado's "clear voice" sings joyously of "the relief she felt at the removal of one of her tormentors" (81). Clearly, Frado's prank against the willful sheep is meant to suggest her wish for revenge against her abusive white sister, Mary — her wish to "cure" Mary by exposing her persistence "in being first served" (54). Yet vindication of this sort requires the presence of someone to act as witness, someone to expose one's tormentor to. In the sheep episode, Frado's sense of revenge is contingent upon the approving audience of hired men who watch her perform. Unlike Mr. Bellmont and Jane, these observers are entertained by Frado's performance because they are able to see what lies behind it — the exposure and punishment of one who had "thrown her down."

Frado similarly "exposes" her other tormentor, her mistress Mrs. Bellmont, in a later episode, which takes place at the family dinner table. Mrs. Bellmont allows Frado to sit at the table for the first time when her visiting son James insists that "while I stay, she is going to sit down *here*, and eat such food as we eat" (68). While Mrs. Bellmont is not pleased by James's "innovations of table discipline" (70–71), she is powerless to oppose her son and a "few sparks from

[her] black eyes" are her "only reply" to his request (68). But Mrs. Bellmont's rage is ignited when she enters the dining room one day to find Frado reaching for a dessert plate while seated in "her mistress's chair" (71). When Mrs. Bellmont commands Frado to eat from her mistress's dirty plate rather than take a new one, Frado deliberately insults her by calling her dog Fido to lick the plate clean. After hearing "the kitchen version" of this story from his brother Jack, James chastises his mother for provoking Frado's "impudent" actions: "You have not treated her, mother, so as to gain her love; she is only exhibiting your remissness in this matter" (71–72).

Unmoved by James's speech, Mrs. Bellmont waits until she is alone with Frado and threatens that if she ever again "exposed her to James" she would "cut her tongue out" (72). Again Frado's "tongue," a metonym for the girl's outspokenness and by extension for the outspokenness of Wilson herself, is the focus of Mrs. Bellmont's wrath. Moreover, Mrs. Bellmont makes it clear that she does not want her servant (and, we might assume, the autobiographer Wilson) to profit from the incident when she explains that the beating is a way "to bring up arrearages" (72). Yet this is just what Frado manages to accomplish. Despite her mistress's threat and beating, Frado not only succeeds in "exhibiting her remissness," but she does so in such an entertaining manner that Jack offers to pay Frado for her prank. After Jack tells James the plate-licking story, he throws a silver dollar to Frado and says, "There, take that; 't was worth paying for" (72). Wilson hoped that her prospective readers would deem her own story, which also sought to expose "remissness," not only morally instructive, but also entertaining enough to be considered worth paying for.

Frado's victory over Mrs. Bellmont in this scene is short-lived, for it costs her her voice. When James finds her alone and sobbing after her beating, "she dared not answer his queries" (72) for fear that Mrs. Bellmont would act upon her earlier threat. While James is able to guess the reason for Frado's crying, the risk of inciting Mrs. Bellmont's revenge prevents her from speaking out. And Frado's loss of voice is enduring. When James becomes seriously ill in a later episode Frado breaks this silence, but only briefly. While others in the family know that a jealous Mrs. Bellmont is behind Aunt Abby's absence at James's bedside, only Frado is brave enough to tell James the truth and risk Mrs. Bellmont's wrath. But while Frado's truth telling results in Abby's return to James's sick room, Frado is soon "seized" by Mrs. Bellmont who places the wedge of wood between her teeth and threatens to "cure her of tale-bearing" (93). Frado remains in this position until Mr. Bellmont enters and begins to ask her questions that, because her mouth is gagged, "she did not, because she could not, answer" (94).

While her heroine is thus again physically prevented from speaking,

Wilson deliberately chooses not to speak. Refusing to narrate the ensuing exchange between Mr. Bellmont and his wife, Wilson explains: "Their conversation we will omit; suffice it to say, a storm raged which required many days to exhaust its strength" (94). Wilson's reasons for remaining silent in this passage are unclear. Did she deem the substance of this conversation irrelevant to the narrative as a whole? Did she feel that revealing this conversation would have posed some unnecessary risk? Whatever her motive, Wilson's silences in this episode — both enforced and deliberate — underscore not only the dangers of "tale-bearing," but also her own need to balance self-expression with self-protection in the text as a whole.

As the episode with James shows, Frado is willing to break her silence to defend the interests of others who need her help. This is evident in another episode when Frado again risks Mrs. Bellmont's censure and abuse to help Jack's new wife, a kind-hearted orphan named Jenny. Disapproving of her new daughter-in-law's lack of money and property, Mrs. Bellmont attempts to drive Jenny away by spreading a rumor that Jenny "had formed an illegal intimacy with [Jack's] cousin," while falsely telling Jenny that Jack is in love with another woman (113). When Mrs. Bellmont then prevents Jenny from traveling to see Jack in Baltimore, where he has a job, Jenny writes a desperate letter to Jack to come and rescue her. Jack fails to reply, but one "watchful and friendly" neighbor understands that Mrs. Bellmont has intercepted Jenny's letter (115). Devising a plan to elude Mrs. Bellmont, this neighbor calls upon Frado to mail the letter from outside the Bellmont home. Frado not only succeeds in reconciling Jenny and Jack, who comes home "angry, wounded, and forever after alienated from his early home and his mother" (115), but she also manages to comfort the distraught and victimized Jenny by sharing her own story of abuse: "Many times would Frado steal up into Jenny's room, when she knew she was tortured by her mistress' malignity, and tell some of her own encounters with her, and tell her she might 'be sure it wouldn't kill her, for she should have died long before at the same treatment'" (115).

The risks Frado takes by mailing Jenny's letter in this episode are suggestive of Wilson's larger project. Like the letter, Wilson's narrative is a written document that she deployed as a call for help, a cry for rescue. And like Frado and Jenny, Wilson had good reason to fear that her own "letter" to the world would fall into the hands of ill-meaning persons such as Mrs. Bellmont, whose own interests could prevent her narrative from being circulated and read by those more sympathetic to her plight. When Frado reaches out to comfort Jenny, Wilson further suggests that the content of such a "letter" — the story of abuse and survival that her narrative tells — has value beyond just rescuing its author. Telling this story entailed risk, but it was a worthwhile endeavor because it could serve to comfort and inspire others who had suffered similar abuse. While Jenny shares Frado's status as a poor orphan, the fact that she is white reinforces Wilson's claim for her story's universality. As a tale of abuse that transcends racial lines, Wilson's narrative implicitly calls for a diverse audience to purchase and read the book. Wilson may have hoped that these readers would do so not only out of charity, but because they could relate aspects of her story to their own lives and thus profit from its message.

The boldness Frado exhibits in the episode with Jenny marks the last moment of girlhood risk taking in the novel. As Wilson notes, "Frado had merged into womanhood" (115), and while she continues to struggle to achieve self-reliance through education, religious faith, and work, her chronic illness is suggestive of the larger burden this burgeoning womanhood has begun to inflict upon her. As a girl, Frado's emerging sexuality is perceived as a threat by Mrs. Bellmont, who cuts off her servant's long curls because she is "getting handsome" (70). By the end of the novel, as these "shining curls" are "toyed" with by the prospective husband who is destined to leave her (126), Frado's sexuality suggests not power but vulnerability. Transformed from the outspoken and fearless girl of the earlier chapters into an abandoned wife, Frado now bears the burden not only of race but of motherhood.

In this light, Frado's earlier relationship with Jenny becomes significant not only because of their similar background as orphans and shared abuse at the hands of Mrs. Bellmont, but because of the difference in their ages. As a girl, Frado is free to speak out and take risks in a way that the woman Jenny is not. Gentle and weak, Jenny conforms to the midnineteenth-century feminine ideal that Barbara Welter defined in terms of such "cardinal virtues" as purity and submissiveness.[26] While this ideal insisted upon a view of womanhood that valued passivity, silence, and docility, very young girls of the period were remarkably free from its influence. As an African American girl, Frado would have been even less restricted by this middle-class ideal than would a white girl of her same age. Thus while Jenny is powerless to speak in her own defense, Frado boldly takes action against the manipulations of Mrs. Bellmont and speaks openly about her own suffering.

A similar juxtaposition between girlhood and womanhood is revealed in the chapter that begins with Frado's antics on the roof of the barn and with the willful sheep. After Frado boasts that she was "quick enough to 'give [the sheep] a slide'" (55), the focus of the chapter abruptly shifts to Mrs. Bellmont's invalid daughter Jane and the two suitors who are vying for her hand. Unlike the fearless Frado, Jane is a woman who lacks "the strength to brave the iron will of her mother" (37), who wishes Jane to marry the wealthy suitor with "sinister eyes" (55) instead of the kind-hearted and well-mannered man Jane herself prefers. While Jane "knew that her husband should be the man of her own selecting," she is too weak to fight for what she wants: "She engaged herself, yielding to her mother's wishes, because she had not strength to oppose them; and sometimes, when witness of her mother's and Mary's tyranny, she felt any change would be preferable, even such a one as this" (56). Although Jane finally prevails and (with the help of Aunt Abby and Mr. Bellmont) marries the man she loves, Wilson writes that "[t]o brave her mother's fury, nearly overcame her" (60–61). The stories of Jenny and Jane foreshadow Frado's own emerging womanhood, which is similarly marked by invalidism and weakness. Indeed, after Frado "merges into womanhood" in the novel's last full chapter, her physical collapse is paralleled by the collapse of the narrative itself into a brief two-page description of her marriage and subsequent abandonment.

That the bulk of the narrative focuses on a young Frado, however, attests to the literary possibilities Wilson saw in the figure of the disorderly young girl, a figure who is able to act and speak in a manner in which women such as Jenny, Jane, and even Wilson herself cannot. Although she borrows from a genre whose plot structure insists upon the girl's development into a conforming woman, this fictional genre nevertheless allows Wilson to express, surreptitiously, her own true story through the girl's trangressive antics and disruptive speech. Indeed, despite Wilson's use of the first-person in the early chapter titles, the characterization and events in these early chapters are precisely those most likely borrowed from fiction. As Gates explains, "Since these early chapters describe events far removed from the author's experiences closest in time to the period of writing, the first-person presences perhaps reveal the author's anxieties about identifying with events in the text that she cannot recollect at all."[27] Gates' speculation that Wilson "fictionalized" her autobiography in these early chapters, chapters in which Frado is still a young girl, supports my point that Wilson was borrowing from an established literary construction—that of the figure of the disorderly girl—in her characterization of her alter-ego Frado.

Eric Gardner's research on the reception and readership of the first edition of *Our Nig* further supports a reading of the novel that emphasizes the theme of girlhood. Gardner not only discovered that many of the original owners of *Our Nig* were middle-class whites but that a number of these owners were under the age of twenty when the novel was first published in 1859. The fact that many of these extant first edition copies belonged to young people leads Gardner to speculate that "the book's purchasers either interpreted or deployed *Our Nig* as a book geared toward the moral improvement of young readers."[28] Indeed, while Gardner calls the novel "a young black woman's bildungsroman," he notes that these first readers may have been less interested in *Our Nig*'s representation of race than in its theme of "a child's search for a self and a God."[29]

That *Our Nig* may have attracted the same white, middle-class readership as did Warner's *The Wide, Wide World* and Cummins's *The Lamplighter* attests to Wilson's success at appropriating the standard characterization and plot of these best-selling novels. And while Gardner notes that *Our Nig* "was not designed to become a best-seller," Wilson was clearly concerned with attracting as large and diverse an audience as possible.[30] By reworking her brutal true experience as an indentured black servant in antebellum New Hampshire into a popular tale of girlhood development, Wilson hoped she could earn enough money to extricate herself from the legacy of her servitude and make a better life for her young son.

But while Wilson was able to "fit" her girlhood persona into this standard plot, she could not appropriate its requisite happy ending. Indeed, Frado's status at the end of *Our Nig* as a poor single mother, abandoned by her black abolitionist husband, undercuts not only the happy ending of the typical sentimental novel, but any conclusion at all. As Gates writes, "The desertion of [Frado's] husband opens, rather than ends, the text, preventing the sort of closure we expect in this genre of the sentimental novel" (xlviii). And while the story of the novel ends ambiguously, the real-life story that prompted the writing of the book ended with tragedy: *Our Nig* was a failure in that it did not provide Wilson with the financial resources she needed to save her son, who died of fever in the County House for the poor in 1860, "only six months after the publication of the book intended to raise money for his support."[31]

But if Wilson's book failed as a financial enterprise, it succeeds as a work of literature. Among the many qualities that contribute to the book's literary richness is Wilson's adept borrowing from established generic traditions. Through her use of one of these traditions — the conventional midnineteenth-century sentimental novel of girlhood development — Wilson legitimized and made palatable a story that few readers of her day wanted to hear. And by appropriating from this popular genre the figure of the disorderly girl, Wilson has constructed a nonthreatening, because fictive, alter-ego through which she not only represents her mistreatment but directs her prospective readers' responses and dramatizes the very risks she faced in telling her story.

NOTES

1. Henry Louis Gates, Jr., "Introduction," in Harriet Wilson, *Our Nig; or, Sketches from the Life of a Free Black* (New York: Vintage Books, 2002), li. Further

references to *Our Nig* are from this edition and will be noted in parentheses within the text.

2. Beth Doriani Maclay, "Black Womanhood in Nineteenth-Century America: Subversion and Self-Construction in Two Women's Autobiographies," *American Quarterly* 43 (1991): 207. Other essays that explore these issues include: P. G. Foreman, "The Spoken and the Silenced in *Incidents in the Life of a Slave Girl* and *Our Nig*," and Claudia Tate, "Allegories of Black Desire: Or, Rereading Nineteenth-Century Sentimental Narratives of Black Female Authority," in *Changing Our Own Words: Essays on Criticism, Theory, and Writing by Black Women*, ed. Cheryl A. Wall (New Brunswick: Rutgers University Press 1989).

3. Barbara A. White, "'Our Nig' and the She-Devil: New Information about Harriet Wilson and the 'Bellmont' Family," *American Literature* 65 (1993): 38.

4. See Nina Baym, *Woman's Fiction: A Guide to Novels by and about Women in America, 1820–70*, 2nd ed. (Urbana: University of Illinois Press, 1993), 30–31.

5. Elizabeth Fox-Genovese, "'To Weave It into the Literature of the Country': Epic and the Fictions of African American Women," in *Poetics of the Americas: Race, Founding, Textuality*, ed. Bainard Cowan and Jefferson Humphries (Baton Rouge, LA: Louisiana State UP, 1997), 189.

6. Wall, *Changing Our Own Words*, 113.

7. John Ernest, "Economies of Identity: Harriet E. Wilson's *Our Nig*," *PMLA* 109 (1994): 426.

8. Eric Gardner, "'This Attempt of Their Sister': Harriet Wilson's *Our Nig* from Printer to Readers," *New England Quarterly* 66:2 (1993): 243.

9. Henry Louis Gates, Jr., *Figures in Black: Words, Signs, and the "Racial" Self* (New York: Oxford UP, 1987), 137.

10. Wall, *Changing Our Own Words*, 114.

11. White, "'Our Nig' and the She-Devil," 40.

12. Gates, *Figures in Black*, 148.

13. White, "'Our Nig' and the She-Devil," 38.

14. Gates, *Figures in Black*, 149.

15. Baym, *Woman's Fiction*, 37.

16. Barbara A. White, *Growing Up Female: Adolescent Girlhood in American Fiction* (Westport, CT: Greenwood Press, 1985), 26.

17. Susan Warner, *The Wide, Wide World*, 1850 (New York: Feminist Press, 1987), 63.

18. Warner, *Wide, Wide World*, 145.

19. Maria Susanna Cummins, *The Lamplighter*, 1854 (New Brunswick: Rutgers University Press, 1995), 11.

20. With its focus upon the girl's transformation from wild child to virtuous woman, the plot of woman's fiction spoke to the larger concerns of middle-class American society during the period. While the advent of industrialism required boys to internalize qualities such as ambition and competitiveness, which were considered essential for success in the "public sphere," it was believed that girls had to

inculcate the traits needed to preside over the domestic realm of home and family, which, in the words of the historian Carl Degler, was "but the state writ small." *At Odds: Women and the Family in America from the Revolution to the Present* (New York: Oxford UP, 1980), 97. Since, by the beginning of the nineteenth century, the mother was at the head of this microcosm of the state, the proper rearing of girls, who would eventually become mothers themselves, became the focus of increasing attention and anxiety.

21. Nathaniel Hawthorne, *The Scarlet Letter* (Boston: Ticknor, Reed, and Fields, 1850), 137.

22. Ibid., 217.

23. Ibid., 319.

24. Ibid., 312.

25. The use of the phrase "shut up" to signify "hold one's tongue" or "compel silence" dates from the sixteenth century. Among the texts that include examples of the phrase "shut up" in this context are Shakespeare's *King Lear*, Dickens's *Little Dorrit*, and Kipling's *Barrack Room Ballads*. See John S. Farmer and W. E. Henley, eds. *Slang and Its Analogues Past and Present* (New York: Routledge and Kegan, 1965).

26. Barbara Welter, *Dimity Convictions: The American Woman in the Nineteenth Century* (Athens: Ohio UP, 1976), 21–31.

27. Gates, *Figures in Black*, 147.

28. Gardner, "'This Attempt . . . ,'" 228.

29. Gardner, "'This Attempt . . . ,'" 242, 238.

30. Gardner, "'This Attempt . . . ,'" 232.

31. White, "'Our Nig' and the She-Devil," 21.

Beyond the Page

Rape and the Failure of Genre

Cassandra Jackson

SINCE THE REDISCOVERY of *Our Nig*, critics have attempted to classify
Harriet Wilson's novel, tracing its generic contours and naming the literary
traditions that inform it. This approach has advanced the critical interpretation of the novel, illuminating its complex artistic and political maneuvers by
placing it among its literary relations. But while *Our Nig* often evokes familiar
traditions, naming its own extended literary family, it just as often denies its
own kith and kin, carefully dodging any attempt to neatly place it within any
single tradition. Indeed, the cacophony of interpretations of genre suggests
that this novel confirms what such critics as Gabrielle Foreman have argued,
namely that *Our Nig* often stretches the boundaries between genres.[1] To some,
the work is a slave narrative without the slaves.[2] To others, it is a conversion
narrative that fails to convert.[3] It is a domestic novel[4] whose domestic spaces
are not cozy kitchens, but rather hellish sites of torture.[5] It is a love story in
which love is rarely mutual, sometimes contractual, and frequently ends in
abandonment. All of these generic possibilities and more emerge within Wilson's text, and like the seduction story that initiates the novel, it also seduces
its reader, only to refuse the satisfaction of generic formulae. Indeed, this generic slipperiness is what compels the critic to chase one or many of these
strands that link the book to particular literary traditions.

In this essay, I explore the relationship between genre and silence to suggest that this collision of generic practices is indicative of an unutterable
narrative that these conventional formulae fail to contain. Indeed, this ever-
present silence in *Our Nig* emerges as the single interpretation upon which
critics of the novel agree. R. J. Ellis argues that the text "acquires its greatest weight through . . . meaningful moments of half-stated or unstated com-
munication."[6] Foreman suggests that we might think about these moments
of muteness as part of Wilson's manipulation of genre, arguing that, though

Wilson evokes the sentimental, her mute male characters are part of a gender inversion that is not in keeping with that tradition.[7] Foreman's reading illuminates the peculiar antagonism between the novel's silences and the generic formulae that narrate — and at times fail to narrate — Frado's story. One might think of the novel's use of generic formulae as overlapping circles, never entirely complete, because none of them can express the particular narrative of abuse that lies buried in the novel's undertext. Each of the genres evoked imposes a certain silence that its own generic conventions require and thus each remains incomplete.

I theorize these peculiar generic fractures as signs of same-sex sexual abuse that can never be candidly related in the novel. Thus, I seek ways of entering Our Nig's many silences, chasing the shadows behind the veil that Wilson draws. My intention here is not to claim that something is there because it does not appear to be there, but rather to carefully explore the contours of that silence, its causes, and its forms of expression. If this approach seems counterintuitive, perhaps this is because I am seeking to examine what might be best described in novelist John Irving's language as "a sound like someone trying not to make a sound."[8] Ultimately, silence has sources, forms of expression, and ways of meaning in the novel. Here, I argue that silence is shaped by generic failures to express same-sex child rape.

Wilson traces the novel's silences in her preface, in which she pointedly directs the reader to the novel's omissions: "I have purposely omitted things that would most provoke shame to those good anti-slavery friends at home" (3). Circling the unspeakable, Wilson begins the novel by calling our attention to the problems of telling, the distance that lies between language and experience, voice and phenomena, literature and being. She compels the reader to consider the novel that Our Nig is not, another text that hovers silently between the pages of this one. Thus, Wilson performs a peculiar disappearing act by investing the reader with the power not only to search for the signs of that other novel, but to create that other novel through some combination of interpretation and speculation. In this essay, I am admittedly attempting to interpret beyond the margins of the novel, to accept what I see as Wilson's invitation to consider the limitations of the novel and its conventions.

In some ways, Wilson's exploration of the coming of age of a brutally abused child might be said to inscribe the text with the mark of the unspeakable from the outset. Indeed, to represent the bodily experience of such a child poses its own risks. As Diane Price Herndl points out, Wilson had to negotiate her novel within the larger context of conflicting pro-slavery arguments: A black heroine represented as ill or as an invalid might be interpreted as evidence of unfitness for freedom, while a resilient black heroine might foster interpretations of blacks as fit for slavery's abuses. Indeed, to represent black women's physicality at all, according to Herndl, was to risk supporting ideological projections of black women as "only physical."[9] Wilson's stated reluctance to reveal the intimate details of the abuses she suffered suggests her awareness of these ideological pitfalls and the ways in which the representation of Frado's contested body might participate in these debates.

At the same time, Wilson does not fail to expose Frados's brutalized body. Indeed, the author provides us with agonizing descriptions of the dreadful thrashings the child receives. She places Frado's physicality on display, thoroughly demonstrating the vulnerability of her body. The novel's silence, then, does not emanate from the problem of exposing Frado's body; neither does it seem to be connected to the inability to express bodily pain. As Cynthia Davis notes, though critics often point to the antithesis between pain and language, in *Our Nig*, language "serves to make pain and even 'our nig' [Frado] herself intelligible."[10] It is through speaking the pain, Davis argues, that Frado makes the transition from object to speaking subject.[11] By prefacing her novel with a description of the bodily feebleness brought about by abuse and asking her reader to participate in the alleviation of that condition by purchasing the book, Wilson uses the intersections between the autobiographical and the fictional to invite the reader to consider the painful consequences of the bodily violence she endures. In this way, Wilson not only expresses her pain, but makes it present for the reader. Moreover, she invests the reader with the responsibility to palliate that pain.

While Wilson and Frado give voice to bodily pain, the recurring image of Frado gagged suggests that there is still more to be told. Indeed, the practical reasons why Mrs. Bellmont repeatedly silences Frado are never entirely clear. Their purpose cannot be to hide her beatings, since everyone in the household is already aware of them. Even family members who no longer live in the household know about the violence; Jack writes letters about them to his brother James. Both the reader and the Bellmont family are aware of Frado's most private suffering; Jack overhears her expressing her desperation and her attendant inclination toward suicide. Given everyone's knowledge of the abuse, the question arises as to what, in effect, must be silenced.

My approach to this question is twofold, both psychoanalytical and historical. I am interested in the modes of desire that inform what I read as the need to name sexual abuse. I am equally interested in the social formations articulated through the representation of such abuse. I would argue that these categories are inseparable to the degree that human desire is inextricable from the power of social formations. In *Psychoanalysis and Black Novels*, Claudia Tate offers a framework that facilitates an examination of this silence in Wilson's novel. Examining how black texts encounter the "tension between the public, collective protocols of race and private, individual desire," Tate outlines three modes of discourse in the novel: conscious, preconscious, and unconscious. While "conscious discourses" are informed by the explicit social content of the novel, "preconscious discourses" include stylistic modes (such as figurative language) that communicate implicit meaning. Finally, "unconscious discourses" are "those longings that are inscribed in the novel's most deeply encoded rhetorical elements." According to Tate, "unconscious discourses" might be interpreted like dreams, "deciphered within the dynamics of its representational design."[12]

My reading of *Our Nig* is primarily concerned with the first two forms of discourse. I read the generic frameworks in the novel as part of the conscious discourse, and as evidence of the social formations that Wilson sought to confront in the novel by disrupting the neat social worlds that emerge in these literary traditions. In keeping with Sabine Sielke's theory that "narratives of sexual violence ponder . . . the power dynamics of a particular culture" (3), I read Wilson's evocation of rape as an attempt to narrativize historically specific social formations and ideologies that informed the lives of free blacks in the antebellum North. If, as Sielke argues, rape has its "history, its ideology and its dominant narratives that . . . are nationally specific," then certainly the suggestion of rape in *Our Nig* engages this discourse as well.[13] More specifically, rape narrativizes the racially informed power dynamics of the national culture, expressing the racial hierarchies that determine power and facilitate the exploitation of black bodies and black labor. As Hazel Carby points out, the novel's title, *Our Nig; or Sketches from the Life a Free Black, In a Two-Story White House, North. Showing that Slavery's Shadows Fall Even There by "Our Nig,"* demonstrates its concern with the nation's social and political landscape.[14] Thus, I read the individual experience of rape in the novel not only as an exploration of these national power dynamics, but as inseparable from them. The "preconscious elements" correspond, then, to the symbolic gaggings and penetrations of Frado's body that allude to the thing that cannot be told here. Finally, the driving desire to name same-sex sexual abuse in the novel might be read as both "preconscious" and "unconscious" desire, shifting between mindful design and more mysterious and subterranean patterns of representation.

Still, since *Our Nig* never names rape specifically, how do we read it? I submit that if we read Wilson's scenes of torture in relationship to more common representations of rape in the nineteenth century, the implications of sexual violence come into focus. Indeed, it is important to consider that the representation of rape—or even consensual sex—in the nineteenth century was subject to powerful social constraints that required rhetorically coded language. Torture was commonly used as a sign of rape in antebellum literature. Certainly, in the slave narrative, such brutal beatings as the torture of Aunt Hester in Frederick Douglass's narrative, functioned as the sign of rape. The ritualized torture that Frado suffers, followed by the repeated penetration of the child with wood, borrows from the tradition both of the slave narrative and of the anti-slavery novel by metaphorizing sexual violence.

Frado's subsequent alienation from her body in the form of her question, "Oh why am I black?" also implies that sexual violation has taken place. This question not only suggests alienation from her body, but locates the social context that informs her vulnerability. We know that, whatever took place between Mrs. Bellmont and the many girls she had hired prior to Frado's indenture, all of them quit. We also know from the family's discussion of whether Frado's blackness was too offensive for her to become a household servant that none of the past servants were black. Trapped by a web of cross-fertilizing factors, including childhood, blackness, and indentured servitude, Frado has no means to leave, and indeed has nowhere to go. Left without a protector, Frado is exposed to the brutal designs of Mrs. Bellmont, whose expression of racial hatred is targeted squarely at Frado. I submit that Wilson codes the scenes of torture to indicate rape as the expression of Mrs. Bellmont's antipathy. The gaggings — usually with a piece of wood — that follow the torture, are also symbolic of rape, as well as the silencing that such an abusive encounter would necessitate.

Mieke Bal argues that "rape is the body speech act par excellence" and that the act — in both its heterosexual and homosexual manifestations — is motivated by hatred of the object rather than lust.[15] Thus, in Wilson's novel, rape is socially motivated, made possible through racialized social structures, and caused by racial hatred implanted by those social configurations that deem black bodies unworthy of dignity or integrity. Like the sun in which Frado is forced to work without a bonnet, rape blackens Frado, marking her, naming her condition as the victim of a crime that because of factors related to race and gender does not exist — and therefore cannot be named — even if social codes permitted. More specifically, such a violation committed by a woman against a girl is culturally and legally invisible in the period. As John D'Emilio and Estelle Freedman point out, until the 1880s even romantic same-sex relationships were assumed to be devoid of sexual content, and early laws against same-sex sexual contact largely applied to men.[16]

The nonexistence of this crime socially, legally, and rhetorically is central to the novel's silences and generic fractures. Thus, the limitations of genre for Wilson are larger than available conventional modes, but instead indicate the broader limitations of expression that shape genre. More specifically, there is no discursive space, linguistic unit, or legal idiom with which to name the sexual violation of a child by a woman. Therefore, the signs of this violation seem to lie deep in the subterranean layers of the novel. When Frado considers departing from the Bellmont household, for example, the narrator remarks that Mrs. Bellmont "felt that she could not well spare one who could so well adapt herself to all departments — man, boy, housekeeper, domestic etc." (116). By depicting Frado as one who fulfills the services of a man, Wilson relies on heterosexual norms and gender expectations to represent the sexual implications of Mrs. Bellmont's misuse of Frado's body.

Interestingly, numerous critical treatments of *Our Nig* note that it is quite deliberately a non-sexual narrative. According to Elizabeth Breau, *Our Nig* is unusual because its mixed-race heroine is not sexually victimized by white men, thus forcing readers to focus on social problems exposed in the novel, rather than indulging in sexual prurience.[17] Davis adds that, in light of the prevailing preoccupation with black sexuality, "Harriet Wilson's *Our Nig* becomes all the more conspicuous in that while its protagonist, Frado, is largely defined by and through her body, it is explicitly pain, not sexuality, which delineates her body; pain not sexuality, which threatens to ruin her; and pain not sexuality which eventually compels her to speak out on her own behalf."[18] Perhaps this near consensus is in part due to what Foreman calls the silence in the "terrain of the sexual" in the novel.[19] Even in the context of Frado's marriage, she argues, Wilson avoids any sexual disclosure.

While Wilson certainly imposes a degree of silence in regard to heterosexual relations in the novel, I would suggest that this reticence is little more than would have been expected for a midnineteenth-century novel written by a woman. Indeed, Wilson evokes the sexual in ways that were appropriate for her nineteenth-century audience from the very beginning of the novel, when she describes the seduction of Frado's mother, Mag Smith. Wilson's careful description of this young, inexperienced white woman's attempt to negotiate a heterosexual union in an effort to achieve financial stability demonstrates Wilson's studied entry into the complicated topography of nineteenth-century sexuality. Despite the scandalous material, Wilson describes the consummation of the relationship between Mag and this serial seducer with sentimental finesse: "She surrendered to him a priceless gem, which he proudly garnered as a trophy, with those of other victims, and left her to her fate" (6). Wilson leaves no question about the nature of the relationship, the designs of the wealthy gentleman in question, or Mag's own desire for social elevation that attracts her to him. In addition, the novel's account of Mag's subsequent contractual relationships with men of African descent not only enters the sexual, but boldly defies nineteenth-century codes of literary propriety by situating Mag as no longer a naïve young girl, but instead a shameless young woman concerned only with material advancement. Indeed, Mag's response to Jim's proposal, "I can do but two things . . . beg my living or get it from you" (13), strips the marriage contract down to its ugliest skeletal framework, a sexual and pecuniary agreement. Wilson opens the novel with a series of sexual relationships in which Mag must accept herself as a traded commodity in order to survive, demonstrating that Wilson not only confronts the sexual with the sentimental tools available to her, but also risks abandoning those conventions when they fail to tell her story. Wilson is not so much broadly silent on the sexual as she is strategically reticent about it. Her tactics, therefore, raise questions about what motivates the novel's disclosures and its gaping absences.

Ronna C. Johnson's provocative essay "Said But Not Spoken" stands out among critical treatments of *Our Nig* in that it points to the relationship between the novel's silences and sexual abuse. Johnson argues that *"Our Nig* says figuratively through narrative structure what cannot be confessed in speech: the sexual transgression against the black female."[20] Johnson contends that the novel's elisions point to the sexual transgressions of the Bellmont men and that Wilson's treatment of Mrs. Bellmont as the origin of the abuse serves to displace the men's sexual aggression. However, as R. J. Ellis notes, if Wilson was attempting to indicate that the Bellmont men raped Frado, there were plenty of conventions at her disposal to communicate such a transgression.[21] Not only were there many fictions of rape, especially in anti-slavery literature, but Wilson's own use of the miscegenated figure as her central character, and her choice to open the novel with a tale of seduction, indicates her familiarity with these traditions and her inversions and subversions of them.[22] Here, I am referring to the common use of mixed-race characters in nineteenth-century American fiction to indicate interracial rape. By reversing the racial coding in her own version of the interracial relationship, Wilson evokes and yet sidesteps the conventional tale of interracial rape. In addition, she portrays the seducer of Frado's white mother, Mag, as a white man whose seduction and abandonment of the protagonist's mother leads to her public disgrace and poverty. If we consider that the seduction motif often served to frame sexual violence, Wilson's use of this motif indicates her awareness of how to communicate white male sexual aggression.[23] Thus, Wilson circles these genres of mixed-race fiction and the seduction tale, carefully demonstrating their intersections and divergences, yet never allowing any one of them to come to a neat completion in relation to Frado.

Wilson's use of sexual conventions in the novel, in addition to her precise characterization of Mrs. Bellmont as the perpetrator of Frado's abuse, suggests that not only would such displacement not have been necessary, but the silences in the novel ultimately center on Mrs. Bellmont. Rather than searching for how Wilson's characterization of Mrs. Bellmont functions as a sign of others' transgressions, I would like to explore how Wilson directs our attention to Mrs. Bellmont's baleful abuse of Frado. In some ways this approach seems obvious — perhaps too obvious — because it merely follows the path on which Wilson squarely places the reader, but perhaps its usefulness lies in its ability to do just that — to follow Wilson's most deliberate lead. My intent here is not to dismiss Johnson's approach, but rather to attempt, like Johnson, to accept Wilson's invitation to fill in the blanks of the novel.

Like Johnson, I argue that at the core of what would "most provoke shame" is the specter of sexual abuse. Yet I seek to add another interpretive strand to this already complicated discursive braid by suggesting that to focus on the men in this novel as the sexual abusers is to deny what Wilson's treatment of Mrs. Bellmont vehemently professes: that the notion of a blissful coalition between abolition and feminism is mythical. Her characterization of Mrs. Bellmont as a racist whose sadistic abuse of her mixed-race charge is hardly matched by slaveholders demands that her audience examine skeptically the relationship between the two midcentury political movements. Indeed, the treatment of gender, which diverges so distinctly from many other nineteenth-century fictions, is what makes the novel and the character of Mrs. Bellmont in particular so difficult to confront. Wilson portrays Mrs. Bellmont as one who callously abuses Frado and yet repeatedly characterizes herself as the victim of abuse. When her husband or her sons criticize or merely refuse to participate in her maltreatment of Frado, Mrs. Bellmont repeatedly frames herself as their victim. When her husband accuses her of imprisoning the child, she responds, "I did not think it would come to this; that my own husband would treat me so," and breaks into tears (47). Wilson's depiction of Mrs. Bellmont exposes what Karen Sanchez-Eppler calls "patterns of exploitation, appropriation, and displacement" that often characterize the relationship between feminism and abolition, exploding the neat conflation of woman and slave.[24] My point here is that Wilson carefully resists such conflations by focusing on her "she-devil" figure as the abuser rather than the male characters. In this way, my reading of the novel follows Wilson's lead by also resisting such conflations and conventional gender expectations to consider the sexual threat that Mrs. Bellmont poses to Frado.

This story, however, can only exist within the rifts of generic junctures. Indeed, by beginning her novel with a seduction story, a form which Sielke argues is "the dominant fictional frame for rendering matters of sexuality and sexual violence," Wilson seems to gesture toward the ways in which Frado's story cannot be generically contained.[25] Perhaps this generic failure demonstrates the ways in which rape, as Bal argues, "cannot be visualized . . . it can exist only as experience and as memory, as image translated into signs, never adequately 'objectifiable.'"[26] Still, Wilson's deft deployment of the seduction tale, both in the beginning of the novel and to some extent in the conclusion, when Frado is seduced, married, impregnated, and abandoned by a free black man, envelops Frado's story within the rhetoric of rape. Sielke argues that the seduction tale conveys rape as an invasion of the mind through speech, through coercive language that penetrates the mind, thus overcoming indecision or non-consent.[27] Perhaps, by beginning and ending Frado's story within this context, Wilson circles the violation that lies at the heart of the novel: Mrs. Bellmont's invasion of Frado's body and mind.

The circle of seduction and exploitation that Wilson draws also bears signs of traumatic repetition. That is, the return to the theme of seduction and abandonment in the novel suggests the need to tell, the imperative to evoke the structures that signify sexual exploitation. And yet, the seduction tale never precisely hits the mark. Instead, it faintly gestures toward abuse without exposing sexual violence. Thus, the seduction narrative repeatedly circles back on itself, demonstrating that it cannot perform as a satisfactory telling. Indeed, in the context of the traumatic experience recounted, as Dori Laub points out, "there are never enough words or the right words, there is never enough time or the right time, and never enough listening or the right listening to articulate the story that cannot be fully captured in thought, memory, and speech."[28] Thus, this larger crisis of telling shapes the text's generic mechanisms, conceivably requiring the silence that pervades the novel.

Perhaps the novel's most profound silence is the larger gap that lies between Wilson and Frado, the invented understudy who stands in for Wilson in the autobiographical novel. This fictional projection suggests not only alienation from the self, but also reminds us that the form of the autobiographical novel allows for such distance between self and experience in that it never promises more than partial truths. If the autobiographical novel enters into a compact with the reader, it is an assurance that the reader must accept the half-spoken truths and acknowledge that meaning is interpretive and lies in artistic representation, or what Tate calls preconscious discourse.[29] In this sense, the autobiographical novel is the single genre that remains intact in *Our Nig* because its incompleteness, its commitment to omission, is part and parcel of its generic framework, and is thus in keeping with the impulses of the work.

On the one hand, Wilson's novel demonstrates the search for meaning, but it is also committed to acknowledging unknowability. Thus, I do not want to characterize *Our Nig* as deficient, but rather as a conscious exploration of its own silences that shape meaning as much as expression does. That is, even as the story searches for ways of meaning, the search itself acknowledges the impossibility of telling. Indeed, *Our Nig* points to what Cathy Caruth describes as the "inaccessibility of trauma . . . its resistance to full theoretical analysis and understanding."[30] Ultimately, Wilson leaves the reader to follow her trail, veering off the page to the place where "slavery's shadows" fall.

NOTES

1. See Gabrielle Foreman, "The Spoken and the Silenced in *Incidents in the Life of a Slave Girl* and *Our Nig*," *Callaloo* 13.2 (Spring 1990): 313–24.

2. Hazel Carby convincingly interprets *Our Nig* as an allegory of a slave narrative in *Reconstructing Womanhood: The Emergence of the Afro-American Woman Novelist* (New York: Oxford University Press, 1997), 43.

3. Elizabeth West, "Reworking the Conversion Narrative: Race and Christianity in *Our Nig*," *MELUS: Journal of the Society for the Study of Multi-Ethnic Literature of the United States* 24 (Summer 1999): 3–27.

4. In his introduction to *Our Nig* Henry Louis Gates, Jr., discusses the ways in which the narrative coincides with the traditions of the domestic novel, though he acknowledges its many departures from that form. "Introduction" in Harriet E. Wilson, *Our Nig; or Sketches from the Life of a Free Black* (New York: Vintage Books, 2002), xli–liii. Further references to *Our Nig* are from this edition and will be noted in parentheses within the text.

5. Julia Stern argues that to read *Our Nig* as a domestic novel is to overlook Wilson's portrayal of the domestic space as the site of brutal violence. "Excavating Genre in *Our Nig*," *American Literature* 67.3 (September 1995): 441.

6. R. J. Ellis, "Body Politics and the Body Politic in William Wells Brown's *Clotel* and Harriet Wilson's *Our Nig*," in *Soft Canons: American Women Writers and Masculine Tradition*, ed. Karen Kilcup (Bloomington: University of Iowa Press, 1999), 112.

7. Foreman, "The Spoken and the Silenced," 320.

8. John Irving, *A Widow for One Year* (New York: Random House, 1998), 14.

9. Diane Price Herndl, "The Invisible (Invalid Woman): African-American Women, Illness and Nineteenth-Century Narrative," *Women's Studies: An Interdisciplinary Journal* 24.6 (1995): 558–59.

10. Cynthia Davis, "Speaking the Body's Pain: Harriet Wilson's *Our Nig*," *African American Review* 27 (1993): 399.

11. Ibid., 400.

12. Claudia Tate, *Psychoanalysis and Black Novels: Desire and the Protocols of Race* (New York: Oxford University Press, 1998), 13.

13. Sabine Sielke, *Reading Rape: The Rhetoric of Sexual Violence in American Literature and Culture* (Princeton: Princeton University Press, 2002), 2.

14. Carby, *Reconstructing Womanhood*, 44.

15. Mieke Bal, "The Rape of Narrative and the Narrative of Rape: Speech Acts and Body Language in Judges," in *Literature and the Body: Essays on Populations and Persons* (Baltimore: Johns Hopkins University Press, 1988), 20.

16. John D' Emilo and Estelle Freedman, *Intimate Matters: A History of Sexuality in America* (New York: Harper and Row, 1988), 121–22.

17. Elizabeth Breau, "Identifying Satire in *Our Nig,*" *Callaloo* 16.2 (Spring 1993): 463.

18. Davis, "Speaking the Body's Pain," 392.

19. Foreman, "The Spoken and the Silenced," 321.

20. Ronna Johnson, "Said But Not Spoken: Elision and the Representation of Rape, Race and Gender in Harriet E.Wilson's *Our Nig,*" *Speaking the Other Self: American Women Writers*, ed. Jeanne Campbell Reesman (Athens: University of Georgia Press, 1997), 96.

21. R. J. Ellis, *Harriet Wilson's Our Nig: A Cultural Biography of a "Two Story" African American Novel* (Amsterdam: Rodolpi, 2003), 113.

22. Here I am referring to the common use of mixed-race characters in nineteenth-century American fiction to indicate interracial rape. By reversing the racial coding in her version of the interracial relationship, Wilson complicates this scenario. Thus, she evokes a figure often positioned as the product of rape, as the product of necessity — that is her mother's poverty causes her to marry a black man.

23. Sielke, *Reading Rape*, 22. According to Sielke, the tale of seduction became a dominant mode of framing sexuality and sexual violence in both eighteenth- and nineteenth-century literatures.

24. Karen Sanchez Eppler, *Touching Liberty: Abolition, Feminism, and the Politics of the Body* (Berkeley and Los Angeles: University of California Press, 1997), 13.

25. Sielke, *Reading Rape*, 22.

26. Mieke Bal, "Reading with the Other Art," *Theory between the Disciplines: Authority/Vision/Politics*, ed. Martin Kreiswirth and Mark A. Cheetham (Ann Arbor: University of Michigan Press, 1990), 142.

27. Sielke, *Reading Rape*, 17.

28. Dori Laub, "Truth and Testimony: The Process and the Struggle," *American Imago* 48.1 (1991): 77.

29. I borrow Phillip Lejeune's concept of the autobiographical pact, in which the author makes a commitment to the reader to come to some understanding of his/her own life. Lejeune, however, makes little distinction between autobiography and the autobiographical novel in that he reads autobiography as a type of fiction. For more, see Phillip Lejeune, *On Autobiography* (Minneapolis: University of Minnesota Press, 1989).

30. Cathy Caruth, "Introduction," *American Imago* 48.1 (1991): 9.

Miss Marsh's Uncommon School Reform

Eve Allegra Raimon

It is time we had uncommon schools, that we did not leave
off our education when we begin to be men and women.
—HENRY DAVID THOREAU, *Walden*[1]

IN THE THIRD CHAPTER of *Our Nig*, "A New Home for Me," a "lengthy
discussion" occurs among Mr. and Mrs. Bellmont and their offspring, Jane
and Jack, over whether to send the seven-year-old Frado to school. The narrator recounts that, predictably, "Mrs. Bellmont was in doubt about the util-
ity of attempting to educate people of color, who were incapable of elevation."
Mr. Bellmont is forced to adopt an uncharacteristically patriarchal and au-
thoritative manner in "declar[ing] decisively that she *should* go to school. . . .
The word once spoken admitted of no appeal; so, not withstanding Mary's ob-
jection that she would have to attend the same school [Frado] did, the word
became law."[2] Most readers attribute Mrs. Bellmont's hostility to Frado's education to her generally baleful disposition and to her surprise at Mr. Bellmont's unusual determination to help his hapless charge. However, the fact
that public schooling was even available to "Nig" represents a rarity in the period. Despite the ascendant influence of the common school movement, which
sought to extend free education to a broader range of social classes and ethnic groups, the notion of racially integrated schooling was beyond imagining
for many, even among the most progressive reformers of the day. Yet a racially
inclusive education is precisely what Harriet Wilson depicts in this novel and
what she champions in the singular figure of Miss Marsh, the schoolteacher.
The portion of the narrative describing Frado's experience in Miss Marsh's
classroom has been under-examined, yet it is pivotal in appreciating Wilson's
artistic and political vision. In her portrait of public school progressivism,

Wilson offers a fictional exemplar of the progressive impulse that typified the nineteenth-century movement for education reform but that too often failed to be realized in practice.

The common school movement that swept from New England westward in the antebellum years was coincident with the rise of such other social movements as the struggle for emancipation and women's rights. State and local governments, confronting an emerging industrial economy and a rapidly diversifying population, faced the necessity of educating a broader range of the populace than ever before if the new republic was to flourish. Led by such figures as Horace Mann, who became Massachusetts's first secretary of education in 1834, and by leading educator Henry Barnard in Connecticut and Rhode Island, the common school design was a response, in part, to the deficiencies typical of earlier "charity" or "pauper" schools. Its goal was to offer "scholars" — as students were then called — a free, "universal" experience of public education. To Mann and others, state-supported schools were essential to the future of an increasingly pluralistic republic, in both religious and ethnic terms: "The establishment of such common schools would reduce poverty and crime," writes Stanley William Rothstein in *Schooling the Poor*; "it would prevent pauperism and widespread social and economic distress." The forerunner of the educational progressivism of the early twentieth century, the movement gained influence from Jacksonian Democrats and speakers on the popular lyceum circuit. The common school model required professional educators who prepared and made public annual school reports that began to create standard expectations for schooling and that made schools directly accountable to their communities. Gradually, because of these reforms, free education for U.S. schoolchildren came to be seen as a birthright — indeed a duty — at least if one was born white. Rothstein continues:

> Ignorance was the enemy of republican government. It was also the enemy of business, which sought more and more skilled and literate workers for factories, retail outlets, and offices. What free schools could do best, however, was to assimilate the new immigrants from Ireland and Europe, to establish the new U.S. nation from the diverse populations that were now spreading quickly westward.[3]

New Hampshire was an early advocate of the broader New England effort to assimilate European immigrants by introducing greater systematization and regulation into public schooling. In 1827 it passed an act establishing school districts and requiring them to be supported by yearly tax assessments. It also raised the qualifications for teachers and required students to be "well supplied with books at the expense of parents, masters, or guardians, and, in case they were not able, at the public expense." In addition, the act mandated the appointment of a "superintending school committee" whose charge included, among other tasks, "to use their influence and best endeavors to secure a full and strict attendance upon school of the youth in the several districts, to direct and determine the text-books without favoring any religious sect," and to report yearly to the town the numbers of children between the ages of four and fourteen who had failed to attend their district school.[4] The statute's language makes clear its intent to further the cause of republican virtue and moral rectitude. It declares that the obligation of teachers is to "preserve and perfect a republican form of government and to secure the blessings of liberty as well as to promote [students'] future happiness." Still more grandly, it calls on teachers to

> impress on the minds of children and youth committed to their care and instruction the principles of piety and justice, and a sacred regard to truth, love of their country, humanity, and benevolence, sobriety, industry, and frugality, chastity, moderation, and temperance, and all other virtues which are the ornaments of human society.[5]

The significance placed here on the duty of the granite state's teachers to embrace such democratic, protestant virtues and to imbue their pupils with them typifies the literature of the period. For example, in *Common Schools, Their Present Conditions and Future Prespects, by a Teacher* (1844), New Hampshire educators John F. Brown and Asa McFarland assert that, "Without good teaching, a school is but a name. We want better teachers, and more teachers for all classes of society; for rich and poor; for children and adults."[6] Whether or not New Hampshire's common schools routinely welcomed students from diverse class backgrounds in actuality, educators' public pronouncements make effusive promises regarding social inclusiveness.

If anything, the educational establishment of Milford, New Hampshire, where Wilson was placed into domestic service, expanded and strengthened the state's ambitious mandate for moral and social reform in the schools. For example, the Rev. Humphrey Moore, a prominent local Congregational minister from 1802 to 1836 — and afterward a regular member of the school committee — was explicit in his desire to extend universal schooling to children of all classes. He declared in an 1845 annual school report that

> this school system, carried into operation, is adapted to the intellectual wants of every class of children, whether they belong to parents, who are paupers of the town. The laws are generous on this subject, and give equal scope to all the unfolding minds, and tend to establish and sustain all that equality in society, which is desirable and practicable.[7]

Moore, who presided over the Congregational services during the decades when Wilson would have attended school in Milford, further insisted that, "In order to produce the best condition in a town, state, or nation, in respect to its pecuniary, political, and religious interests, it is necessary that the whole population be brought under the influence of intellectual education. Knowledge is power."[8]

Yet power for whom remained an issue. Moore exemplifies the expansive rhetoric typical of the common school movement in pointing to each of its threefold goals of advancing the smooth functioning of the republic, quelling religious factionalism, and increasing educational access across class lines. One question such rhetoric begged, however, was whether it was "desirable and practicable" to consider black children as part of the "whole population" to be "brought under the influence of intellectual education." Typically, the answer was no. Though contemporaneous declarations such as the foregoing are rhetorically ecumenical and condemn discrimination, in fact children of color were routinely excluded from "universal" schooling. Moore, himself elected to both houses of the state legislature under the auspices of the anti-slavery party, may have proved an exception to such racially exclusive norms, thus helping to create the conditions that would have made Wilson's attendance at school possible.[9] However, more generally speaking, segregation was standard practice in most places from the outset of public education in the nineteenth century, especially in urban areas. In Boston, for example, a segregated subsystem for black children dated back to 1806.[10] In Salem, Massachusetts, African American children were ousted from all public schools in 1807. True, rural districts tended not to have the means or the enrollment to segment their student populations to the same degree, and could boast substantially higher participation rates overall than their urban counterparts. However, even in rural New England communities "local school committees usually assigned Negro children to separate institutions," according to educational historian Leon Litwack. Moreover, he reports, "By the 1830's, statute or custom placed Negro children in separate schools in nearly every Northern community."[11] Indeed, no less a figure than Horace Mann, a vocal opponent of slavery, balked at the notion of blacks and whites being educated together.[12] Joanne Pope Melish notes the irony in inherent in the fact that, "as the movement to make at least some public schooling available to every child spread throughout New England after 1800, children of color were routinely excluded from most schools. Where some *were* allowed to attend classes with whites, their treatment elicited strenuous complaint."[13]

David Watters documents this history of prejudice in his discussion in this volume of a 1937 case in Boscawen, New Hampshire, in which a school dis-

Schoolhouse in District No. 3 (the school Wilson attended). Closed in 1891, it was first moved to Pine Valley and then to its present location at 54 Union Street, where it is a part of the house. *Courtesy of JerriAnne Boggis*

trict called a meeting to ban a black family from sending its children to a local school. The effort succeeded, and the family was forced to send their offspring elsewhere.[14] The most notorious and violent instance of the municipal expulsion of black students and educators in the state's history occurred in Caanan in 1835, when a committee of the town council literally dragged the abolitionist and interracial Noyes Academy off its foundation. Both students and founder were forced to flee; the schoolhouse was later destroyed in a suspicious fire.[15]

The situation in Milford itself was complex in the 1830s with respect to educating its small black population. As Reginald H. Pitts reveals, some black families, including the Blanchards and the Parkers, were allowed to send their children to the district schools. At the same time, at least in the latter case, such students were ostracized when it came to social activities.[16] In fact, Pitts and Gabrielle Foreman argue that the brutal attack on Noyes Academy provides the historical backdrop for the racial intimidation Frado initially experiences on her first day of school. While Wilson may have been recalling that incident she may also have endeavored to portray a counterpoint to it if we take into account the whole of Frado's encounters at school. Indeed, it can be argued that Wilson fashions a liberatory experience out of the scenes of her heroine's schooling under the influence of Miss Marsh, the white schoolteacher.

In fact, the schoolhouse represents the only location in the novel where "Nig" finds true respite from abuse and where she gains the respect of her peers and her teacher. Moreover, the assembly of scholars Wilson portrays approaches the Christian community-minded ethos the common school movement espoused. Indeed, Miss Marsh embodies the best ambitions of the movement for universal schooling, and is the sole character in the novel who possesses the genuine authority to alter Frado's abject circumstances — at least within the finite environment of the classroom. While she is never described directly, Frado's teacher serves an extraordinary function that critics often overlook. Appearing only briefly, Miss Marsh is perhaps Frado's most effective ally, and the only meaningful character during the period of Frado's servitude to operate outside the private sphere of the Bellmont family. Wilson's portrait of Miss Marsh acts as an entreaty to the common school movement to live up to its stated egalitarian ideals. As the only personification of the public sphere illustrated in the narrative, the teacher and her school embody the community's great potential to enact a more expansive conception of social justice to include "Our Nig." If Frado's schooling does reflect Wilson's own experience, then it can be read as the author's and Frado's great good fortune *and* as an appeal for education reformers to include African American children. Whether the scenes under Miss Marsh's tutelage are fiction or embellished autobiography, they reflect the same profound desire for racial equality in the classroom.

In the narrative itself, Wilson inserts drama to highlight Miss Marsh's uncommon response to Frado. Unlike her counterparts elsewhere, Frado enjoys "three months of schooling, summer and winter . . . for three years," alongside her white classmates (37). When the child first leaves the Bellmonts' for school, we are led to believe that she will meet with a similar reception to that which she daily endures at the hands of Mary and her mother, the "she-devil." Indeed, we are told that, "Frado sauntered on far in the rear of Mary, who was ashamed to be seen 'walking with a nigger.'" What is more, her classmates gather to heap scorn upon her when she does arrive: "'See that nigger,' shouted one. 'Look! Look!' cried another. 'I won't play with her,' said one little girl. 'Nor I neither,' replied another" (31). Such sentiment lends credence to the idea that the appearance of students of color was less than a common occurrence in the Milford district schools in the 1830s, likely attributable both to prejudice and to the small population of black families then residing in rural New Hampshire.[17] As readers expect, "Mary relished these sharp attacks," and looked forward to "lowering Nig where, according to her views, she belonged." Frado herself is "chagrined and grieved" that her "anticipations of pleasure at such a place" appear to be dashed (31).

Just when the child has all but decided to turn around and return "home,"
enter Miss Marsh, who surprises both the novel's readership and the protagonist herself with a singular act of welcome: "[O]bserving the downcast looks
of the child, [she] took her by the hand, and led her into the school-room."
Once inside, the schoolteacher delivers a lecture to her students that consti-
tutes the only explicit condemnation in the novel of "all prejudice," and thus
merits quoting in full:

> She then reminded them of their duties to the poor and friendless; their cow-
> ardice in attacking a young innocent child; referred them to one who looks
> not on outward appearances, but on the heart. "She looks like a good girl;
> I think *I* shall love her, so lay aside all prejudice, and vie with each other in
> shewing kindness and good-will to one who seems different from you," were
> the closing remarks of the kind lady. Those kind words! The most agreeable
> sound which ever meets the ear of sorrowing, grieving childhood. (31–32)

This speech is remarkable in several ways, and proves to be a crucial turning
point in Frado's developing agency. As we have seen, references to students'
"duties to the poor and friendless" are integral to common school ideology.
However, with its suspenseful buildup and its emphasis on disregarding "outward appearances" and rejecting prejudice, this scene goes as far as is possible
in the context of its production explicitly to advocate for racial equity. It also
underscores the author's placement of the female teacher as the spokeswoman
for educational and social reform.

The As a woman, Miss Marsh reflects the emerging view that female teachers were naturally better suited than men to educate the nation's young. Such
gendering of the profession goes back at least as far as Horace Mann, who favored this approach both because of women's perceived inherent maternal na-
tures and also because they could demand less compensation than men and
would therefore place less strain on local budgets. One New Hampshire education commissioner's report concluded, "That the female character is, by nature, better adapted to guiding and unfolding the mind of the young child, is
not to be questioned."[18] As was commonplace in the 1830s, Miss Marsh taught
the summer term rather than the winter session, since until the latter decades of the century it was believed that male teachers could better handle the
higher population of boys who attended during the winter months.[19]

The real-life inspiration for Miss Marsh may well have been a woman
who challenged the common school movement to consider the rights of African American children. In their introduction to the 2004 Penguin edition of the novel, Foreman and Pitts contend that Miss Marsh was probably
based on Abby A. Kent (1802–57), a teacher from neighboring Amherst,

New Hampshire. Kent was the best friend and cousin of President Franklin Pierce's future wife, Jane Means Appleton. Abby Kent taught school in New Hampshire until her marriage in 1834 to Robert Means, Jr. (In the narrative, a charming suitor, George Means, marries Jane, the invalid Bellmont daughter.) The real Abby Kent visits Mrs. Pierce in Washington D.C.; while there, both ride in the presidential carriage to help teach at Myrtilla Miner's famed School for Colored Girls.[20] As recounted in a memoir of the school (later the University of the District of Columbia), Abby Kent Means "was attracted by Miss Miner's enthusiasm."[21] Thus, through her presidential relative, Means gained access to an important figure in the history of black education. In fact, the "enthusiasm" Minor and Means shared for teaching girls of color prior to the Civil War almost cost Miner her life. According to her biographer, Miner's school—which doubled as her home—was frequently the target of mob violence. After one such incident, the school's founder is reported to have exclaimed: "Mob my school! You dare not! If you tear it down over my head I shall get another house. There is no law to prevent my teaching these people, and I shall teach them, even unto death."[22] While Abby Kent Means's attraction to the antebellum D.C. school for black girls postdates her tenure as teacher in the District Three school in Milford, it affords us a glimpse of her political and philosophical zeal for radical school reform in general and meaningful educational opportunities for blacks in particular. The figure of Miss Marsh, then, may well be inspired by a woman who cared deeply and for many years about educating black girls.

If Abby Kent Means went on at midcentury to work for social justice and black children's education she was not alone. By 1870, according to Foreman and Pitts, Wilson had established herself as a leader in Boston's Lyceum movement, a progressive effort aimed at a "'drawing out' of the powers within the child [rather] than the choking of its individual growth." In numerous Spiritualist gatherings in Boston and elsewhere in the postbellum years, she championed early education and the "capacities of her race."[23] Clearly, Wilson's interest in the education and welfare of children of color grew out of her own background, including the probable early death of her own mother and the death in poverty of her son, George, at age seven.[24] Wilson's own troubled history augments the importance of the benevolent Abby Kent, perhaps the sole maternal surrogate in the author's young life. Likewise, it affords more context for Wilson's portrayal of a reformist Miss Marsh and her schoolyard exhortation for "all citizens" to "shew kindness and good-will" by promoting race and class equity.

Perhaps the novel's most significant enactment of the potential inherent in a truly progressive public school system occurs in Wilson's description of the virtuous community of scholars that includes Frado herself. In these scenes, it becomes clear that Miss Marsh's guidance has immediate and profound effects in promoting a schoolhouse whose egalitarian social order is designed "to produce the best condition in a town, state, or nation." The narrator documents that, "Example rendered her words efficacious. Day by day there was a manifest change of deportment towards 'Nig.' Her speeches often drew merriment from the children; no one could do more to enliven their favorite pastimes than Frado." Under the empowering influence of Miss Marsh, then, Frado thrives, transforming herself not just from silent object to speaking subject, but also to a position of community leadership. As Frado's stature increases, Mary's social capital correspondingly declines: "Mary could not endure to see [Frado] thus noticed, yet knew not how to prevent it. She could not influence her schoolmates as she wished. She had not gained their affections by winning ways and yielding points of 'controversy'" (32–33). In this way, school is figured as the place where Frado is given the fullest license to employ her manifest skills at social interaction and rhetorical proficiency. The once abject servant has now achieved a central position among her peers through the authority of a reformist public school teacher. Also, in Wilson's vision of the common school, distinctions between the feminine private sphere and the masculine public sphere become blurred. The female teacher represented by Miss Marsh acts in the public domain of the schoolhouse to promote an idealist republican government. Students — both male and female — learn by example to demonstrate civic virtue — a value associated with the common good rather than the domestic hearth.

Indeed, proponents of common schooling had huge ambitions for what the institution could accomplish in the public sphere. For example, in the chronicle of their experiences in rural New Hampshire schools, Brown and McFarland remark upon the influential and transformative impact of a local schoolhouse: "Its influence upon a single individual can not be estimated," they write. "Its influence upon a whole community is *unlimited*."[25] In *Our Nig*, Mary's attempt to use violence to recover her lost social status fails as a direct result of Miss Marsh's lesson in social justice. Mary, not satisfied with the "abuse and taunts" to which she subjects Frado on the way home, resolves to use physical force "'to subdue her,' to 'keep her down'" (33). Wilson's introduction of quotation marks around these two phrases underscores their use as stock vocabulary in the Bellmont household and all it represents about race and class subjugation. In the episode that follows, Mary attempts to tyrannize Frado by forcing her to cross the stream on "a single plank." The scheme backfires, however, when Mary herself loses her footing and falls in. More significant than Mary's blunder itself is her classmates' response to the incident. The narrator records that,

"Some of the larger scholars being in sight, ran, and thus prevented Mary from drowning and Frado from falling" (33). In this scene, Mary's attempt to exert class and race dominion over Frado falters twice—once in the actual execution, and again because the children, now transformed by Miss Marsh's influence, rescue both playmates at once rather than making distinctions based on social ranking or race. In this small schoolhouse, at least, the ideals of the common school movement seem to have been realized. Moreover, Miss Marsh's students demonstrate the import of enacting school reform that goes beyond the republican individualism of some antebellum common school ideology to advance the principle of equal treatment on the basis of race as well as class difference. Following the grand principles set out in the New Hampshire statutes, these scholars take seriously the principles of "piety and justice," "a sacred regard to truth," and a duty to "humanity and benevolence."

Significantly, Frado's classmates continue to identify with her and to demonstrate their appreciation of her newfound social status even after Miss Marsh's disappearance from the narrative. During the three months of the winter school session, Mrs. Bellmont forces her servant to wear only "a cast-off overcoat, once worn by Jack, and a sun-bonnet." Though her attire is "a source of great merriment to the scholars," they attribute its selection to "Old Granny Bellmont," so that their glee "was not painful to Nig or pleasurable to Mary." Indeed, the narrator underscores the contrast between the protagonist's deportment in Mrs. Bellmont's presence, when she is "under restraint," to her behavior in class, where "the pent up fires burst forth":

> She was ever at some sly prank when unseen by her teacher, in school hours; not unfrequently some outburst of merriment, of which she was the original, was charged upon some innocent mate, and punishment was inflicted which she merited. They enjoyed her antics so fully that any of them would suffer wrongfully to keep open the avenues of mirth. She would venture far beyond propriety, thus shielded and countenanced. (38)

Here, Frado adopts the social persona of the mischievous rebel precisely because she is "shielded and countenanced" by a public institution where acceptance and equality are expected. Frado's social confidence persists under the tutelage of a male teacher identified only as "master." She outwits him by hiding a lit cigar in a drawer of his desk, provoking his frightened screams of "Fire, fire!" Again, instead of eliciting anger and retribution, which would be the consequence at home, the male teacher becomes the object of the youngsters' merriment: "The scholars shouted with laughter to see the terror of the dupe, who, feeling abashed at the needless fright, made no very strict investigation, and Nig once more escaped punishment" (38–39). Twice in four pages of text, then, Wilson narrates scenes associated with school wherein the heroine not only avoids persecution but triumphs over established authority—exactly the opposite result to that which she continues to endure at the hands of her mistress. The stark juxtaposition in Frado's treatment between domestic and educational arenas accentuates the reader's sense of the classroom as a place of relative security, freedom, joy, and achievement. While it could be argued that such schoolhouse escapades possess elements of minstrelsy, I would contend that such a claim is more valid in episodes where Frado entertains James and Jack, such as in the dinner table scene when Jack, "boiling over with laughter," throws "Nig" a silver half-dollar after she defies Mrs. Bellmont by offering the mistress's plate of food to Fido. Here, social hierarchies are accentuated rather than discouraged, as they are in the schoolyard. Scenes that feature Frado entertaining James and Jack invoke a slave atmosphere, whereas her schoolyard antics position her as a social equal protected by her community (72).

Finally, toward the end of the novel proper, Frado's literacy promises further to raise her social standing. Commentators have noted multiform ways in which *Our Nig* follows in the slave narrative tradition, not the least of which is the importance the girl places on her developing literacy. In much domestic fiction, alternatively, the sexual threat the mulatta figure supposedly poses to the mistress is paramount; here, the threat is more muted. While Mrs. Bellmont does react to Frado's physicality, it is her growing Christian literacy that provokes greater outrage. Mrs. B. "seemed to have great aversion to the notice Nig would attract should she become pious." The servant's moral rectitude would be hard to dismiss. Moreover, her literate—and therefore her Christian—status would threaten her abject social caste. At one point, the matriarch catches her servant reading scripture and reacts with her trademark fury: "She ordered her to put up the book, and go to work, and not be snivelling about the house, or stop to read again." Next, Mrs. Bellmont complains to John about what she'd seen, and laments that "it was just as though [Frado] expected to turn pious nigger, and preach to white folks." The mistress concludes, darkly, "So now you see what good comes of sending her to school" (86–89). As Frado "merge[s] into womanhood" and the end approaches to "the term of years which Mrs. B claimed as the period of her servitude," the young scholar revels in the fruits of her education: "Her school-books were her constant companions, and every leisure moment was applied to them. . . . She had her book always fastened to her, where she could glance from toil to soul refreshment" (115–16). Here, Frado exemplifies the common school tenet that the Milford Congregational minister espoused when Wilson lived in that town. She embodies the Rev. Humphrey Moore's imperative that for the sustenance of the republic "it is necessary that the whole population be brought under the influence of intellectual education" — even if Moore himself had not meant to extend his decree to blacks. Indeed, by this measure, at least, Frado matures into a better, more virtuous member of her civic community than Mrs. Bellmont.

In her descriptions of Frado's literal attachment to her books, Wilson not only recalls common elements of the slave narrative but also honors the familiar theme of literacy in Frado's intensely personal, overtly reverential relationship to learning. Her education constitutes the promise of a better life even as Wilson's literacy offered her the chance, through the publication of *Our Nig*, she believed, to save her son from the kind of persecution and destitution she suffered. Later, in one of several "towns in Massachusetts," the protagonist is taught by "a plain, poor, simple woman" how to make straw bonnets and how to appreciate "the value of useful books." Soon, Frado feels herself "capable of elevation; she felt that this book information supplied an undefined dissatisfaction she had long felt, but could not express" (124). At novel's end, she assures her readers that, "Nothing turns her from her steadfast purpose of elevating herself" (130). In scenes such as these that follow Frado's formal schooling, Wilson honors the venerable African American literary tradition of extolling self-education. Moreover, in this context, such tributes also act as a corrective to the hypocrisy and racism endemic to the supposedly liberatory system of "universal" public education. Here, literacy serves not only as a vehicle for self-advancement but also as a tool to articulate social and political "dissatisfaction" and resistance.[26] Twice, Frado pledges to herself and to her readers that despite her physical limitations and the limitations placed upon her by Northern prejudice she will "elevate" herself. Wilson's most formidable impediment, of course, is the neglect of the masses of "professed abolitionists" that Frado decries at the end of *Our Nig* — the same audience that failed to recognize the author's achievement as she made her way through New Hampshire and Boston after publishing her singular work.[27]

Nevertheless, one of Wilson's many thematic innovations and narrative achievements is to focus on the emerging institution of the public school as the place where Frado is allowed entry into a community that offers a model of a republican government founded on principles of genuine equality. In brief but pivotal scenes featuring Miss Marsh and her school, the author extends common school doctrine to include a rare vision of a racially inclusive republic. Thus, at the center of *Our Nig* is rendered a truly progressive image of the public sphere in general and a genuinely transformative role for the public school in particular. To borrow from Thoreau, Frado's unusual common school education together with her own impulse to become an autodidact helped her develop into an "uncommon" woman. Would that the racial history of public schooling in the United States had lived up to Miss Marsh's ideals.

NOTES

1. Henry David Thoreau, *Walden* (New Haven: Yale University Press, 2004), 106.

2. Harriet E. Wilson, *Our Nig; or, Sketches from the Life of a Free Black*, ed. and intro. by Henry Louis Gates, Jr. (New York: Vintage Books, 2002), 30–31. Further references are included in parentheses within the text.

3. Stanley William Rothstein, *Schooling the Poor: A Social Inquiry into the American Educational Experience* (Westport, Conn.: Bergin and Garvey, 1994), 5–6.

4. Quoted in George Gary Bush, *History of Education in New Hampshire* (DC: Government Printing Office, 1898), 16–17.

5. Quoted in Bush, *History of Education in New Hampshire*, 16.

6. John F. Brown and Asa McFarland, *Common Schools, Their Present Conditions and Future Prospects* (Concord: N.H. imprints, 1844), 14.

7. Humphrey Moore, *Report of the Superintending School Committee of the Town of Milford* (Nashville: printed by Albin Beard, 1845), n.p.

8. Ibid., n.p.

9. George Allen Ramsdell, *The History of Milford* (Concord: The Rumford Press, 1901), 88.

10. Robert L. Osgood, "Undermining the Common School Ideal: Intermediate Schools and Ungraded Classes in Boston, 1838–1900," *History of Education Quarterly* 37.4 (Winter 1997) n.10, 381. Osgood traces the history of segregated "intermediate schools" aimed primarily at children of European immigrants. He reports that in the 1850s the Boston School Committee "distanced itself further from a common school ideal by establishing the single-sex intermediate schools but also one solely for children of African descent" (381).

11. Thanks in part to a lawsuit brought by African American John Remond, father of prominent future educators and abolitionists, the Salem school committee voted in 1844 to integrate the schools. See Rebecca R. Noel, "Salem as the Nation's Schoolhouse," in *Salem: Place, Myth, and Memory*, ed. Dane Anthony Morrison and Nancy Lusignan Schultz (Boston: Northeastern University Press, 2004). On urban/rural enrollments, see Carl F. Kaestle and Maris A. Vinovskis, eds., *Education and Social Change in Nineteenth-Century Massachusetts* (Cambridge: Cambridge University Press, 1980), 117. On separate schooling by immigrant status and race, see "Education: Separate and Unequal," in *Education in American History: Readings on the Social Issues*, ed. Michael B. Katz (New York: Praeger Publishers, 1973), 254.

12. John L. Rury, *Education and Social Change* (Mahwah, N.J.: Lawrence Erlbaum Associates, 2005), 115. Rury writes that reactions to black education were sometimes violent compared to the ongoing debate about women's education.

13. Joanne Pope Melish, *Disowning Slavery: Gradual Emancipation and "Race" in New England, 1780–1860* (Ithaca: Cornell University Press, 1998), 188. Melish attributes the increasing "racialization" through scientific racism (and the resultant segregation) in nineteenth-century New England to "whites' need to resolve post-Revolutionary uncertainty over susceptibility to enslavement and eligibility for citizenship" (6).

14. David H. Watters, "'As soon as I saw my sable brother, I felt more at home': Sampson Battis and the Place of New Hampshire African American History," in this volume.

15. Craig S. Wilder, "'N——— School': The Plight of Noyes Academy in Canaan, New Hampshire," paper delivered at conference on Black New England, University of New Hampshire, June 23, 2006. Also see Douglas Harper, "Slavery in New Hampshire," www.slavenorth.com/newhampshire.htm.

16. Reginald H. Pitts, "George and Timothy Blanchard: Surviving and Thriving in Nineteenth-Century Milford," in this volume.

17. In "*Our Nig* and the Politics of Recovery, or, Sketches of the Life of a Free Black and Eloquent Colored Spiritualist," unpublished paper, P. Gabrielle Foreman notes that there is only one free woman of color recorded in the 1840 and 1850 censuses in Milford (12). Reginald H. Pitts documents members of the Blanchard family attending District School Number Four.

18. J. Cummings, *Report of the Commissioner of Common Schools for the County of Hillsborough* (Concord: Barton and Hadley, 1856), 18.

19. Rury, *Education and Social Change*, 78; Kaestle and Vinovskis, *Education and Social Change in Nineteenth-Century Massachusetts*, 122.

20. Foreman, introduction to *Our Nig; or Sketches from the Life of a Free Black* (New York: Penguin Books, 2005), n. 11, p. 88. While Foreman and Pitts identify Abby Kent and Jane Means Appleton as cousins, Ellen O'Connor calls Kent "an aunt of Mrs. Pierce." Myrtilla Miner and Ellen O'Connor, *Myrtilla Miner: A Memoir and The School for Colored Girls* (1885, 1854, respectively; repr., New York: Arno Press, 1969), 56–57.

21. Miner and O'Connor, *Myrtilla*, 56–57.

22. Ibid., 56.

23. *Religio-Philosophical Journal*, October 10, 1874, 6, quoted in P. Gabrielle Foreman, "*Our Nig* and the Politics of Recovery," 22; *Banner of Light*, September 14, 1867, 5.

24. Foreman, "*Our Nig* and the Politics of Recovery," 10–11. Henry Louis Gates, Jr., was the first to document the death of Wilson's son in his introduction to the 1983 edition of the novel.

25. Brown and McFarland, *Common Schools*, 4.

26. For a classic example of literacy's liberatory and subversive potential in the slave narrative tradition see Frederick Douglass's *Narrative of the Life of Frederick Douglass, an American Slave* (1845; repr., New York: Penguin Classics, 1986), 78–79.

27. The racial hypocrisy she decries at the close of *Our Nig* is matched by her

later experience in the spiritualist movement. The *Religio-Philisophical Journal* re-cords that Wilson spoke "at some length of her own grievances at the treatment she received from Boston Spiritualists." *Religio-Philosophical Journal*, October 10, 1874, 6, quoted in Foreman, "*Our Nig* and the Politics of Recovery," 22.

Fairy Tales and *Our Nig*

Feminist Approaches to Teaching Harriet Wilson's Novel

Helen Frink

IN DESCRIBING APPROACHES to Harriet Wilson's *Our Nig*, the first African American novel published in the United States, several authors follow the lead of Henry Louis Gates in pointing out similarities to slave narratives and sentimental novels.[1] In their introduction to the 2005 Penguin edition, P. Gabrielle Foreman and Reginald H. Pitts add "the seduction novel and the captivity narrative" to the popular genres they find referenced in *Our Nig*.[2] While modern-day readers of *Our Nig* may not be familiar with these popular nineteenth-century genres, most of us are familiar with fairy tales, which offer a revealing window into understanding this text as a *gendered* narrative. In this paper I propose first to explore the novel's connections to some of the best known fairy tales about girls' development, and second to interpret the novel as a primarily *girl's and young woman's* narrative of struggle against poverty and oppression, a struggle predetermined by the economic conditions facing New Hampshire working women in the midnineteenth century. This twofold approach facilitates teaching the novel to college undergraduates while placing it in a feminist context.

I

In *Our Nig* we recognize important themes from classic fairy tales such as "Snow White," "Cinderella," "Rapunzel," and "Hansel and Gretel." Such tales, like *Our Nig*, describe the maturation of a girl from childhood through adolescence and contain themes such as learning how to work, rivaling an older woman, choosing a marriage partner, and founding a home.[3] In exploring these parallels, I do not suggest that Wilson read fairy tales, although Gates's "Introduction" asserts that Wilson read "broadly" in " nineteenth-century American and English literature (xxxix). Rather I trace in both *Our Nig* and in fairy tales elemental patterns of human behavior and conflict and the transparent images storytellers used to depict them in what Wilson herself calls "crude narrations."

Numerous fairy tales begin with a daughter whose real mother has died or disappeared from the scene, thrusting her out of her home and making her vulnerable to wrongful exploitation.[4] Gretel, Snow White, and Cinderella must endure hard labor and unjust humiliation for a period of testing and trial, before finding lasting happiness. The instrument of their rescue at first glance may appear to be a prince, but in reality is often the girl herself (Gretel, Cinderella, or Rapunzel) and her own resourcefulness. Sometimes seduction by and reliance on a prince proves to be a mistake, and the girl is subjected to wandering and trials even after the birth of a child, e.g. "Rapunzel," "The Maiden Without Hands," "Brother and Sister," or "Rumpelstiltskin."

Frado's struggles as she labors in the Bellmont household from the age of six until eighteen replicate this classic fairy tale pattern.[5] Frado's African American father, Jim, dies, and her impoverished white mother, Mag Smith, abandons her at the Bellmont house. Mrs. Bellmont, "self-willed, haughty, undisciplined, arbitrary and severe," rules over a household that encompasses her mild-mannered husband, John, his sister Aunt Abby, and the three Bellmont children remaining at home: the semi-invalid Jane, the playful Jack, and Mary, her mother's namesake and favorite.

Most of the fairy tales named above feature a subtext that we might call the evil stepmother; if there is a father present, he fades from the scene like Frado's father, Jim, who dies, and like the passive Mr. Bellmont. Aunt Abby urges her brother to defend Frado against his wife's cruelty, but he replies, "How am I to help it? Women rule the earth and all in it" (44). Throughout the novel, he repeatedly fails to help Frado just as Cinderella's biological father fails to defend her against his new wife and her daughters. Hansel and Gretel's father does not resist his wife's insistence that they abandon their children in the forest, although he is glad to see them when they return home. The fathers of Snow White and Rapunzel also fail to prevent their daughters' expulsion from the childhood home.

The stepmother, who should provide the girl with a role model and should nurture and guide her, instead engages in a power struggle against her, as Mrs. Bellmont does with Frado. The wicked stepmother's daughters, like Cinderella's stepsisters, ally themselves with their mother in tormenting the girl. As soon as Frado appears in the Bellmont household, Mary, who is closest to her in age and will become her rival for popularity among schoolchildren in chapter 3, opposes her by suggesting she be sent to the County House and insisting "I don't want a nigger round *me*" (26). In Mrs. Bellmont's marked favoritism for Mary, who resembles her in "disposition and manners" more than any of her other children, Wilson demonstrates the value of a "good" mother's love for her daughter, highlighting by contrast what Frado has lost when Mag Smith abandons her. Fairy tales like "Cinderella" and "Mother Holle" also employ such contrasts between the mother's protection of her biological daughter(s) and her hatred for her stepdaughter. Similarly "The Juniper Tree" contrasts a mother's love for her own daughter with hatred of her stepson. And in "Brother and Sister" the evil stepmother whose cruelty forced the siblings to leave home reappears after her stepdaughter's marriage to a king, determined to kill her and place her own daughter in the marriage bed.

Subjected to Mrs. Bellmont's ferocious cruelty, Frado is sustained and protected by an older wise woman, Aunt Abby. Later other motherly women such as Mrs. Walker and Allida, whom Frado calls Aunt J., offer her a temporary home and help support her. In Grimms' tales a fairy godmother rescues Sleeping Beauty from a prospective death; in their "Cinderella" the helpful spirit is not a fairy godmother, but rather Cinderella's dead mother. Both the fairy tales and *Our Nig* pose the question how a girl like Frado is to grow to maturity and assume her own identity as a woman without a caring role model to guide her. As we shall see, both Frado's and Harriet Wilson's experiences of marriage and motherhood appear to replicate the failures of Mag Smith.

A common feature of numerous fairy tales is the lesson that girls have to labor at endless domestic chores. Spinning, tending animals, carrying firewood or water, cooking, and cleaning figure among the tasks that the miller's daughter must perform for the king in "Rumpelstilskin," Snow White for the seven dwarfs, Gretel for the witch, or Cinderella for her stepmother and stepsisters. These other women may torment the girl with meaningless extra labor. Cinderella's stepmother, for example, throws peas and lentils into the ashes and insists that she pick out every one before she can go to the ball. In much the same way Mrs. Bellmont insists that Frado bring in smaller kindling wood and threatens to beat her for not finding it even when there is none to be had.

In fairy tales such as "Hansel and Gretel" and "Cinderella," animals often figure as helpers; here it is the dog Fido who proves to be Frado's most faithful companion and comforter. In one important scene, Mrs. Bellmont, who resists James's insistence that Frado sit and eat like a member of the family, orders the girl to eat from her own used plate as a way of humiliating her. Fairy tales such as "Goldilocks," "Frog King," and "Snow White" use eating from another's plate as a symbol of joining a household, or attempting to do so.

Here Mrs. Bellmont purposely subverts James's intent to have Frado join the family and insists on denigrating her by forcing Frado to take her used plate. Frado, sensitive to the insult Mrs. Bellmont intends, cleverly turns the tables by having Fido lick the plate clean first. In so doing she demonstrates that her cruel mistress is more distasteful and revolting to her than a dog.

Often the wicked stepmother's struggle against a girl is exacerbated or triggered by the older woman's reaction to the girl's beauty or youthful vigor. Snow White and Rapunzel, for instance, are thrust out of their homes when they reach puberty. In *Our Nig* the sadistic torture Mrs. Bellmont inflicts upon Frado encompasses a current of sexual rivalry. Frado's beauty strikes men at once. First Seth Shipley (the partner of Frado's widowed mother) appraises her value: "Frado's six years old and pretty . . . and white folks'll say so. She'd be a prize somewhere" (17). Jack Bellmont is aware of Frado's girlish attractiveness as soon as she arrives in his home. When family members debate what to do with this abandoned child, he says: "She's real handsome and bright, and not very black, either" (25).

To mask the beauty of this girl who intrudes into her home, the stepmother tries to make her ugly, though the girl's virtue and goodness shine through, as does Cinderella's beauty beneath the ashes and soot of the hearth. A similar fate befalls the haughty princess in "King Thrushbeard," who is punished for rejecting marriage suitors by being given to a beggar. Dressed as a kitchen maid, she toils in a palace until her beggar-husband, perceiving that she has learned humility, throws off his disguise and acknowledges her publicly as his queen. In "All Fur" (sometimes called "Donkey-Skin") a princess whose father desires her incestuously escapes and cloaks herself in fur and soot to disguise her beauty until she can choose a suitable marriage partner. Likewise in *Our Nig* Frado's beauty and growing sexual attractiveness become the target of Mrs. Bellmont's determination to destroy her girlhood. She purposely insists that Frado work outdoors without shielding herself from the sun, in order to darken her skin. She dresses Frado in rags; the girl begins school barefoot and wearing a cut-down overcoat of Jack's. The clothing suggests that she and Jack are kindred spirits, within the limits of gender and race. Both succeed in defying Mrs. Bellmont, and Jack clearly admires Frado's courage in doing so.

Later Frado is forced to wear inappropriate clothing to evening religious services with Aunt Abby and is mocked by the neighbors at James's funeral because his widow, Susan, can only find a bonnet with an inappropriate pink ribbon for her to wear. Wrong clothing masks her loyal and loving nature, so that others think ill of her, and she is forced to doubt herself. After Mary's death in Baltimore, Frado considers leaving the family, but reflects, "Who would take her? Mrs. B. had always represented her as ugly. Perhaps everyone thought her so. Then no one would take her. She was black, no one would love her" (108). After a decade in the Bellmont household, she has internalized their conception of both her outward appearance and her own worth. During the first summer of her freedom from servitude with the Bellmonts, Frado, who has only "one decent dress," studies "what poor samples of apparel" she owns, and uses her first wages for "garments necessary for health and cleanliness" (117). Acquiring better clothing revives her self-esteem, albeit only briefly, as her health fails again, ruined by years of overwork and beatings at the hands of Mrs. Bellmont.

The stepmother's treatment of the girl in fairy tales demonstrates that, as an aging woman, she feels threatened by this young beauty and is determined to punish her by destroying her sexual allure. Julia Stern writes, "Frado's erotic desirability threatens to destabilize her mistress's position as the most compelling female in the household."[6] Fairy tales represent sexual allure in symbolic terms. For example, the wicked queen tempts Snow White with a comb, then with the stay laces needed for a corset to cinch her growing womanly figure. Hair is the most powerful symbol of sexual attractiveness in fairy tales, and in Our Nig. After Rapunzel lets down her hair to bring up the young prince who becomes her lover, the old sorceress cuts it off. Frado is first described at the age of six as "a beautiful mulatto, with long, curly black hair, and handsome roguish eyes, sparkling with an exuberance of spirit almost beyond her years" (17). Frado's school companions, with the notable exception of her rival, Mary, admire and like her for her cheerfulness, her daring, and her pranks. So too do the Bellmonts' farm workers: "The men employed on the farm were always glad to hear her prattle; she was a great favorite with them" (37). As Frado grows into puberty, her black curls seem to symbolize her pert, defiant demeanor, so Mrs. Bellmont shaves her head, not only as a way of humiliating her, but as a way of reducing her attractiveness to men. When Jack Bellmont returns home after a long absence, he says,

"Where are your curls, Fra?"
"Your mother cut them off."
"Thought you were getting handsome, did she?" (70)

Jack's comment demonstrates that he is still aware of Frado's attractiveness and realizes that her youth, her strength, and her beauty threaten his mother, who feels age undermining her own power and dominance. Consistent with Aunt Abby's role as the archetypal Christian, she sees not the shorn head or the latent sexual being in Frado, but "a soul to save," when she beholds the child: "Many of lesser piety would scorn to present so doleful a figure; Mrs. B. had shaved her glossy ringlets; and in her coarse cloth gown and ancient bonnet, she was anything but an enticing object" (68–69). True to her interest in the soul, "Aunt Abby looked within" beyond the inappropriate, demeaning clothing and the shorn head.

When Frado meets Samuel (an abolitionist lecturer who claims to be a former slave), Wilson writes, "Was it strange . . . that he should toy with her shining curls, feel proud to provoke her to smile and expose the ivory concealed by thin, ruby lips" (126). This description echoes that of Snow White's hair, skin, and lips. It is worth remarking that the recipe which later helps Frado earn a living is a hair dye, restoring gray hair to its earlier color. Jane, the invalid daughter who opposed her mother's wishes to marry for love, reappears years later with "silver locks in place of auburn tresses" but retains the love of her husband (130). Thus hair in this novel, as in fairy tales, symbolizes a woman's power and sexual attraction.

Finally, like a fairy tale, Frado's story nears its conclusion assuring the reader that the villain has been justly punished; Gretel pushes the witch into her own oven, and Snow White's wicked stepmother attends her wedding and is forced to dance in shoes that have been heated over red hot coals "until she fell down dead." We read that Mrs. Bellmont became so irritable not even her own children could stand her, and finally died "after an agony in death unspeakable" (130).

II

The similarities between fairy tales and Harriet Wilson's novel — girls' labor, the stepmother figure, the importance of hair and appearance — highlight the importance of gender in *Our Nig*. As Jack Zipes demonstrates in his introduction to Grimms' fairy tales, final versions of those tales revised by Wilhelm Grimm throughout his lifetime were purposely reshaped to highlight the Protestant work ethic. Their moral teachings, often directed at girls, were intended to prepare them for a lifetime of duty and hard work. Similarly, in the real world of midnineteenth-century New Hampshire, gender and the vulnerability of growing up female were the determining factors in girls' development. In insisting on the centrality of gender, I diverge from Henry Louis Gates, who writes in his Introduction that, "The subplot of love, marriage, childbirth, and betrayal" — features shared with the sentimental novel — only appear in the novel's last chapter, 'The Winding up of the Matter'" (xxviii). Gates's emphasis on race, which is undoubtedly the locus of oppression in the novel, causes him to underestimate the importance of gender.

In fact, the novel begins and ends with parallel stories of *women's* poverty

that shape the plot of "love, marriage, childbirth, and betrayal." Wilson herself calls attention to the similarities between Mag Smith and her daughter
in the epigraph for the chapter containing Frado's marriage and motherhood: the epigraph cites the Book of Ecclesiastes: "Nothing new under the
sun" (126). Just as Mag Smith, a single mother, abandons Frado, hoping that
the child can grow up in the hostile environment of the Bellmont household,
Frado, whose identity dissolves into that of Harriet Wilson, has to make the
same decision twenty years later, and leaves her son with a white family: nothing new indeed. Although Allida's letter in the appendix says that Frado's son
is kindly treated, Barbara White's research into Harriet Wilson's biography
shows that "the Wilson boy" was supported by the town of Milford between
1857 and 1859.[7] He was living at the Hillsborough county farm in Goffstown
(Wilson's native Milford lies in Hillsborough county), an environment at least
as harmful as the Bellmont household, when he died in 1860 at the age of
seven — fewer than six months after the novel was published. In short, despite
her courage, her literacy, and the milestone achievement of publishing the first
African American woman's novel in the United States, Harriet Wilson succeeded little better than Mag Smith in supporting herself and her child.[8] The
fact that she both begins and ends her story with the desperate plight of wid-
ows unable to provide for their minor children calls us to look more closely at
the link between *gender* and poverty as a central issue in the novel, and in Harriet Wilson's life.

It's true that neither Harriet Wilson nor her narrator Frado explicitly mentions gender as an obstacle or as a determinant of Frado's hardships, probably
because the most powerful figure in the novel is a white woman, Mrs. Bellmont. Given her dominance over her household, it would be hard to make a
case for women as the weaker sex in this setting, although she is forced to ca-
pitulate when her husband insists Frado attend school. Mrs. Bellmont ma-
nipulates younger women — who clearly are the weaker sex — throughout the
novel. First she tries to persuade her invalid daughter Jane to marry a wealthy
neighbor, Henry Reed, whom Jane does not love. And when Jack Bellmont
marries an orphan, Jenny, his mother schemes to separate her from him, ma-
nipulating events to create the appearance that Jack had courted another
woman and that Jenny is unfaithful to Jack with one of his nearby cousins. Although both of these schemes ultimately fail, and Frado sees through them,
Mrs. Bellmont's machinations effectively counteract the appearance of wom-
en's helplessness or subordinate position in this milieu.

Yet outside the Bellmont household, midnineteenth-century New Hampshire afforded girls and unmarried women only a precarious livelihood. Wilson's autobiographical novel offers eloquent testimony about living conditions

for women in small-town New England. For both Frado and her mother, Mag Smith, being a woman means being poor. The greatest predictor of poverty in nineteenth-century New Hampshire was gender. That is, women were more likely to be poor and to become town paupers than men. There were five reasons for this difference: first, at every stage of life, daughters were worth less than sons. When family resources were scarce, boys were better fed, better educated, and better provided for through property ownership. Second, when work was available to women either before or during marriage, they earned half or less than half of what men earned, even for the same work, such as teaching school. Third, women outlived men, outlived adult children who might have provided for them, and fell into poverty in old age. Fourth, sons inherited property, like John Bellmont, who owns the family homestead, while his unmarried sister, Aunt Abby, is only entitled to live there, with no provision for making a living from the farm itself.[9] Fifth, the greatest risk factor for poverty was unmarried motherhood, either out-of-wedlock births, abandonment, or widowhood, the trap that seals the fate of both Mag Smith and Frado herself. At every turn, Wilson expresses women's fate in economic terms.

Men, even those who are black (both Jim and his work-mate Seth Shipley) are able to support themselves, Mag Smith, and Mag's two children — at least until a period of uncommon hardship. Julia Stern observes that "a free black male, . . . though socially degraded by his color, is nevertheless empowered by his sex. Economically, such a man would outrank almost any Caucasian female."[10] Thus gender, rather than race, is the key determinant of poverty.

Harriet Wilson begins her narrative with Frado's white mother, Mag Smith, who has an affair with a white man "far above her" whose voice is "alluring her onward and upward." "She thought she could ascend to him and become an equal." She surrenders to him "a priceless gem," which he "garners as a trophy"—her virginity (6).[11] When he leaves her unmarried and pregnant—her child dies shortly after birth—she has fallen even further down the social ladder than where she ranked before. The loss of her sexual value, her virginity, is suggested in her name Mag, which may allude to Magdalene, or Mary Magdalene, whose Biblical name usually evokes promiscuity. In her devalued condition as fallen woman, she descends to a status within reach of a black man, who would earlier have been considered far beneath her. Note here the ironic discrepancy between social status — white woman outranks black man — and economic status — she must depend on him for support.

The black man, Jim, who takes pity on Mag Smith supplies her with food and firewood, as Wilson deliberately frames their relationship in economic terms; hunger and cold weather overcome Mag's initial resistance to his black skin. His opener in proposing marriage to her is "How's the wood, Mag?" Followed by "Anything to eat in the house?" hardly a romantic overture. "You's down low enough," Jim asserts, as he suggests, "'Sposin' we marry!" (12). The narrator names Mag's marriage of necessity "another step down the ladder of infamy" (13). Jim nonetheless considers Mag "a prize" and "his treasure — a white wife" (14). Their children, "two pretty mulattos," represent "an additional charge" that "time levied" upon him (14). When he became ill, Mag fulfilled her contractual responsibilities and "cared for him only as a means to subserve her own comfort; yet she nursed him faithfully and true to marriage vows until death released her" (15). Wilson's language: "treasure," "charge," "levied," — underscores the economic basis of Mag's marriage contract. We never learn Jim's last name, nor Frado's, and Mag Smith has no other name. Unlike Mrs. Bellmont or later characters known as Mrs. Hoggs and Mrs. Walker, Mag Smith gains no status through her marriage with Jim, and never attains the respectability of being called Mrs.

Again, a black man, Seth Shipley, appears after Jim's death to offer Mag "a weekly allowance," and they pool their meager resources to live together. Mag does not marry Seth, perhaps because he is black and marriage to him would not elevate or benefit her in any way. Mag "asked not the rite of civilization or Christianity" before living with Seth; their co-habitation is described as "perpetual infamy." Mag herself refers to her own children as "the black devils" (16). We hear almost nothing more of Frado's sibling, neither name nor gender, but Frado is abandoned to the "right she-devil" Mrs. Bellmont, and Mag Smith deceives her as well as her own daughter with the expectation that she will return to fetch her child.

Within the Bellmonts' white world, too, marriage is framed as a financial transaction that increases a woman's power and status. Aunt Abby as a "maiden sister" is always referred to by her first name, because she remains single, and her dependency appears reinforced by "Aunt," the term identifying the relationship that allows her to live in her brother's house. Because she occupies such an inferior position, she seldom dares to challenge her sister-in-law, *Mrs.* Bellmont.

Jane Bellmont, a semi-invalid daughter of the house, is courted by a wealthy neighbor, Henry Reed. Mrs. Bellmont encourages the match, although Jane does not love Henry: she "knew there was silver in the purse; she would not have Jane too sentimental" (56). Money triumphs over feeling in choosing a spouse. Jane defies her mother's materialism, secures the support of her father and Aunt Abby, follows her heart, and marries a newcomer, George Means, introduced into the household through Aunt Abby.

When Frado's best ally, Jack, gets married, he does so away from home, perhaps because he chooses a penniless orphan. The title of this chapter,

"Marriage Again," prompts us to consider earlier marriages in the book, most directly Jane's marriage to George Means. We might also look back to Mag Smith's economic alliance with Jim, and reflect upon the marriage between the Bellmont parents, where the wife clearly rules the household, and the loving marriage between James Bellmont and his wife Susan. Mrs. Bellmont scorns Jack's marriage to the orphan Jenny as a bad bargain:

> "Hadn't she any property? What did you marry her for," asked his mother. "Oh, she's worth a million dollars, mother, though not a cent of it is in money."

To Mrs. Bellmont, the bride's lack of wealth is even grounds for dissolving her son's marriage: "Jack! What do you want to bring such a poor being into the family for? You'd better stay here at home, and let your wife go" (111–12).

While Mrs. Bellmont's materialism is one of her many repugnant characteristics, Frado's vulnerable situation at the end of the book reminds us that marrying *without* thought of financial security can increase her hardship. Like her mother, she too is seduced by hope. She meets and falls in love with a black man who presents himself as a fugitive slave and abolitionist speaker. He marries her, fathers a son, leaves her, returns briefly, and then leaves again and dies of fever in New Orleans. Like Mag Smith, Frado, with a child to provide for, is weaker and more vulnerable after this marriage than she was before.

Outside marriage, what other means of earning a livelihood were open to Mag Smith or to Frado? As Harriet Wilson relates her struggles with women's economic choices, she abandons the role of Frado, and the fictional guise of *Our Nig* fades. Building upon the biographical research of Barbara A. White, P. Gabrielle Foreman, and Reginald H. Pitts, and my own work as a town historian, I will explore Wilson's dilemma as a working woman in small town New Hampshire.

For nineteenth-century New England women, property ownership, as well as a stable marriage, was the key to economic security. Wives often kept the income from sales of butter they made themselves, mittens or stockings they knitted at home, or eggs from their own chickens, while the larger sources of farm income, such as sales of livestock, firewood, maple syrup, and crops, were considered men's property. We learn that Frado has made butter and cheese that supplied the physician (Mrs. Bellmont's brother) who later attends her when she is sick, but of course Frado has no claim to the profits of this labor (120).

One of the common occupations for unmarried girls was teaching school. (Until after the Second World War, New Hampshire women who married forfeited their positions to men.) Teachers might be as young as sixteen, and needed just an eighth-grade education during this time period. According to an 1848 report by the Commissioner of Common Schools in New Hampshire, male teachers were paid an average of $13.56 per month, while women received an average of $5.59. More women taught in the summer terms when men worked as farm laborers, while in wintertime the genders were about evenly balanced. Frado meets a kind-hearted young teacher, Miss Marsh, in the summer school, but in winter a master, whose cigars she uses to fill his desk drawer with smoke and amuse her companions. In Milford as in most rural towns, far more "scholars" attended school in winter (493) than in summer (232), and problems with rowdy boys provided some rationale for hiring more male school*masters* to discipline them. Thus six men and four young women taught in Milford's eight school districts in winter, but only nine young women in the summer. Milford's schoolteachers enjoyed higher than the state's average earnings, probably because the town's mills and other industries competed for workers. Yet the wage gap between men and women remained high: average monthly earnings for men were $19.36, compared to around a third that amount, just $6.63 per month, for women.[12] Frado attends only three three-month terms of school before Mrs. Bellmont declares it enough, effectively closing the door to this livelihood.

Frado cycles in and out of poverty after ending her servitude with the Bellmonts at the age of eighteen. She works briefly for a Mrs. Moore and in the home of a clergyman. This occupation, "domestic," the most common for undereducated young women, paid significantly better than teaching, though the work was more laborious and lasted far longer than the school day. According to wage data from the 1860 census for Goffstown (where Wilson gave birth to her son at the county farm) a "female domestic with board" earned average weekly wages of $3.25. In comparison, a male laborer with board earned one dollar a day, a male carpenter without board earned $1.75 per day, and a male farmhand with board earned $23 per month. At $13 a month, a female domestic earned just over half as much as a farmhand, but more than a female teacher ($7.83 per month without board in 1855).[13]

Mag Smith's work, when she has any, is domestic work or washing for families such as the Bellmonts. "Foreigners who cheapened toil and clamored for a livelihood competed with her," Wilson writes, shortly before Mag accepts marriage with Jim (8). An economic depression struck New England during the presidency of Andrew Jackson (1829–1837) and lasted for several years. In his *History of the Town of Milford* George Ramsdell notes for 1837 "Very hard times. But little business being done, prices of necessaries of life high and large numbers of people out of employment."[14] The term "foreigners" in Mag's usage probably connotes people from other states rather than the French Canadians and Irish who arrived after 1850 to work in Milford's textile mills.

Ramsdell's *History of the Town of Milford* lists numerous manufacturers and mills in Harriet Wilson's hometown in the early 1850s: textile mills, saw and grist mills, mills manufacturing axe helves, Eagle plows, carriages, boots and shoes, furniture, and North Star cooking stoves.[15] *Our Nig* tells us nothing about these industries. Instead Frado learns sewing after leaving the Bellmont household, and makes better clothing for herself as well as working for others. The U.S. census for Milford does not identify tailors there in 1850, but two appear in nearby Goffstown, where Wilson gave birth to her son in 1852. Wages there were considerably higher than those of mill workers. W. S. Richards of Goffstown paid the six women in his tailor shop eight dollars a month, while William Thorp paid $12.50, a handsome sum, until we compare it to the $27.50 he paid each of his two male employees per month.

While dressmaking appears a good livelihood for women, Frado experienced her greatest prosperity while making straw hats. The letter from Allida published in the Appendix says, "Through the instrumentality of an itinerant colored lecturer, she was brought to W———, Mass. . . . where women work straw with their hands" (133). In the home of Mrs. Walker she learns the trade of "straw sewer" and the "art of making hats." The "Chronology" accompanying the 2002 Vintage edition of the novel offers information about the locations of straw sewing but few details about the trade itself (lxxiii–lxxiv). Hats were sometimes made of rye straw from local farms. The straw had first to be flattened with a knife against a hard surface, then braided and sewn into concentric circles and shaped into hats. Since the flat straw braid was only about an eighth of an inch wide, it took countless yards to make a woman's bonnet or a man's broad-brimmed hat. In some towns, local stores sold palm leaf to women sewers and took finished hats in trade for other goods.

The advantage of this type of cottage industry was that it kept the woman at home, under the social protection of a father or husband. At the same time, her work could be combined with traditional women's tasks such as baking or minding children. The disadvantages were eyestrain, repetitive motion problems, sitting for long periods of time indoors, and a low rate of pay that could be augmented by working faster or longer hours through the piecework system. The owners who brought women straw to braid or braided straw to sew into hats were all men, and they returned at regular intervals to collect the finished work. In other words, men owned the means of production and profit while women did the labor.

Women braiding and sewing straw hats in Alstead and Swanzey (both in Cheshire county in southwestern New Hampshire) earned 90 cents to $1 for finished hats, but their income varied with the pace of their work. Nevertheless, the livelihood was one of the most lucrative available to New England women who were Harriet Wilson's contemporaries. Sally Loomis, an impoverished widow with five children who lived in Alstead, wrote to her daughter Mary in 1835, "You could clothe yourself well if you like to braid." Her daughter took up the craft, and her mother wrote later, "Mary has got her five new dresses and a new cloak . . . and six pair of shoes. Her cloak coast eight dollars and her black silk dress eleven dollars."[16] These were considerable riches for women at this time period, as we can see by comparing clothing prices to weekly earnings. Mary Loomis used her fine clothes to best advantage, marrying a successful farmer and breaking out of poverty for good.

At the end of chapter 11 Harriet Wilson briefly describes Frado's work in straw sewing, but devotes more space to the satisfaction she gains from living with the woman who teaches her to make hats and their sharing reading and learning together. It is unclear how much time passes before Samuel, the black man whom she marries, arrives and seems to present a secure future in marriage, which turns out to be a vain hope. In any case, marriage and the move back to Milford put an end to her self-sufficiency and relative prosperity. By the end of her novel, Harriet Wilson reveals herself as one and the same with Frado, and has fallen upon such hard times that she gives birth to her son at the county farm. Frado follows in her mother's footsteps, along a path of marriage, pregnancy, birth, and destitution.[17]

Her arrival at the county farm marks a return to the desperate poverty of Frado's earliest years and calls us to explore pauperism and welfare in mid-nineteenth-century New Hampshire. When Mag Smith abandons Frado at the Bellmonts', they discuss what to do with the child. "Send her to the County House," says Mary (25). Instead, Frado endures twelve years of brutal drudgery in the Bellmont household, and is forced to return there after a few years of independence because her health is broken. Mrs. Bellmont's own brother, a doctor, is called in to attend her. Mrs. Bellmont neither thanks him in a sisterly manner, nor offers any money. Instead she says, "We shan't pay you for doctoring her. You may look to the town for that, sir," indicating that she will report Frado as a town pauper (120). If paupers were physically able to work, their board was struck off to the lowest bidder, meaning that the town paid a minimal sum to a homeowner who agreed to provide food, shelter, and some clothing for the paupers in exchange for their labor.

Next Frado lives with "two maidens (old) who had principle enough to earn the money a charitable public dispenses" (122). Such arrangements enabled unmarried women to earn some income, provided they owned their own house. After two years in their home, these women grow weary of caring for

her and request that Frado be moved. She spends a year under similar conditions with Mrs. Hoggs, "a lover of gold and silver" whose name suggests her
greed (122). Frado recovers enough to move to Massachusetts where she learns
to make straw hats, enabling her "to cast off the unpleasant charities of the
public" (124).

Left destitute and pregnant after Samuel abandons her, Frado has no
choice but to return to Milford. In New Hampshire towns, paupers left without family or wealth were supported at the expense of the town where they
were born. Selectmen "warned out of town" anyone suspected of becoming
a town charge, and went to great lengths, including lawsuits, to return likely
paupers to the place of their birth to avoid the costs of their upkeep. Because
of these welfare arrangements, Frado is forced to return to Milford (Singleton) to claim support from her native town.

To provide for the elderly and the mentally or physically disabled who
were unable to earn their daily bread, or whose condition made it unlikely
that any homeowner would take them in, towns and later counties operated
poor farms, as Milford did between 1831 and 1868. The town or county poor
farm operated as subsistence agriculture, where inmates cut firewood, raised
livestock and gardens, produced their own food, and exchanged any surplus
for the purchase of clothing and other essentials. The 1850 roster of the Milford poor house affirms that the feminization of poverty was not a twentieth-
century phenomenon; the institution housed four elderly women, one elderly
man, one male laborer, a ten-year-old mulatto, Henry Blanchard, and a thirty-
five-year-old mother with her two children. The cost of maintaining a pauper, either at the county farm or in a private home, at this time was figured
at about $1.50 to $2 per week, which towns paid to county farms or to private
homeowners. When we compare this cost of maintaining paupers to women's
wages for teaching school or domestic labor, we see that even when unmarried
women did find work, they were barely able to support themselves above the
poverty line.

Frado/Harriet Wilson gave birth to her son at the county farm in Goffstown in 1852. Far larger than a town poor farm, the county institution supported about two hundred paupers in 1860, although only eighty-five lived
there in June of 1860 when the census counted them. These statistics remind us
that work was a seasonal activity, and that monthly wages earned in the summer had to support workers through the winter as well. Farm laborers were
thrown out of work in the winter, except for those cutting firewood or gathering maple syrup in early spring. Some men could then fall back on teaching school for the winter term, displacing young women. On a larger scale,
mills like those described in Ramsdell's Milford history fell idle in winter, be-

cause their water wheels iced up and ceased to run. Mill hands were simply laid off. (Not until the mid to late 1860s did mills install turbines, which were somewhat better protected from ice.) For these reasons, the threat of poverty loomed larger in the winter.

An examination of the 1860 census figures for the Hillsborough county farm in Goffstown shows that it was a catch-all for people who were blind, deaf, injured, insane, "idiotic" (mentally disabled), and intemperate (alcoholics). In June it housed only eight men of working age (twenty to fifty) but twenty-one women. Over a third of its residents were children like George Mason Wilson. Barbara White's valuable research details what life would have been like for Harriet's son, who lived much of his seven years at the county farm in Goffstown, where he died in February 1860.

New research by Foreman and Pitts locates Harriet Wilson nearby in June of that year, living in the adjacent city of Manchester in the boardinghouse of Mrs. Sophia Young, and suggests that she may have been employed in a cotton mill (the census lists her occupation as weaver).[18] Further examination of the 1860 Manchester census furnishes additional details about textile mill work, which had become one of the most common forms of employment for young unmarried women. Let us assume that this Harriet Wilson, weaver (no notation appears for race), is indeed Harriet E. Adams Wilson. If so, she reduced her age from thirty-five to twenty-eight, undoubtedly to fit in with the other twenty-four unmarried women living in the boardinghouse, who ranged in age from sixteen through their twenties, with only a handful above the age of thirty. The largest employer of female weavers in Manchester's Ward 2, where the boardinghouse was located, was the Amoskeag Manufacturing Company, whose huge complex of red brick buildings still stands beside the Merrimack River. The 1860 industrial census tells us that this mill wove cotton fabrics: sheeting, drilling, ticking, denim, and flannel. It also manufactured steam fire engines, castings, and machinery; we can assume that most of the 525 men employed by the company worked in this branch of the factory, where they earned an average of $38 per month. By comparison, the 1,600 women and children who tended the looms and spindles earned average wages of $18.75 per month. Again, these figures highlight women's weaker earning power and hence their greater vulnerability to poverty. The price of board to a laboring man (no figures are given for women) was $2.50 per week. Even assuming that women could board somewhat more cheaply, and that average wages of $18.75 per month are skewed by the census inclusion of children in this category, we see that women earned only half as much as men, and that about half their income went immediately to boardinghouse expenses. No wonder then that employment at the Manchester cotton mill did not enable Harriet Wilson to take her son out of the county farm in adjacent Goffstown and bring him to live with her, where he might have escaped disease and an early death.

Although critics' enthusiasm for her milestone achievement has led them to praise Wilson's success, her effort to rescue her son through her writing proved a failure, a failure that hinges upon gender.[19] Wilson appeals to her "colored brethren" to buy the book to rescue her from poverty, yet surely she knew she would need to sell the book to white women. They had more leisure than blacks of either gender and were more likely than white men to read a woman's story, patterned to some extent on sentimental novels. But Wilson alienated the segment of the book-buying public most crucial to her financial success by making the most significant white woman in the book, Mrs. Bellmont, into a real "she-devil," thus violating any tendency of white women readers to identify with her. In the final analysis, her attempt to support herself and her son by selling her novel failed because of the deep scars left by the very experiences she wished to narrate.[20]

NOTES

1. Henry Louis Gates, Jr., "Introduction" to Harriet E. Wilson, *Our Nig; or, Sketches from the Life of a Free Black* (New York: Vintage, 2002): lx–lxi. Subsequent references to the text of the novel come from this edition.

2. P. Gabrielle Foreman and Reginald H. Pitts, "Introduction" to Harriet E. Wilson, *Our Nig; or, Sketches from the Life of a Free Black* (New York: Penguin, 2005), xxxi.

3. For a discussion of the didactic purpose of the Brothers Grimms' reworking of such tales, see Jack Zipes, "Once There Were Two Brothers Named Grimm," which appears as "Introduction" in *The Complete Fairy Tales of the Brothers Grimm* (New York: Bantam, 1987): xxii–xxiii.

4. Bruno Bettelheim's *The Uses of Enchantment* (New York: Random House, 1975) includes helpful interpretations of the stepmother theme and of "Hansel and Gretel,""Snow White," and "Cinderella."

5. In the novel Wilson gives Frado's age as six at the time of her abandonment. However, if Foreman and Pitts's assumption is correct that the Margaret Ann Smith who died in Boston on March 27, 1830, after a drunken brawl with her husband was indeed the mother of Harriet E. Wilson, then Frado/Harriet would have been scarcely five years old when her mother abandoned her. See their "Introduction," xxviii.

6. Julia Stern,"Excavating Genre in *Our Nig*," *American Literature* 67 (September 1995): 444.

7. Barbara A. White, "Afterword," to Wilson, *Our Nig* (Vintage, 2002): x–xiii.

8. Recent research by Foreman and Pitts in the 2005 Penguin edition traces

Harriet Wilson's eventual success as an entrepreneur selling hair dye and as a Boston Spiritualist lecturer who later married a white man eighteen years her junior. Nevertheless, she wrote her novel as a widow and a single mother and according to Foreman and Pitts continued to speak out about children, poverty, and education throughout her career as a lecturer (xl, xli).

9. The model for Aunt Abby was not in fact an unmarried sister but the widow Sally Hayward Blanchard.

10. Stern, "Excavating Genre," 458.

11. Foreman and Pitts note the "economically deterministic" tone of *Our Nig*, but without connecting it to gender-specific issues such as virginity and marriage (xxxii). For a discussion of women's chastity as property, see Laurel Thatcher Ulrich's *Good Wives* (New York: Vintage, 1991), 93–94. In insisting on the sexual liaison as an economic transaction, my interpretation differs from that of Cynthia J. Davis, who observes that Wilson represents a white woman (Mag Smith) rather than a black woman as sexual in order to challenge "the widespread racist notion that black women, and only black women, were innately promiscuous." "Speaking the Body's Pain: Harriet Wilson's *Our Nig*," *African American Review* 27 (1993): 395.

12. *Report of the Commissioner of Common Schools to the Legislature of New Hampshire June Session 1848* (Concord: Butterfield and Hill, 1848): 58, 43.

13. Original handwritten New Hampshire census ledgers are kept in the state archives in Concord, N.H.

14. George Ramsdell, *A History of the Town of Milford* (Concord: Rumford Press, 1901): 196–97.

15. Ibid., 212.

16. Helen H. Frink, *Alstead Through the Years* (Alstead: Alstead Historical Society 1992): 92.

17. John Ernest finds in Frado's story of love and marriage echoes of her mother's: "But whereas Mag's love led her to the hope of transcending class divisions, Frado's *extends from* what proves to be an equally naive belief in the inherent community of race." "Economies of Identity: Harriet E. Wilson's *Our Nig*," *PMLA* 109 (1994): 429. Angelyn Mitchell describes the novel as "a maternal text" because of its "concern for and characterization of women and children of all races." "Her Side of His Story: A Feminist Analysis of Two Nineteenth-Century Antebellum Novels," *American Literary Realism* 24 (1992): 16.

18. This identification of Wilson's whereabouts seems more plausible than the Gates edition's identification of a black fifty-two-year-old Boston widow born in Fredericksburg, Virginia (xvii). Harriet Wilson often represented herself as younger than her true age, but not older. Furthermore, Manchester borders Goffstown, where her son lived at the county poor farm.

19. Claudia Tate views Wilson's asserted purpose in publishing her novel somewhat differently, as "a rationale for the self-assertion of writing—which even white women of this era were anxious about claiming" and suggests instead that Wilson cloaks "the self-interest of professional literary creation" in "the selflessness of

mother love" (*Domestic Allegories of Political Desire: The Black Heroine's Text at the Turn of the Century* (New York: Oxford, 1992): 42.

20. Foreman and Pitts's discovery of Harriet Wilson's later career as a seller of hair dye and a Spiritualist lecturer provides an epilogue to her story in which she finally transcended, at least partially, the limits of gender. They write that she ultimately found success in Spiritualism, a radical movement "that appropriated space for *women's* expression and leadership" [italics mine], xxxix.

PART III

"A Faithful Band of Supporters and Defenders": Personal Reflections

Losing Equilibrium

Harriet E. Wilson, Frado, and Me

John Ernest

I

I FIRST MET Harriet E. Wilson far from New Hampshire — sometime between 1989 and 1992, when I was an assistant professor at Florida International University in Miami. Through the years (well over a century) and across the miles, her book came to me, and it is safe to say that I began my relationship with *Our Nig* and its author in ignorance. I valued greatly the detailed introduction to the book provided by Henry Louis Gates, Jr., but I still felt that I knew next to nothing about either Wilson or her narrative of "the life of a free black, in a two-story white house, north." The book was unlike any other I had read by that point, and all of my training as a literary scholar should have prepared me to dismiss the book, as one scholar did, as subliterary.[1] The writing seemed rough, the point of view shifted, the narrative of Frado's life was at times detailed and at times barely suggestive, and the book seemed a confusing blend of some conventions one would usually encounter in fiction and some that were associated with slave narratives. But although I have no clear memory of my first reading of the book, I don't think I was inclined to dismiss it, for the book soon captured all of my attention. I wrote and presented a conference paper on the book in 1992, that paper developed into an essay that was published in 1994, and that essay led me to write a book that was published in 1995. Along the way, I had redefined myself from a scholar in nineteenth-century American literature (with almost an exclusive focus on white writers) to a student of African American literature, history, and culture.

My relationship with Harriet Wilson began, then, as the most important relationships generally do, in ignorance. I understood very little about the experiences and the world her book portrayed, and I found myself at the beginning of a gradual realization that I didn't really learn *how* to read this book and countless others until *after* I completed my formal education. After all, I received a Ph.D. in American literature without ever being asked to read more than a handful of African American writers. As is often the case, my students proved to be the best teachers, and the teaching I did as a graduate student convinced me that my education was woefully incomplete. And so I began to read on my own. My teachers were writers from the nineteenth century: Frederick Douglass, Frances E. W. Harper, Martin R. Delany, Harriet Jacobs, William Wells Brown, and Harriet E. Wilson. And as I learned to read the many books, poems, essays, speeches, and newspaper articles these writers produced — and as I discovered that I had much to learn in this regard — I came to appreciate my self-conscious ignorance as a much better guide than my earlier appreciation for the security of knowledge. Eventually, I came to appreciate the guidance, the demands, of ignorance in the way that Barbara Johnson presents it in her book *A World of Difference*. "If I perceive my ignorance," Johnson explains, "as a gap in knowledge instead of an imperative that changes the very nature of what I think I know, then I do not truly experience my ignorance."[2]

If I have succeeded thus far in being a responsible student of African American literature, history, and culture, as I hope I have, it is only because I began what amounted to my second graduate education, the one that followed my degree, with a strong sense of my own ignorance — the confusion I felt when I was so deeply drawn to Wilson's book and so initially incapable of explaining my response. My education in African American literature has led me to question almost everything that I have been taught; it has led me to distrust much of what we call knowledge; and it has led me to stray from the well-marked map of American literary history that I had, in effect, received with my degree. For I do not believe that we basically had the story right and that now we simply need to add to the mix white women writers, African American writers, Asian American writers, or any of the wide world of writers so long omitted and neglected. I do not believe that the interpretive tools I've acquired over the years are always useful for or even appropriate to the task at hand; I do not believe that my well-marked map of the literary landscape will serve me well, and I find myself trying to piece together a map without knowing quite either where I am or where I want to go.

In *Our Nig*, Wilson provided me with a different kind of map, one that I'm still learning how to read.

II

Reading *Our Nig* always takes me back to a few central questions. Is this a novel? Is this an autobiography? Do we even have terms to describe the genre of this book? My point is not simply to question whether this is to be identified as a work of autobiography or as a work of fiction. Rather, my point is to note that the text itself blends the two genres. In other words, this is not merely a matter of deciding, through research, whether this book is an autobiography or a novel, but rather of noting the narrator's own shifting focus and voices throughout the text. Chapters narrated in the third person are headed by chapter titles that identify this as another episode in the life of the writer of this narrative — so that chapters about Frado's experience carry titles that refer to "my mother" or "my father," and the chapter about Frado's entrance into the Bellmont household is headed by the title "A New Home For Me."[3] The narrative tells of the experiences of Frado, Wilson's representative in this story; but Wilson never allows us to view Frado as simply a character in a work of fiction. This is, in other words, a book about the need to turn to fictional representations in order to construct an autobiography. And these questions are important because they have a lot to do with how and why we read this book — for questions about what kind of book this is are also questions about audience, about readers and how they read. Today *we* are the readers of this book, we are its audience, and we are the ones who carry the responsibility for Wilson's commentary on racial identity and social injustice in New Hampshire.

At a very fundamental level, questions about autobiography have to do with the concept of race — not just in *Our Nig* but in any autobiography written in the United States — so it is important to be clear about what race is. Race is a cultural construction based on superficial, observable differences that are given significance over time to serve the economic, political, and social order. That is, race is not biological, and it is not simply a matter of skin color or of general cultural affiliations; it is something that is created and enforced through the manipulation of law, science, politics, history, the media, and every other aspect of society. Of course, one needs to add that race is not simply defined by the dominant culture, for race is also the developing and dynamic response to that complex construction — the traditions, the rhetorical maneuvers, and the ideological methodologies of survival, resistance, and collective self-definition that have developed in certain communities over time. In our culture today, we have a habit of saying that this person or that person just happens to be black, or that someone just happens to be white. But racial identity doesn't just happen. It has been created with great deliberation, it has been enforced at every level of social life, and it is constantly recreated and revised by those whom it most directly affects.

Even in New England, often considered the center of anti-slavery activity, white Americans who resisted the anti-slavery movement (and even many who supported it) tried to contain or, in various ways, eliminate African Americans as a significant presence in the region. As James Brewer Stewart has noted, many of Boston's most prominent white families added "new fortunes to old by linking their assets with those of 'king cotton.' By developing sophisticated textile factories outside Boston that processed vast amounts of raw cotton, these powerful entrepreneurs linked their city's banking, shipping, trading, and investment enterprises to the economy of the slave states." "By the 1840s," Stewart observes, "it had become common to equate Boston's 'lords of the loom' with the 'lords of the lash' who held sway in the Deep South."[4] Not incidental to this economic connection to the South was the developing selective memory and vision by which the presence of slavery and of African Americans generally were removed from New England's vision of itself as a region.

Historian Joanne Pope Melish is particularly instructive on this point in her book *Disowning Slavery: Gradual Emancipation and "Race" in New England, 1780–1860*. "New England whites," Melish notes, "employed an array of strategies to effect the removal" of people of color "and to efface people of color and their history in New England." Melish looks at a wide range of measures by which New England whites tried to render African Americans, along with the history of slavery in New England, invisible:

> Some of these efforts were symbolic: representing people of color as ridiculous or dangerous "strangers" in anecdotes, cartoons, and broadsides; emphasizing slavery and "race" as "southern problems"; characterizing New England slavery as brief and mild, or even denying its having existed; inventing games and instructional problems in which the object was to make "the negroes" disappear; digging up the corpses of people of color. Other efforts aimed to eliminate the presence of living people of color: conducting official roundups and "warnings-out"; rioting in and vandalizing black neighborhoods. Finally, some efforts involved both symbolic and physical elements, such as the American Colonization Society's campaign to demonize free people of color and raise funds to ship them to Africa.[5]

I present this long list of the "array of strategies" employed by white New Englanders in order to indicate the complex cultural theater in which African Americans were forced to perform in writing their autobiographies. As Melish notes, many of these strategies involved the representation of black character and of the black presence in national history (which was, for many, *white* national history). Even those who escaped from slavery to tell their stories in the North found that the white North had stories of their own to tell.

It is important, then, to place *Our Nig* within the absurdities of nineteenth-century American culture, for this was a nation that regularly proclaimed its devotion to liberty even though every aspect of the nation—political, economic, social, legal, even theological—was devoted to slavery. This was a nation that regularly celebrated a founding document proclaiming that all men are created equal even as that same nation was devoted to creating the fictions of race so as to enforce unjust, enslaving, and even murderous social distinctions. This is a nation whose champion of liberty, New Hampshire's Daniel Webster, helped to craft a political compromise in 1850 that violated the rights of African Americans, both those who had escaped from slavery and those who were nominally free. This was a nation whose highest legal authorities declared in 1857 that black Americans had "no rights which the white man was bound to respect."[6] This was a nation whose most popular and influential form of entertainment was blackface minstrelsy, and indeed a nation almost obsessed with defining and controlling the terms of black identity.

Constantly confronted by violations of celebrated national principles, by white supremacist legal practices, and by popular caricatures, even African Americans who were born and grew up in the North understood all too well that the white people of the North had stories of their own to tell about black identity—at their occasional best, seemingly sympathetic stories that demonstrated white benevolence, but at their more frequent worst, overtly racist stories. All of white culture seemed devoted to creating fictions about what it means to be black—and accordingly, the interest of even the most trusted white Americans in the life-stories of black Americans was almost always a mixed blessing. Many of Sojourner Truth's speeches, for example, were later misremembered and misrepresented, as white writers not only put words in her mouth but also presented Truth's speech patterns in stereotypical black Southern dialect, even though Truth was raised in a Dutch-speaking area of New York.[7] Sarah Bradford, looking to help Harriet Tubman, wrote a biography that begins by having the young Tubman engaged with "a group of merry little darkies," a biography that also praises Tubman by distinguishing her and her family from other African Americans, asserting that "all should not be judged by the idle, miserable darkies who have swarmed about Washington and other cities since the War."[8] Such well-intended but prejudiced misrepresentations were not unusual, and almost all African American public figures of the time demonstrate a keen understanding of what it means to live in a white supremacist culture.[9] African American narrators accordingly were cautious about the prospect of revealing the details of their lives even to benevolent white readers, who were simultaneously being influenced by a culture bent on trivializing, eliminating, and otherwise controlling the

African American presence in the North. To tell your story is to give some-one control over your life, unless they are willing to reveal just as much about themselves. As Wilson's Northern-based *Our Nig* suggests, to tell the truth of African American life in the United States was to tell a story that might alienate those white readers upon whom one relied, at least in part, for one's readership.

Wilson's intriguing mix of autobiographical assertions with the conven-tions of storytelling associated with sentimental fiction suggests the dilemma Wilson faced in trying to tell her story. The truth of one's life was bound in-timately with questions about *how* to tell that truth, how to relate one's ex-periences; and the question of *how* to tell one's story was shaped in part by the audience for whom one was writing. How could one tell the story of one's life, then, through straight autobiographical narration? How do you tell a true story in a land devoted to falsehoods? How does one give a realistic account of one's life, one's character, one's nature in an absurd social environment? One needed to account for these fictions, these absurdities, as being the primary forces shaping one's life. One needed to represent the fictions of the larger cul-ture in order to get at the realities of one's life.

Because Wilson attempted to represent the world of her life as well as her life in the world, *Our Nig* cannot be comfortably classified as either novel or autobiography. Perhaps we should think of this as a novel about autobiog-raphy—or as autobiographical reflections on social fictions. In constantly drawing attention to her blending and *bending* of literary genres, then, Wil-son indicates to her readers that the story she has to tell is both inside and outside the story they are reading. Wilson's concerns extend beyond the par-ticular family implicated by the title page, for she never allows readers to set-tle in to a familiar genre and in that way to determine their relation to this story. The narrative leads, finally, to a direct appeal to the reader for financial aid—payment for the labor of the book, and for the instruction provided by that labor, the lessons to be learned from Wilson's experiences, lessons avail-able only from Wilson's perspective but vital to the moral health of the nation. Wilson's story of Frado's struggles—including her struggles with a religion that has itself been corrupted by white supremacist ideology—leads finally to an appeal to her readers to continue the moral work begun by Frado's own dif-ficult conversion. This book that seems to challenge one's sense of what consti-tutes literary writing builds to a challenge to the reader's own moral literacy. The question of how to respond to this book, in other words, seems ever more urgent as one actually learns how to *read* this book, a process that includes learning how to read the world of the book—indeed, the world that made this book necessary.

III

It would be a comfort to know more about Harriet Wilson — that is, to have hard facts about her life, a clear story to tell. But it would be a deceptive comfort. We know so little about nineteenth-century African American lives, individual and collective, and much of what we think we know often proves to be wrong. Sojourner Truth, as her most recent biographers demonstrate, was a more complex figure than we have generally assumed, though many still hold to comforting myths and legends. William Wells Brown, the social activist and writer born in slavery, published about a dozen narratives of his life, and he drew from his life in his fiction as well. The various versions correspond generally but sometimes contradict one another in their details — and often they present inaccurate information. At times, one cannot even be sure whether Brown intends any given narrative to be taken as fact or as fiction. Many other African Americans of the nineteenth century similarly represented their lives in multiple narratives, and, as I have noted, many had their lives represented by white writers whose attitudes about race are all too apparent in even their most well-intentioned narratives. In all of these narratives, one is forced to reflect upon the comforts of a settled story, a clear biography, or a familiar legend — and one can only realize that the story one is most eager to hold onto and define in unchanging form is one's own. When we're uncertain about what to make of someone else, we can easily find ourselves wondering what to make of ourselves.

My relationship with Harriet Wilson, then, is productively unsettling and spiritually challenging. Early in *Our Nig*, readers witness a conversation between Frado's mother, Mag, and Seth, the man Mag takes up with following the death of Frado's father, Jim. Seth is suggesting that they leave Frado with a white family, and as he speaks, we are told, he is "tipping his chair back against the wall, and placing his feet upon the rounds, as if he had much more to say when in the right position" (17). Most people, it seems to me, draw authority and confidence from placing themselves "in the right position." When told of the plan, though, Frado's response is instinctive and dramatic: "'No!' screamed she; and giving a sudden jerk which destroyed Seth's equilibrium, left him sprawling on the floor, while she escaped through the open door" (19). *Our Nig* itself was just such a response to the world that shaped the life of Frado and of Harriet Wilson — destroying the equilibrium of the fictions we live, the racial fantasies we have come to accept, the unjust order that gets but a chapter or a page or a paragraph in a history textbook, or that disappears altogether from our national memory or from our sense of ourselves.

Close to the end of *Our Nig*, the narrator informs the reader that "enough has been unrolled to demand your sympathy and aid" (130). What was true in 1859 remains true in the twenty-first century. The social conditions behind this sacred demand — for this is not a request, and the demand is not simply Wilson's own — still stand, and that moral work remains. As we look back at *Our Nig*, we are looking at a national history in which the very terms of identity have been complicated by racial ideology. We're looking at a nation that sacrificed its dearest principles not only to support the system of slavery but also to support the system of racial inequality that slavery required. And as we look back at the racial concerns that shaped Frado's life, and Wilson's life, and the life of Wilson's lost son, we are looking not simply at black history in New Hampshire but also, and more significantly, at white history in New Hampshire, the whiteness of an unjust system, the whiteness of an ideological imperative that shaped the lives of all U.S. citizens. This is the whiteness of the two-story house that houses this narrative — and the two stories we face today remain quite urgent: the story of the past, and the story of the present as shaped by the past. After being ignored for so many years, *Our Nig* has finally found its readers. Now the question remains: how will we, the readers of this book, respond to its appeal for a moral response to an unjust social system? If we respond by saying that these problems are in the past, then we violate Wilson's achievement even as we celebrate it. The choice is ours, then. When we write our own stories in relation to this book and to our national history, will we write fiction or autobiography? If we are to honor Wilson's achievement, then perhaps the time for fiction is over.

NOTES

1. See Lawrence Buell, *New England Literary Culture: From Revolution through Renaissance* (Cambridge: Cambridge University Press, 1986), 301.

2. Barbara Johnson, *A World of Difference* (Baltimore: Johns Hopkins University Press, 1987), 16.

3. Harriet E. Wilson, *Our Nig; or, Sketches from the Life of a Free Black, in a Two-Story White House, North. Showing that Slavery's Shadows Fall Even There. by "Our Nig"* (New York: Vintage Books, 2002), 5, 14, 24. All quotations from *Our Nig*, hereafter cited parenthetically, are taken from this edition.

4. James Brewer Stewart, "Boston, Abolition, and the Atlantic World, 1820–1861," in *Courage and Conscience: Black and White Abolitionists in Boston*, ed. Donald M. Jacobs (Bloomington: Indiana University Press, 1993), 107.

5. Joanne Pope Melish, *Disowning Slavery: Gradual Emancipation and "Race" in New England, 1780–1860* (Ithaca: Cornell University Press, 1998), 2.

6. I'm referring, of course, to the Dred Scott Supreme Court decision in 1857, in

which Chief Justice Roger B. Taney, speaking for the majority decision, made this statement.

7. For biographies that challenge our received image of Sojourner Truth, see Carleton Mabee, with Susan Mabee Newhouse, *Sojourner Truth: Slave, Prophet, Legend* (New York: New York University Press, 1993); and Nell Irvin Painter, *Sojourner Truth, a Life, A Symbol* (New York: W. W. Norton, 1996).

8. Sarah Bradford, *Harriet Tubman: The Moses of Her People*, 2nd ed. (1886; rpt. New York: Citadel Press, 1991), 13 and 69.

9. For a more extensive discussion of the white presence in African American life stories, see John Ernest, *Liberation Historiography: African American Writers and the Challenge of Fiction, 1794–1861* (Chapel Hill: University of North Carolina Press, 2004).

Discovering Harriet Wilson in My Own Backyard

William Allen

WHEN I WAS A BOY, I built a miniature version of the Boston Red Sox's Green Monster, which leaned against a granite foundation that edged my yard. There, I often found bits of china or broken bricks that got churned up in the dirt nearby, but I never really understood the significance of the old wall. I lived in a new home, one that was built near the foundation site in 1991. I know now that this foundation is the former location of the Milford Poor Farm, which was once situated at the corner of Stable Road and Town Farm Road in Milford. According to historian Winifred Wright in *The Granite Town*, Milford purchased a piece of property from Isaac Lund, which was used to establish a home for the town's paupers. The Milford Poor Farm existed between 1831 and 1868, just about the same time that Harriet Wilson, the first female African American novelist to publish in the United States, lived in Milford. The poorhouse system in Milford changed at the end of the 1860s, when many of Milford's town paupers were sent over to the Hillsborough County Farm in Goffstown. One of the themes in *Our Nig* is how Wilson worked as a domestic rather than live on the poor farm. Through my work with the Harriet Wilson Project, I learned the significance behind the remnants from the past that I found in my own yard.

I had heard the story of Harriet Wilson early on because my parents have an interest in history and literature, and *Our Nig* was often a topic of conversation around our dinner table. When I was a sophomore at Milford High, Peggy Miller, a reporter at the *Milford Cabinet*, wrote a story about Wilson and her novel *Our Nig*. One of the questions she asked in her article was, "If the novel was so important to American literature, why wasn't it taught in Milford High School?" After the article appeared, a teacher at Milford High wrote a letter to the editor saying that the book was inappropriate for students, and that male students in particular would not have any interest in it.

As a member of the History Club then, I was approached by the Harriet Wilson Project and asked to join a roundtable discussion of Wilson's book. I was excited because it gave me a chance to learn more about this story, and I would actually have the chance to read Wilson's book. Despite the controversy in the newspaper, students were interested in the novel and I enjoyed listening to my classmates talk about how they understood racial tensions in the North before and after the Civil War. After the discussion, I spoke to members of the Harriet Wilson Project and told them I was interested in helping out their cause. As a result, I served as the student representative on a panel of readers and scholars and made my first presentation at an event sponsored by the Portsmouth Black History Trail. After that, I participated in several discussions in libraries that were hosted by Harriet Wilson Project members. There, I was able to listen to members of my community talk about the book and how they view race, gender, and the indentured servant experience in the free North.

As I became more involved with the Harriet Wilson Project, I decided that I had to stop stealing my parents' copy and get one of my own. When I walked into a local Barnes and Noble store, the woman behind the reference desk looked at me impatiently, almost as if she were checking to see if the little hoodlum standing in front of her had a parent. Finally, she asked, "How can I help you?" I told her I was looking for a book written by Harriet Wilson. She rolled her eyes and asked for the title, and in my hesitant, young voice I replied, "Our Nig." Silence followed my request. Before I knew it I was being hustled out the door for using inappropriate language in public. The woman was so flustered that she may have used some disparaging language toward me herself. I was shocked at the initial response, but even more shocked when I learned that, in the following weeks, Barnes and Noble would be hosting a book discussion on the same Harriet Wilson! I returned to the project chuckling with amusement from my encounter at the chain store. I was reassured that small, locally owned bookstores were more understanding about the value of a book like Our Nig.

Election time followed shortly thereafter, and Harriet Wilson Project Director JerriAnne Boggis asked me to stand outside polls and hand out flyers for an upcoming book discussion on Wilson at the University of New Hampshire in Durham. I stood outside the gymnasium of Milford Middle School approaching adults who, for the most part, seemed willing to listen. Unfortunately, there were also many grownups who walked away, avoiding me at all cost. They made no eye contact. Mothers grabbed their children and hurried them off, fearing that I would speak to them and cause a commotion. Others didn't speak to me because they thought I was trying to solicit money. One man stopped to listen to my pitch. He asked, "Why are you, a white boy, help-ing to advance this black person's agenda?" I looked at him in amazement; clearly he had just heard me talking about Wilson's story and how she had tried to overcome racism in the North. In that moment, I felt a small taste of the ignorance and intolerance that Wilson must have felt.

The effort to get Harriet Wilson's message out to the people of Milford, her hometown, and to New Hampshire more broadly was long and taxing. I decided the best way to educate people was to make a documentary for the National History Day Competition, where my work could be shown in Wash-ington to students all across the nation. I spent months preparing the docu-mentary, but it didn't gain as much attention as my opponent's project did. A glamorous and glitzy documentary on Jackie Robinson beat my project, and that was when I really understood that Harriet Wilson's life was truly invisible or unimportant to most people, including most of New Hampshire's teachers. I knew by then that Wilson's story was every bit as valuable as Jackie Robin-son's. And although I wasn't able to reach a national audience as I had hoped, making the documentary showed me the important connections between sto-ries like Wilson's and Robinson's. My experience taught me that most people are comfortable hearing an uplifting story about how a baseball player bridges the gap between the races. At the same time, we are not comfortable with Wil-son's story of racism when we are confronted with it in our own backyard.

Still, our local community has made progress toward accepting and under-standing Harriet Wilson's story. In May of 2004, the Harriet Wilson Project, along with the New Hampshire Humanities Council, held an event to kick off a series of statewide lectures and readings about Wilson. The event fea-tured Professor Henry Louis Gates, Jr., who spoke about finding *Our Nig* in the bookshop of a good friend and about his research in the early 80s to learn all he could about Wilson. More than five hundred people attended, packing Milford's Town Hall. One of the things I fondly remember about that day was the tremendous welcome I received from Dr. Gates when I introduced him to the audience. On stage, Dr. Gates jokingly asked me for the name of a scholar on Wilson, and I surprised myself when I provided him with the correct an-swer! I'll never forget the encouragement and advice he gave me to work hard and keep studying.

One of the goals I had when I volunteered for the Harriet Wilson Project was to educate those who live in the area about Wilson. Even though her novel is not yet taught on a regular basis in Milford's public schools, I think the community is finally approaching that goal. For example, the Milford Board of Education is now willing to accept the term "nig" as it is applied to Wilson's writing. Unfortunately, though, Milford's students and others across New

Hampshire are still not getting the information they need to understand the impact of slavery in the North. The lessons that can be learned from Wilson's story should be a part of every student's high school curriculum. One of the lessons that I learned from this experience is that even as a sixteen-year-old high school sophomore, I was capable of understanding the history and the literature that shaped our state's history. Wilson's groundbreaking work also taught me to have empathy and understanding for the tragic life of a young girl who lived in my hometown more than 150 years ago. And at the election polls, I learned that despite the strides we've made in the Civil Rights Movement, deep down, many people are still uneasy about giving up what they perceive to be power over one another.

Although I've left Milford to attend college, I have not left Harriet Wilson behind. Wilson's story has shaped my understanding of race relations in New Hampshire. Hers is the story of a young girl forced into child labor, abused by her caretakers and forsaken by her community. Ironically, this story happened in the most unlikely of places — Milford, New Hampshire — a place that was a key stop on the Underground Railroad and home to the Singing Hutchinsons, a famous group of abolitionist performers working to spread the word against slavery. Wilson's novel tells a story of the racism that took place in our own backyard. Even in the twenty-first century, that knowledge is still very hard for people to accept. However, I believe that ultimately Harriet Wilson will be remembered as the kind of figure who unites a community like Milford. Her story will gradually rise to the top, just like the little bits of china and pieces of brick that rose to the top of the soil in my yard — treasures from the past that tell us who we have been, who we are, and who we will become as a culture and as a people.

A Conversation with
Tami Sanders

Gloria Henry

I FIRST MET Tami Sanders in 2003 before she joined the Harriet Wilson
Project as the National Public Affairs Coordinator. How she came to connect with us was pure serendipity. A friend of a friend told us about a Native
American woman who had studied Wilson's work and might have some information that could be useful in our research. Though that information was not
what we had hoped for, what we discovered was a woman whose own life story
paralleled Wilson's in many ways.

At our first meeting, I was struck by Tami's calm nature as well as her profound knowledge of her Native American heritage. Tami was well versed in
her people's way of passing culture, mores, and history from one generation to
the other through storytelling. And although by profession she is a community organizer and advocate with a B.S. in Human Services, it is storytelling
that is closest to her heart. Tami has refused to allow the majority culture to
marginalize her people and her history or invalidate their contributions to our
country as the original developers of North America.

What follows is a conversation we had about Harriet Wilson's *Our Nig* and
Tami's Native American heritage. The idea to include our conversation in this
collection came about because of the unique perspective and uncanny similarities Tami shares with Wilson. Throughout our discussion I could feel Tami's
conflict when presenting her story. Her answers were slow, careful, and deliberate. In retrospect, this tension of wanting to honor her tradition yet not
appear to be a spokesperson for her people, reminds me of the theme of "two-
ness" Du Bois describes as black Americans try to reconcile their African heritage with their pride in being U.S. citizens.

GLORIA: Tami, I first want to ask you about your background; what is
your heritage?

TAMI: My heritage is both European and Native American. Ancestors on both sides of my family originally came from around Nova Scotia. They are Mi'Kmaq and Cree Nation, Scotch and Irish.

GLORIA: Given your mixed ancestry, how do you identify yourself?

TAMI: Well, my values, my culture, my belief, my upbringing and ways with my family make me mostly Native American. Yet, as you can see, my Scotch and Irish ancestry are evident. I'm truly a product of both cultures, the living story of the history of North America. I am a *metis*, a mixed blood, the real result of those people and the impact they had in shaping the American way of life.

GLORIA: A mixed blood like Harriet Wilson.

TAMI: Yes, a *metis*.

GLORIA: Were the similarities between you and Wilson your reason for joining the Harriet Wilson Project?

TAMI: When I heard that a group of people was working to get Wilson's story acknowledged in New Hampshire, I felt I had to be a part of that history. I wanted to be part of making sure her story was told. And, I wanted to let people know that her story is not a thing of the past. The issues of racism and violence that Wilson highlights in her book are current issues.

GLORIA: When did you first hear about Harriet Wilson and her book *Our Nig*?

TAMI: I think I read an article in *Essence* magazine sometime in 1983 when Dr. Henry Louis Gates received recognition for republishing the book. I was living in Nashua, New Hampshire, by then. I was studying African American history at the time, and I was also in a relationship with an African American man, my daughter's father. I remember we had several conversations about the book, which I purchased but did not read until 1984.

GLORIA: And when you read *Our Nig*, what were your thoughts?

TAMI: I was really excited! Being Native American and of mixed ancestry, I was thrilled to read a story that was New England–based and about a person of color. I also saw that Wilson's story was a native story, my story; another half-breed that wasn't treated well by her community. Interestingly enough, Wilson's novel reads like one of "our" stories. It is filled with ambiguities and sketchy details — places, dates, family identifiers, aren't always important in our story. For me, *Our Nig* validated the voice and experiences of people of color. Here was evidence that we have a story, a history in New Hampshire. I'd learned in school that I did not exist. It was almost a mantra: no people of color, no people of color.

GLORIA: You learned you did not exist?

TAMI: Yes, I grew up hearing my white teachers reiterate that all the Native Americans were dead. I'm not sure if they considered those statements as a victory, but I heard this from the first grade on. I would sit in class and wonder if I should raise my hand and say "I'm here!" But I was only a child, I couldn't. Teachers would tell us that the Europeans did not kill the Native Americans and that we just died from some natural selection or "manifest destiny" or we weren't fit enough to survive. They never mentioned that the Europeans brought the diseases with them that afflicted my people. Some teachers even stressed that the Europeans were empowered by God and therefore prevailed. Knowing that my heritage was Native American, I remember feeling very strange when I heard this. I felt that if all my ancestors had been wiped out in the early 1600s, as they said, then how could I possibly exist? That type of propaganda repeatedly invalidated my existence and that of my people. Those statements by uninformed teachers always made me feel invisible.

GLORIA: Can you talk about the impact growing up feeling invisible had on you?

TAMI: I was made invisible because people did not see me as a Native. That lack of acknowledgment made me nonexistent. If the dominant community refuses to see or acknowledge people of color, they are undervalued. I became whatever they wanted to identify me as. I knew I looked different from my classmates. I knew my features weren't completely Irish or Scotch. I was round faced with long black hair. Wilson's protagonist was never acknowledged and was kept invisible. Every effort was made to destroy her self-worth and self-esteem.

Similarly, a woman's worth as a homemaker and child raiser was not valued until the 1970s when the women's movement attached a monetary value to her various tasks. If one counted all the jobs that the homemaker did, then one could not afford her. Throughout history women were somewhat undervalued, unappreciated, and invisible until their worth was validated by an auditing process. Although in most cases no monetary compensation is made to the homemaker, she is at least made visible by appreciation and acknowledgment of her important role in society.

GLORIA: As a complement to the previous question, how did you relate to the theme of invisibility in *Our Nig*?

TAMI: I felt a kinship when I read the incidences of abuse and racial meanness incited on Frado. I think somewhat morosely, I was validated by the more negative parts of her story. It is a sad type of affinity one has to have in order to survive and deal with that isolation. Having experienced Northern hypocrisy firsthand, I also connected with the hypocrisy Wilson revealed. I had been repeatedly told that my native heritage was nonexistent, which further confused me. I knew this to be untrue. This fostered a sense of mistrust towards whites and their ambivalence towards me. Most of my people had been isolated to reservations and seldom acknowledged except in relationship to the pilgrims and the Thanksgiving experience.

In *Our Nig*, Wilson called attention to the hypocrisy of the North. We had Northerners criticizing slavery in the South, yet all the cotton mills were here in the North. The North also profited from slavery, but most people are not aware of this duplicity. In Frado's struggle for survival, she seldom rose above basic subsistence. That's a story I knew very well from my own experience and my family's story of survival.

GLORIA: Was Frado's struggle for survival the most poignant aspect of the novel for you?

TAMI: Well, that was one aspect. At the time I read the novel, I had just become a mother and the abandonment by the white mother in the novel of her mulatto daughter deeply affected me. Knowing how fulfilling and powerful my own motherhood experience was with my girl child, I could not fathom how Mag could hand over her daughter to members of a community she knew would look upon her child as chattel. Even carrying a child and giving birth was not enough to erase the mother's sense of her child's invisibility. To me this reflected the white mother's feeling of racial superiority. She definitely did not bond with her child or she could never have abandoned her.

GLORIA: Does that mean you did not sympathize with Mag?

TAMI: No, I did not sympathize with Mag. Actually very little was revealed in *Our Nig* about her, but I surmised she lacked maternal affection. I definitely connected more with Frado. As I discussed earlier, I felt a deep sense of invisibility because my Native existence was seldom affirmed. Wilson, however, acknowledged her multi-ethnicity. From my own experience, I know that individuals of multi-ethnicity in childhood and adolescence often exist in cultural limbo — a state of not fitting in or belonging to any group. It's hard to find your voice in that place. We are always clarifying ourselves. We often stand back and observe our not being drawn into either group. We are always waiting to see how people respond to us. We are generally not enough of one or the other to fit in either. I know that *Our Nig* is loosely autobiographical. Therefore, Frado was real to me. She would often cry over her color, maltreatment, and disenfranchisement, but I believe that Wilson eventually accepted her uniqueness. She affirmed her self-worth when she wrote her story. She had a spiritual awareness that overcame the abuse and perils placed upon her. After I participated in different book discussions of *Our Nig,* it was remarkable to see the different responses and what each group got from reading the book. I think how one interprets *Our Nig* is predicated by one's culture and belief system.

GLORIA: How do you think a young woman of color living in New Hampshire today could interpret Wilson's story?

TAMI: I think Wilson's story would explain that their feeling of being invisible is not new. It puts a voice and identification to what one is experiencing. This is very important to one's self-esteem, especially for young people of color. To know you are experiencing invalidation, realizing that invisibility is not simply imagination is helpful. Knowing what you perceive is true despite everyone trying to deny it, is the essence of human survival. You can deal with it. You can voice it and move on.

I recall a visit to the New Hampshire History Museum in Concord where a photograph of a New Hampshire Union Army battalion was displayed showing the soldiers prior to going off to fight in the Civil War. In the photo, all the names of the individuals in the picture were listed except the name of the black battalion drummer in the same uniform. I asked the curator if she knew the name of the black Union soldier. She indicated she had no idea who the black soldier was. This speaks to the reality of the invisibility of people of color. No one took the time to acknowledge the black soldier by recording his name when the photograph was taken. This simple documentation would have been the writing of his story. If people of color are not historically chronicled in books and periodicals, then their contributions to building our country are forever forgotten, diminished, and marginalized. The black battalion soldier could have saved the whole battalion for all we know. Yet because no one took the time to document his story, he is just another invisible black victim caught in an inconsequential existence.

GLORIA: How do you think Wilson deals with the theme of silencing?

TAMI: Wilson makes a strong statement about silencing with her metaphorical use of the piece of wood stuffed into Frado's mouth. For me, she showed the great lengths a culture will go to in order to silence people of color and deny their existence. Almost every government policy placed on the Native American was a form of genocide. The common theme of the government in most dealings with Native people was that to save the man you must kill the Indian. Which meant it was necessary for the Native culture to be destroyed in order to assimilate them into the majority culture. After all, we were savages, right?

One of the most famous attempts at acculturation happened in the 1800s when Army Captain Pratt founded the Carlisle Indian School. His mission was to completely strip his Native American students of all their culture and history. Likewise, Native children from almost every tribe were subjected to inhuman maltreatment at Christian missionary Indian schools. Native children were forcefully removed from their families and placed in schools far from their family and culture. An army of teachers were hired to eradicate their so-called barbarism and instill the white Christian way of life. The children were forced to take European names; cut their hair (cutting hair was only done when a family member died to show grief); give up their sacred objects, native clothing, and their native language. Many Native children were hit in the mouth or severely beaten if they were caught speaking their native tongue. Here again, I am reminded of Mrs. Belmont's attempt to silence Frado with the piece of wood.

I'm reminded of the quote by Kent Nerburn in *The Wisdom of the Native Americans* that poetically captures the essence of indigenous people. "The Spirit of the Native people, the first people, has never died. It lives in the rocks and the forests, the rivers and the mountains. It murmurs in the brooks and whispers in the trees. The heart of these people was formed of the earth that we now walk, and their voice can never be silenced."

Native people had to be silent about their existence in order to survive. All sorts of genocidal practices, from mass murder to sterilization, were done to wipe out our Native population. Everything was done to silence and destroy us. There is the saying that the more you try to silence someone the lower they become. The fact that Native people still exist is the ultimate act of resistance. The fact that Wilson survived to write her story was also an act of resistance and self-empowerment.

GLORIA: How do you think Wilson and her protagonist overcome their invisibility?

TAMI: Wilson's writing of *Our Nig* validated her existence, which removed the shadow of invisibility. I believe Wilson tried very hard not to personalize her experience. She wrote very detached in a lot of ways, which is quite remarkable. Once you have experienced overwhelming abuse, how could you not put your own self in the center? People who have lived through oppression usually express themselves in a more personalized manner.

Wilson's satirical use of the pen supported her powerful anger and indignation toward Northern racism. Personally, I think her spiritual essence made her stay detached from the hypocrisy of the dominant Christian religion. Yet, it is evident she had a belief in something bigger that sustained and empowered her to tell her story. In sharing her story she was not seeking revenge but enacting a teaching experience.

GLORIA: New information published by P. Gabrielle Foreman and Reginald Pitts in 2005 has Wilson living in Boston in later life and becoming a Spiritualist. What do you think of Wilson's involvement with Spiritualism?

TAMI: It didn't surprise me to discover that Wilson found solace in Spiritualism. From her documented life experiences one can easily see that she would not be involved in the hypocrisy of traditionally organized religion. Despite the obstacles and active resistance she faced, Wilson had a strong belief in her self. This allowed her to forge ahead in her life's journey. I believe Wilson was used in a spiritual sense. Out of the chaos and trauma of her life came a story that continues to teach and enlighten many individuals even today.

GLORIA: What can we learn from Wilson's book?

TAMI: The universal spiritual truth that there is right and there is wrong; there is kindness and there is meanness; there is truth and there is lying. Life is duality. This fact is absolute. Just as the early mythologies continue to be used as teaching tools, *Our Nig* gives us an opportunity to learn from our past. And most importantly, *Our Nig* is a book that speaks loudly to the ability of the human spirit, to survive. It is not a story about what can or can not be proven but the human story of a woman of color who lived in a small New Hampshire town.

GLORIA: Do you have any final thoughts?

TAMI: I believe Wilson wrote *Our Nig* in order to give voice to her story. And what a powerful act of defiance that was! Writing her story not only freed her from oppression, isolation, and invisibility, but it dealt a huge blow to the status quo. It was the ultimate act of defiance, for a woman of color, to use the written word to unveil and chastise the community in which she lived. Even more so, the fact that she self-published her work was the final blow to the status quo. We can clearly hear the echoes of Wilson and the ancestors. "Yes, I did exist. I was here!" On another level, a metaphysical level, I believe that Wilson's desire to write her story was more powerful than she could deny. She was driven by a higher power.

In my Native culture oral sharing of history is the preferable form of teaching and it is the most reliable. Writing has its place, but the translation is not always quite the same from reader to reader. Oral storytelling is at the core of our family, our community. It is the essence of our existence. Even when our culture was forced underground our history survived. We survived as whole families the oral sharing of our stories.

GLORIA: Can you tell us a story that would sum . . .

TAMI: What a surprise, a request for a piece of Indian wisdom and teaching! In our way storytelling is a spontaneous, fluid event, arising out of the moment. I can't really think of a story from my own tradition that fits this occasion but if you must have a story, there is this muskokee (Creek) story by Adonaset I heard recently.

When the 'others' invaded the land of the People, they settled in and made homes and began to farm the land. For many years the People and the 'others' lived side by side in peace, then something as old as time happened, some of the People took 'others' for wives. These marriages produced children, and soon a problem arose. In the People's tradition, clan is passed through the mothers' family, but since the 'others' did not belong to any clan their children were clanless. It is a bad thing to be clanless. Although the children were well loved by their parents, they were not completely accepted by the community. This made the mothers of the clanless ones very sad. They went to the Elders and asked for advice. The Elders told them to pray to the Creator, and if their hearts were pure the Creator would hear their prayers. The women left the village and went out to a place of prayer. For many days they prayed and prayed until the Creator finally heard their prayers and saw the sincerity in their hearts. The Creator told the women to go to the place of soft ground and black waters and to stay there and search until they found a plant that would cry out to them from under the ground. The Creator told them if they listened to the plant and did as it instructed, they would not only find a clan name for their children, but they would also give the People a gift that would feed the People for ever.

The women left the place of prayer and went back to the village. They said goodbye to their husbands and children and left for the place of soft ground and black waters. The place of soft ground and black waters is a place filled with biting insects, snakes, thorns, mud, spiders, the hungry logs, and strange spirits. This was a place that would test the hearts of the women. For many days they searched and listened for the plant that would call out to them from under the ground. Just as the women were about to give up all hope of finding the plant, they heard the voice of the plant calling out to them. It was difficult to find the plant because it was hidden from view, but they found it and dug it up. The plant told the women that even though it was from under the ground, the Creator had given it the ability to see in every direction at one time. The plant then gave them instruction as to what to do. As instructed, the women took the plant to the village of the People, they took a knife and cut out the eyes of the plant, they planted the eyes on a small mound so that the plant would grow. From then on the clanless children became known as the White Potato Clan, and the plant has continued to feed the People until this very day.

You know what I think, Gloria? Children like Wilson, like myself, have a purpose. We can move among the accepted ones as one of them. We can walk in their world and learn many things. If we combine that knowledge with our ancient ways we survive.

Not Somewhere Else, But Here

JerriAnne Boggis

> We are a people. A people do not throw their geniuses
> away. And if they are thrown away, it is our duty as artists
> and as witnesses for the future to collect them again for
> the sake of our children, and, if necessary, bone by bone.
> —ALICE WALKER[1]

I HAD ALWAYS planned to move. As soon as our sons were finished with school we'd leave. Sell the house. Move somewhere, anywhere but here. Move to a place where there are more stories of us, my sons and me. Move to a town with more history, black history. I have longed for a community I could connect with, a town that could deliver an unshakable sense of belonging. This town of Milford, this State of New Hampshire, is my husband's. One never has to look too far or search too hard for signs of his white history, his heritage. It is written. It is visible. It is concrete. Buildings, parks, and streets all bear witness to the deeds of founding fathers, town benefactors, and prominent landowners. It is a story that is told and retold in the books my sons have read in school since they were six. It is the story of our state that is told and retold through the ubiquitous images of verdant hills, a pastoral setting, and a pure Anglo-Saxon lineage. Yes, I had planned to move until that call came.

"JerriAnne, did you see it? Did you read it? In today's *Cabinet* . . . You won't believe it . . . Born here . . . The first black novelist . . . She. . . ."

"Whoa, Delia," I interrupted, attempting to slow her down.

"Born here . . . A black woman . . . published a book." She plowed on, oblivious to my meager efforts to slow her down.

"That's not news," I chuckled.

"In 1859?"

I went out and got our local paper.

And that was how I discovered that Harriet E. Wilson, the first black woman to publish a novel in the United States and the author of *Our Nig; or Sketches in the Life of a Free Black*, was born and raised here in Milford, the town I've lived in for more than twenty-three years. Actually, it was not the first time I had heard of Harriet Wilson. Years earlier, while doing a research project on African American writing, I had seen a reference to Wilson and her novel in *The Signifying Monkey* by Henry Louis Gates, Jr. Unaware that Wilson was a New Hampshire native, I added *Our Nig* to my when-I-get-around-to-it reading list. As the mother of two teenage sons, I was preoccupied with helping them understand recent history — 1999, Amadou Diallo; 2000, Patrick Dorismond; 2001, Timothy Thomas.[2] My priority reading included such titles as *What's Going On* and *Makes Me Wanna Holler* by Nathan McCall. However, when I discovered that Wilson had been born here in this town, I moved *Our Nig* to my must-read-now list. Here was the history I had longed for. Here was a New Hampshire *Mayflower* story of sorts, roots to pass on to my boys, a history that connected them and their blackness to this, their native town. "A Well Kept Secret," the headline read:

> As Black History Month draws to a close, a local African American author and her book — famous in literary and academic circles throughout the country — remain buried from public view here, as they have been for close to 150 years.[3]

Twenty-three years of living in this town, twenty-five years of Black History Month being recognized in this state, and twenty years since Gates's reintroduction of Wilson's book to the world had not prepared me for the revelations in Peggy Miller's article. Until that day, I never would have guessed that black folks had a history in our town; one that predated the Johnsons or the Burks, two black families who were transplants from Massachusetts in the 1960s. Here was written evidence of a pre-Johnson Burk era. Here was evidence of a black history with roots deep into the nineteenth century.

Reading Miller's article I was shocked to discover that, although our head librarian had known about the book after Gates republished it in 1983, he had not read it and "probably wouldn't," he said, since "it was a genre of literature I don't read much."[4] I was relieved to read that Brad Craven, our high school principal, was determined "to help bring the book to light" and give Wilson and her work the attention that was overdue. "It seems like it definitely has its place," Craven declared. "If it is not in our library, we will get a copy. I intend to have a meeting, and see why I don't know about this."[5]

I immediately went out to purchase Wilson's book, "a piece of local history that (had) been ignored."[6] Finding her work was an adventure. A black

A well-kept secret

Milford author was first African-American published

By Peggy Miller
Cabinet Press staff

MILFORD—As Black History Month draws to a close, a local African-American author and her book — famous in literary and academic circles throughout the country — remain buried from public view here, as they have been for close to 150 years.

Harriet E. Adams Wilson was a Milford author heralded as "one of the first major innovators of the American fictional narrative form" by American Perspectives on Literature, an on-line research and reference guide published by California State University.

But in Milford, where she lived before the Civil War, she is virtually unknown.

The author was the first black person to publish a novel in the United States. She called it "Our Nig; or Sketches from the Life of a Free Black in a Two-Story White House, North. Showing that Slavery's Shadows Fall Even There."

Written in the 1850s, the book is an autobiographical novel of Wilson's life in Milford, according to Harvard University historian Henry Louis Gates. She was the child of an interracial marriage, aban-doned by her mother to a family that routinely over-worked her and beat her. Gates wrote a lengthy introduction to the book's paperback edition, published in 1982.

"Our Nig" is part of the literature curriculum in major universities, a placeholder in the Encyclopedia Britannica, and on lists of prestigious novels — yet it remains virtually unknown and unread in Milford and Amherst.

Students are not taught about the novel in local schools, nor have local historical societies featured it, although it was discussed in a woman's history class at the New Hampshire Historical Society last fall.

"This is a landmark book, but it is a well-kept secret," said Louie Carey, Milford Historical Society member, who has read the book. "Milford wasn't a very large place and the prominent families are very interconnected. One man said there were no black families living here in the 1850's, but there were. There were three."

There might have been some concern about the story, which deals with a black child abandoned by her mother to a local family in a northern town. It is

'OUR NIG' Page 4

Article in the Milford *Cabinet* that led to the founding of the Harriet Wilson Project. *Photo reprinted by permission, Cabinet Press, all rights reserved.*

woman asking for a book whose title was *Our Nig* was an anomaly. I was often asked to repeat my request. When I was finally understood, throats would be scratched, eyes would fall to the desk, and the rapid clicking of the keyboard would fill the silence. "Ahem! Sorry ma'am. We don't have that title," was the invariable refrain from clerks. It turned out that none of our major booksellers had Wilson's book — not Borders, not Barnes and Noble, not Booksmith. And remember, this was Black History Month, a month when black books were featured prominently in window cases and on the front shelves of book-stores. I would later discover that not even our State Library had *Our Nig*; their copy had fallen victim to a Yankee swap, traded in a book exchange pro-gram with the Vermont State Library. Thank heavens for our little indepen-dent bookshop, The Toadstool, which ordered several copies. I had the book in a couple of days.

That night, I read *Our Nig* as a seasoned artist would when making a sketch of a fascinating landscape — quickly and effortlessly. I was totally engaged, from the mystery implied in the opening lines — "Lonely Mag Smith! See her as she walks with downcast eyes and heavy heart. It was not always thus" — to the ominous overtone of reckoning suggested in the closing sentence — "Frado has passed from their memories, as Joseph from the butler's, but she will never cease to track them till beyond mortal vision."[7] And as I read, an unimagined and more complex picture of our town's history began to form. The myths I had accepted began to crumble. First, Milford's history was not "lily-white." In fact, Milford might have had a black community! If indeed *Our Nig* was a complex reconstruction of Wilson life, with Frado, the protagonist, repre-senting Wilson, as suggested in Miller's article and in Gates's introduction, then there had been at least seven blacks living in town, if not more.[8] Wilson, in her autobiographical novel, introduces us to Jim, "the kind-hearted Afri-can" (9); Pete Greene, who asks Jim, "Where you come from, you sly nigger!" (10); Frado and her sibling, about whom the narrator comments, "Time levied an additional charge upon him, in the form of two pretty mulattos" (14); Seth Shipley (Jim's business partner), and "another little colored girl" (19), a favorite playmate of Frado's, whose introduction implies the presence of another fam-ily, her parents. Small numbers of blacks does not equal no blacks. Who was responsible for this whitening of history?

The second myth that would fade away was the belief that our town, like the rest of the North, had been a safe haven for blacks and that its inhabit-ants were kinder than their Southern counterparts. I had always heard that Milford was a "major stop" on the Underground Railroad and a "hotbed" for abolitionism. This notion was reinforced in George A. Ramsdell's book, *The History of Milford*. He wrote, "It can truthfully be said that in no town in New

Hampshire were the seeds of opposition to the institution of African slavery earlier planted than in the town of Milford."[9] But here was a second story of our town, a story that could have come from the slaveholding South. I was horrified by the extent of the brutality Frado experienced and was even more dismayed that sympathetic observers had not intervened on her behalf. "How could a town have been so blind?" I wondered. As I pondered that question, I realized just how easily it could happen today. Just how easy it is to be invisible in plain sight. For what do I know of my neighbors? What do I know of the family that owns the Asian restaurant in town where we buy Chinese food every Friday night? Nothing. What more did I know of Atli the tailor, who has altered my husband's uniforms every few months for over five years, other than his name and Turkish origin? Nothing. If I were still living in Jamaica, the land of my birth, I would have asked him his story. The neighbors would have known about his family. In fact, as a newcomer to our town, his "business" would have been "in the street" and all over the community. Yes, I would have known more. How I have changed since my move to this cold climate. How easy it is to remain uninvolved, anonymous.

I would read Wilson's book a second time that week, but then as a detective searching for clues to the places in town Wilson might have been. I underlined every mention of place, from Mag's "hovel" to Jim's "rude shop," from the house "near by where a family of cousins" lived, to the house "a mile distant," to which Frado moves after leaving the Bellmonts. As I made these marks, I realized just how maddeningly scant her information was. Was this a writer's oversight or a deliberate act to keep the place vague? Thomas Moore once wrote that, "Ultimately, home is the place where our soul is welcomed, settled and cared for."[10] It is clear that Wilson never felt welcomed, settled, or cared for in her hometown, so why would she create in writing a place that is concrete? Those questions would plague me as I viewed all the old bridges in town as possibly the one Frado/Harriet and her family crossed before they abandoned her at the Bellmonts. I viewed every old two-story white house I drove by with Wilson's description in mind. "Was that the one?" I wondered. Our oldest cemeteries were becoming quite familiar. I walked their grounds as Alice Walker did when she went looking for Zora Neale Hurston's unmarked grave, hoping for a revelation.[11] Unfortunately, I had no death record to use as a guide.

Remembering Brad Craven's promise to bring Wilson and her work "into the light," I was patient. I thought now that this gem, this famous "daughter" had been revealed to the town, that the public interest and excitement would create fuel for more research. More information would surely follow. Instead, the following week the paper printed an op-ed response to Miller's report.

'Our Nig' is college-level reading, not for high school

To the Editor:

I am writing in response to Peggy Miller's recent article about the book "Our Nig." As a social studies teacher at Milford High School, I have spoken with Dr. Brad Craven about the topic and feel compelled to write and "set the record straight."

I have not only read "Our Nig," I have also studied it as both history and literature. Although not currently teaching American Studies I (which covers U.S. history from 1789 through about 1900), whenever I have in the past, I have used excerpts from "Our Nig." It is a wonderful book and laden with still recognizable landmarks of Milford. Perhaps the most obvious is the First Congregational Church of Milford where Harriet Wilson attended Bible study and received emotional support from other women. Regretfully, records of her membership,

participation and marriage were lost in a fire that destroyed the interior of the church in 1947.

As Ms. Miller correctly pointed out, the book is part of the literature collection in major universities. What she may not recognize was that the reason it is read at the university level is because the book is difficult to read, violent and insinuates situations of sexual molestation. As in so many powerful situations, what the writer does not say resonates as loudly as what she does. This book, in its entirety, is not age-appropriate for the young people who would be studying the time frame of ante-bellum New England (sophomores). When I have used excerpts from the book, I have always read aloud from it. I have told a bit of Wilson's background and history, and also explained the use of the one offensive title word carefully. When I was a student teaching in Manchester, a young woman of color was horrified by the title as I held the book and I have since kept

her sensibilities in mind and used a photocopy of the pages. Although I believe that Wilson's book is a useful classroom resource, its unedited use might prove difficult. In my humble opinion, reading of the book belongs at the collegiate level. The book is written in the 19th century romance style, making it complicated reading. On another level, it also deserves the respect and consideration that adults can give it as a study in

its genre and as an historical document. While its inclusion in Milford history is important, I believe that I, as an educator, must use careful judgment in its classroom use at the high school level.

This book is neither forgotten nor ignored at Milford High School. Respecting it as the historical gem that it is, we have simply kept it in the appropriate setting.

Article in the Milford *Cabinet* that led to the founding of the Harriet Wilson Project.

Photo reprinted by permission, Cabinet Press, all rights reserved.

The headline read: "*Our Nig* is college-level reading, not for high school." The letter began, "I am writing in response to Peggy Miller's recent article about the book '*Our Nig*.' As a social studies teacher at Milford High School, I have spoken with Dr. Brad Craven about the topic and feel compelled to write and 'set the record straight.'"[12] I was stunned by this teacher's claim that Wilson's work was only read at the university level because, as this teacher wrote, "the book is difficult to read, violent and insinuates situations of sexual molestation." She concluded that it was inappropriate for high school sophomores "in its entirety." I could feel the bile rising in my stomach as I read on. The teacher continued: "When I was a student teaching in Manchester, a young woman of color was horrified by the title as I held the book and I have since kept her sensibilities in mind and used a photocopy of the pages," she added. I was incensed. I was angry at the benevolent teacher who was trying to protect us people of color from ourselves. I was also angered by the irony implicit in her next proclamation. "The book is written in the 19th century romance style, making it complicated reading." I guess that meant that Charles Dickens's *Great Expectations* and Nathanial Hawthorne's *The Scarlet Letter* are less complicated and written in a different 19th-century romance style than *Our Nig*, for they continue to appear as required high school reading.

Ironically, a year later, the same teacher received an award for her work teaching the Holocaust to the same high school students who would have found Wilson's book too traumatic for their young minds. The article covering that story read: "She tries to show how the 'tiny erosion' of rights and freedoms, combined with a campaign of misinformation and a national sense of 'pre-conceived anti-Semitism' slowly, but deliberately led to the death of six million Jews."[13] It concluded with the teacher's observation that if one presented the Holocaust correctly, it would be possible to understand what and how it had happened.

I saw the teacher's op-ed piece as an attempt once again to undermine the significance of *Our Nig*. It was yet another sign of America's reluctance to address the history of abuse and oppression when that abuse and oppression were directed at its own minority groups. We see this historical amnesia around the treatment of Native Americans, Asians (including the Japanese Americans who were held in detention camps during WWII), Latinos, and African Americans. I knew I had to do something. To rally support for Wilson and her work, I approached my colleagues from the Business and Professional Women's Heritage Association, a Nashua, New Hampshire–based organization for professional black women. And that was how the Harriet Wilson Project was born. A nonprofit organization, the project is designed to research and promote New Hampshire's black history through public recognition and celebration of Wilson and other historical African American figures.

Since its inception, the members of the Harriet Wilson Project have worked hard to raise awareness of Wilson and her contribution to the literary and historical fabric of our state. We have held book and panel discussions at area libraries, high schools, historical societies, bookstores, clubs, and organizations. We have brought together scholars and researchers to share their insight on Wilson. Even R. J. Ellis, a Wilson scholar from England, came to New Hampshire to participate in one of our panel discussions. One of our most exciting events occurred in May of 2004, when Dr. Henry Louis Gates, Jr., visited our town. Although Gates had extensively researched Wilson's identity and connection to Milford, this was his first visit. Over five hundred people filled our town hall. I will forever remember not only Gates's moving keynote address but also the rousing applause for the last line of our original play, "Hearing from Harriet." "My name is Harriet E. Adams Wilson and I was here," the actress said emphatically. Wilson would have been proud. My sons were proud. For the first time in their lives, in their hometown, they bore witness to a historical figure of color being honored, celebrated. I have since wondered whether that many people had filled the town hall in 1843, when William Lloyd Garrison, Wendell Phillips, Parker Pillsbury, Nathan Rogers, C. L. Remond, Abby Kelley, Stephen Foster, George Latimer, and Fredrick Douglass attended an anti-slavery convention in town.[14]

It would have been easy to stop campaigning to resurrect Wilson's legacy after the celebration. Mission accomplished; the town now knew about Wilson. However, history has shown us how simple it is for African Americans to disappear from the records of a town and the collective memory of a community. Take, for example, the case of Revolutionary War veteran George Blanchard. In Ramsdell's 1901 *History of Milford*, George Blanchard is described as a "colored man and a veterinary surgeon" who moved to Milford in 1804.[15] Curiously, he disappears from the records seventy-eight years later, when Winifred Wright publishes her book on Milford's history. "There were no veterinarians recorded in Milford before 1899,"[16] Wright wrote. This erasure is not something that happened only in the past, ancient history. An excerpt from a recent cover story in *Hippo Magazine*, a progressive paper in Manchester, repeats the same act of deletion:

> For most of its history, Manchester, like the rest of New Hampshire, has been lily-white in its make-up. Even the immigrants have been white: French, Canadian, Irish, Bosnian, Dutch. For a long time, the concept of a minority population was scarcely more than that — even a wild idea. Minorities, people of color — were in the South or New York, or Boston but not in the Great White North. . . . But my how our hue is changing.[17]

A person unaware of our state's history would logically conclude that this wave of non-white immigrants was a recent phenomenon unique to 2005. This article is a prime example of the way we perpetuate the myth of an all-white state and wipe out a more "color-filled" history, a history of black folks that dates back 360 years with the arrival of the first African immigrant — an immigrant, albeit unwilling.

Since we did not wish the same acts of disappearance to befall Wilson after she had been rediscovered for a second time, the project decided to create a permanent and visual memorial in her honor. We hosted a tri-state artists' competition with the stipulation that the artist read Wilson's book and produce a life-size sculpture that was representational in time, place, and spirit. On March 17, 2005, in an event we co-sponsored with the Center for New England Culture, Professor P. Gabrielle Foreman and genealogist Reginald H. Pitts revealed new information on Wilson, including the location of her burial site.[18] At that event, we unveiled the winning drawing of the Harriet E. Wilson Memorial submitted by Fern Cunningham, a prominent Massachusetts sculptor and the creator of the Harriet Tubman Memorial in Boston. Now installed, this memorial is the first in the state of New Hampshire to commemorate any person of color and give visual testimony to our black history.

Commonwealth of Massachusetts.

No. _192_

RETURN OF A DEATH.

To the Clerk of the City or Town in which the death occurred.

(FILL OUT WITH INK. ALL NAMES TO BE IN FULL.)

Name, _Hattie E. Wilson_   Sex, _F_ Color, _African_

Date of Death, _June 28_ 190_0_ ; Age, _75_ Years, _3_ Months, _13_ Days.

Maiden Name, {If married, widowed or divorced} _Hattie E. Green_

Husband's Name, _____

Single, Married, Widowed or Divorced;   Occupation, _nurse_

Residence, {If out of town, also state fully} _Boston Mass. 9 Pelham St._

Place of Birth, _Milford N.H._

Place of Death, _Quincy Mass. 93 Washington St._

Name and Birthplace of Father, _Joshua Green_ _____

Maiden Name and Birthplace of Mother, _____

Place of Interment, (Give name of Cemetery), _Quincy Mass. Mt Wollaston_

Dated at _Quincy Mass._   Signature and place of business of Undertaker. { _John Hall_
on _June_ 190_0_   _90 Hancock St. Quincy_

PHYSICIAN'S CERTIFICATE.

Name and Age of Deceased,† _Hattie E. Wilson_ Age, _75_ Y. _3_ M. _13_ D.

Place and Date of Death, died at _Quincy 93 Washington St. June 28_ 190_0_.

Disease or Cause of Death,‡ { Primary, _Inanition_   Duration, _two months_
Secondary, _incident to old age._   Duration, _____

I certify that the above is true to the best of my knowledge and belief.

Signature and Residence of Certifying Physician. { _C. W. Garey_   M. D.
"198 Hancock St

Date of Certificate, _June 29_ 190_0_.

* Give also street and number, if any. † Give sex of infant not named. If still-born, so state.
‡ Soldier or Sailor in the War of the Rebellion, give both Primary and Secondary Cause.

Countersign and transmit to the clerk of the city or town.

Agent of Board of Health.

Harriet Wilson's death certificate.

Harriet Wilson's grave. *Courtesy of Gloria M. Henry*

An unexpected result of our work to memorialize Wilson has been the creation and development of a Milford Black Heritage tour. Our research revealed at least eighteen sites in Milford directly relevant to Wilson's life, the Blanchards' homestead, the anti-slavery movement, and the Underground Railroad, all sites that speak to a black heritage.[19] Milford is now officially the second town in the state to offer a black heritage tour after Portsmouth.

Thanks to Harriet E. Wilson, we know now that Milford, New Hampshire, is far more than rolling hills, grazing fields, and white ancestors. Wilson's work stands as testimony to the contrary and holds a society up to self-examination. Wilson's story is only one in the recovery of a lost history, a black heritage in New England. According to Christopher Alexander, "People cannot maintain their spiritual roots and their connections to the past if the physical world they live in does not also sustain these roots."[20] Through our work we are fostering such roots and making our long-denied past visible. It is my hope that my sons and generations to come will no longer have to look too far or search too hard for signs of their black history. I am now very involved in this town of Milford, this state of New Hampshire that is my husband's. And I have learned that the history I have craved is not somewhere else, but here.

NOTES

1. Alice Walker, *In Search of Our Mothers' Gardens* (San Diego: Harcourt Brace Jovanovich, 1967), 92.

2. In 1999, Amadou Diallo, an unarmed West African immigrant, was shot nineteen times at his doorstep in the Bronx, New York, as he tried to identify himself. The four white cops who shot him were acquitted by a majority white jury. Weeks after Diallo's killers were acquitted in 2000, New York City cops killed Haitian immigrant Patrick Dorismond, who had rebuffed an undercover cop's attempt to sell him drugs. In Cincinnati, Ohio, white off-duty cops shot and killed nineteen-year old Timothy Thomas. Thomas had been wanted for outstanding traffic tickets.

3. "A Well-kept Secret," *The Milford Cabinet*, February 27, 2002, 1.

4. Ibid.

5. Ibid.

6. Ibid.

7. Harriet E. Wilson. *Our Nig; or Sketches from the Life of a Free Black*, ed. Henry Louis Gates, Jr. (New York: Vintage, 1983), 5, 131. Quotations used in this essay are taken from this edition. Further references will be noted in the text.

8. I would later read Barbara White's essay where she reveals the true identity of the Bellmonts and confirms the autobiographical nature of Wilson's work. "'Our Nig' and the She-Devil: New Information about Harriet Wilson and the 'Bellmont' Family," *American Literature* 65 (1993).

9. George A. Ramsdell, *The History of Milford* (Concord: Rumford Press, 1901), 106.

10. Thomas Moore, *The Education of the Heart. Readings and Sources for Care of the Soul, Soul Mate and the Re-Enchantment of Everyday Life* (New York: Harper Collins Publishers, 1996), 126.

11. Alice Walker's account of her search for Zora Neale Hurston can be read in her essay "Looking for Zora," *In Search of Our Mothers' Gardens*, 93.

12. *The Cabinet*, March ?, 2002.

13. "Teacher Makes Sense of the Holocaust," *The Cabinet*, August 21, 2003, 27.

14. Ramsdell, *History of Milford*.

15. Ibid., 592.

16. Winifred A. Wright, *The Granite Town: Milford, New Hampshire 1901/1978* (Canaan: Phoenix Publishing, 1979), 108.

17. "Multicultural Manchester: The Changing Faces of the Queen City," *Hippo Press, Manchester*, January 6–12, 2005, 18.

18. See P. Gabrielle Foreman and Reginald H. Pitts, *Our Nig; or Sketches from the Life of a Free Black* (New York: Penguin, 2005, xxiii.

19. Description of the sites can been seen on the web at www.harrietwilson project.org.

20. Moore, *Education of the Heart*, 130.

Contributors

WILLIAM ALLEN, a resident of Milford, New Hampshire, graduated from Milford High School to attend Wheaton College in Norton, Massachusetts. He is currently pursuing a degree in political science and economics. His motivation to lead his peers has resulted in appointment to student government, an internship on Capitol Hill in the U.S. Senate, and his enlistment into the United States Coast Guard. He hopes one day to become an elected official.

JERRIANNE BOGGIS is the founder and director of the Harriet Wilson Project, a nonprofit organization designed to research and promote New Hampshire's black history through public recognition and celebration of Harriet Wilson and other historical African American figures. Boggis has developed and presented several cultural events to the New Hampshire public not only through her work as a community activist but also as the Coordinator for Diversity Educational Programs at the University of New Hampshire. Ms. Boggis received her M.A. in Writing from Rivier College.

VALERIE CUNNINGHAM is a native of Portsmouth, N.H. She is a founder and president of the Portsmouth Black Heritage Trail, Inc., a tour of landmarks representing more than 360 years of African-American history in New Hampshire. Cunningham is the coordinator of Community Black Heritage Partnerships at the University of New Hampshire and was appointed in 2005 to serve on the N.H. Commission on the Status of Women. She is co-author, with historian Mark J. Sammons, of *Black Portsmouth: Three Centuries of African American Heritage* (University Press of New England, 2004).

JOHN ERNEST, the Eberly Family Distinguished Professor of American Literature at West Virginia University, is the author of *Resistance and Reformation in Nineteenth-Century African-American Literature: Brown, Wilson, Jacobs, Delany, Douglass, and Harper* (University Press of Mississippi, 1995) and *Liberation Historiography: African American Writers and the Challenge of History, 1794–1861* (University of North Carolina Press, 2004). His work has appeared in various journals and books, including *PMLA*, *American Literature*, and *American Literary History*.

P. GABRIELLE FOREMAN is Professor of English and American Studies at Occidental College, where she teaches nineteenth-century African American and American literature and culture as well as issues of social justice. She is the editor of the Penguin Classic's reissue of Harriet Wilson's *Our Nig or, Sketches from the Life of a Free Black*, with Reginald Pitts. Foreman has published numerous essays, book chapters, and reviews in anthologies and academic journals and has been the recipient of several academic and professional grants. Her latest publishing projects, *Dark Sentiment: Reading Black Women in the Nineteenth Century* and *Rebellious Desires: Anti-Slavery Literature and Culture in the U.S. and Cuba*, are forthcoming.

HELEN FRINK is Professor and Chair of Modern Languages at Keene State College, where she also teaches in Women's Studies and Holocaust Studies. She is the author, in addition to literary criticism, of two New Hampshire town histories: *These Acworth Hills* and *Alstead Through the Years*. Her most recent book, *Women After Communism: The East German Experience*, was translated into German in 2004. Her latest research focuses on women and the Holocaust.

ERIC GARDNER is the editor of *Major Voices: The Drama of Slavery* (Toby, 2005), an anthology of pre-1900 American plays about slavery. He chairs the English Department at Saginaw Valley State University in Michigan. He has authored articles on figures such as Chloe Russel and Frank J. Webb and is working on two projects — one on rhetoric and race in the St. Louis courts (with some focus on Lucy Delaney) and another on representations of Black fortune-telling (building from his work on Russel).

HENRY LOUIS GATES, JR., is W. E. B. Du Bois Professor of the Humanities at Harvard University. Professor Gates is Editor-in-Chief of the Oxford African American Studies Center, the first comprehensive scholarly online resource in the field of African American Studies and Africana Studies. He is co-editor with K. Anthony Appiah of the encyclopedia *Encarta Africana* published on cd-rom by Microsoft (1999) and in book form by Basic Civitas Books under the title *Africana: The Encyclopedia of the African and African American Experience* (1999). Oxford University Press published an expanded five-volume edition of the encyclopedia in 2005. His most recent books are *America Behind the Color Line: Dialogues with African Americans* (Warner Books, 2004); *African American Lives*, co-edited with Evelyn Brooks Higginbotham (Oxford, 2004): and *The Annotated Uncle Tom's Cabin*, co-edited with Hollis Robbins (W. W. Norton, 2006). *Finding Oprah's Roots*, his latest book, a meditation on genetics, genealogy, and race, was published by Crown in February 2007.

LISA E. GREEN is a graduate of the University of Michigan and the City University of New York Graduate Center, where she earned her Ph.D. in English. Her essay on Harriet Wilson is adapted from her dissertation, "Disorderly Conduct: The Figure of the Girl in Three Mid-Nineteenth-Century American Women's Novels."

She has taught English at Manhattan Community College, Hunter College, and The Masters School.

GLORIA HENRY is a former history teacher. She has an extensive background as an entrepreneur and administrator for a Fortune 500 company where she managed the inaugural national database marketing campaign for the now famous Nicoderm Patch. Currently, Gloria is a writer; a community activist and volunteer child welfare advocate against child abuse; a founding board member and Administrator of the Harriet Wilson Project; a Board member of the New Hampshire Civil Liberties Union; and the proud grandmother of an ever-increasing number of grandchildren.

CASSANDRA JACKSON is an Assistant Professor of English at the College of New Jersey. She is the author of *"Barriers Between Us": Interracial Sex in 19th Century American Literature* (Indiana University Press, 2004). Her research and teaching focus on nineteenth-century American fiction with special interests in African American literature, and visual culture. She is currently working on a book entitled "Body Language: Race and American Photography 1850–1900."

MARY LOUISE KETE is Associate Professor of English at the University of Vermont. Her first book, *Sentimental Collaborations: Mourning and Middle-class Identity in 19th Century America*, was published by Duke University Press in 2000. She is also editor of the nineteenth-century section of the McGraw-Hill *Anthology of Women's Writing World Wide*, to be published in 2007. She teaches and publishes on questions of antebellum literary culture with a special emphasis on the cultural work of non-elite New Englanders.

REGINALD H. PITTS is a professional historical researcher and genealogist. He graduated from Lincoln University (Pennsylvania) in 1977 and subsequently earned his M.A. in American History from Villanova in 1979 and his Juris Doctorate from Rutgers University School of Law in Newark, N.J., in 1982. Principal of Blanket Genealogical and Historical Research Services of Elkins Park, Pennsylvania, Mr. Pitts performs primary source historical and genealogical research services for a host of international, national, and local individual clients and institutions.

EVE ALLEGRA RAIMON is associate professor of Arts and Humanities at the University of Southern Maine, Lewiston-Auburn College. Her book, *The "Tragic Mulatta" Revisited: Race and Nationalism in Nineteenth-Century Antislavery Fiction*, was published by Rutgers University Press in 2004. She has also written about the rhetorical and political history of U.S. miscegenation and, with a biologist, on the interdisciplinary teaching of race.

DAVID H. WATTERS is Director of the Center for New England Culture and Professor of English at the University of New Hampshire. He is the co-editor of

The Encyclopedia of New England and the author of books and articles on New England literature, culture, history, and gravestone art. He serves as a trustee of the New Hampshire Historical Society, the Robert Frost Homestead Foundation, and the Portsmouth Black Heritage Trail.

BARBARA A. WHITE is Professor Emerita and former coordinator of the Women's Studies Program at the University of New Hampshire. She has written or edited several books on American women writers in the nineteenth century. The latest, a biography of the Beecher sisters, was published by Yale University Press in 2003. White also serves as the historian on the board of the Harriet Wilson Project.

Index